The Solution for Marriages

MENTORING A NEW GENERATION

Jeff Murphy • Chuck Dettman

What Marriage Champions Are Saying About
The Solution for Marriages

"With decades of experience in marriage ministry, Jeff and Chuck have written a much-needed book on mentoring. The Solution for Marriages is packed with helpful questions and assessments, giving those just starting the journey the tools they'll need to not only survive, but to thrive as a couple."

JIM DALY
President, Focus on the Family

"Chuck and Jeff have created a wonderful marriage mentor training and support tool. Their many years of mentoring, successful marriages and love of God gives them a unique perspective from which to share practical tips that will enhance any marriage or relationship mentoring process. Refined and comprehensive, I appreciate how they have incorporated a great deal of the PREPARE/ENRICH framework into their work. The Solution for Marriages redefines the art of marriage mentoring!"

PETER J. LARSON, Ph.D., LP
President, Life Innovations, Inc.
Co-Author of PREPARE/ENRICH and
The Couple Checkup

"I believe the key to having strong, happy families starts with strong, healthy marriages. But marriage is not always easy, and when couples struggle, families suffer. That's why it is so important to have leaders like Jeff Murphy and Chuck Dettman to guide us along the marriage journey. The Solution for Marriages is a simple, yet crucial mentoring handbook that provides the tools and topical information any mentor couple might need to confidently lead others in creating healthier marriages."

DAN T. CATHY
President and Chief Operating Officer
Chick-fil-A, Inc.

"How refreshing to discover a marriage resource that is comprehensive, yet so accessible at the same time. Jeff and Chuck deliver practical tools that remind all of us that the hard work of marriage is worth it! Whether you have been a marriage mentor in the past or feel God is tugging your heart in that direction, make "The Solution for Marriages" your road map. You won't regret it."

JULIE SIBERT
Christian Speaker and Writer
IntimacyInMarriage.com

"When it's time for a Pastor's own children to get married, one seeks out the best of the best to offer pre-marriage mentoring for those young adults. I was delighted when my son and daughter –in- law were able to sit with the excellence and passionate personnel represented by these authors. Seeing is believing; there are few people I have found, in 27 years of serving in the Kingdom, more committed to healthy marriages than these men who have made their experience available to you. This material will influence, with high impact, a marriage pleasing to God!"

REV. BRENT K. HAGGERTY
Lead Pastor, Stonecrest Community Church
Warren, NJ

"Marriage is not only the foundation of society, but it is through our community that we learn "how to do it." This marriage mentoring book is an inspiring resource for anyone wishing to help strengthen marriages. The information provided will leave no stone unturned in mentoring couples and the resources they provide for mentors and couples is absolutely fantastic. "

ELIZABETH DOHERTY THOMAS
President, The First Dance

"Dettman's and Murphy's book is a valuable resource for marriage mentors, mentees, counselors or pastors. The advice is practical, Biblically sound and easy to use. It is a great resource for any person who is investing into the lives of couples or investing in their own relationship."

REV. ED LAREMORE
Senior Pastor, Atlanta Road Alliance Church
Seaford, DE

"'Equip God's servants for ministry!' It's a Pastor's calling and this manual is a Pastor's tool! Jeff and Chuck have taken their many years of experience in mentoring couples and put it into a format that can be used to begin a marriage-mentoring ministry in your church or provide ongoing training for one already in place. Given the Enemy's war against godly marriages, this manual is especially timely and will be greatly used by God."

DR. PETER PENDELL
Sr. Pastor (Ret.), Millington Baptist Church
Basking Ridge, NJ

"The Solution for Marriages is hitting the market at just the right time. As our nation's marriage movement gains steam, people will be drawn to more resources like this one. One would be hard pressed to find a more informative and well-researched book on the topic of marriage mentoring than this one. We are excited to recommend it to anyone who cares about seeing marriages thrive."

BRETT & KELLIE HURST
Co-Founders, Home Encouragement Ministries, Inc.

Unless otherwise noted, all scripture verses used are from THE HOLY BIBLE, NEW INTERNATIONAL VERSION®, NIV® Copyright © 1973, 1978, 1984, 2010 by Biblica, Inc.™ Used by permission. All rights reserved worldwide.

Scripture quotations marked (NLT) are taken from the Holy Bible, New Living Translation, copyright © 1996, 2004, 2007 by Tyndale House Foundation. Used by permission of Tyndale House Publishers, Inc., Carol Stream, Illinois 60188. All rights reserved.

ISBN 13: 9780983898702

1. Marriage-Religious aspects-Christianity. 2. Marriage-Biblical teaching. 3. Relationships-Mentoring.

This book is available at large quantity discounts for use in denominational or regional marriage initiatives and can be customized with your organization or denomination's logo. For more information, contact Sales@TheSolutionForMarriages.com .

Printed in the United States of America.

We dedicate this book to marriage mentors—dedicated couples and individuals committed to transferring timeless, practical skills and biblical values to younger couples and those seeking to improve their marriages, all for the good of generations to come and the glory of God.

We also dedicate this book to each of our wives, Glynis Murphy and Mae Dettman, who through their unconditional love, inspiration, and co-mentoring alongside us, have enriched our lives, polished off our rough spots, and blessed us with marriages that have exceeded our hopes and dreams.

For the sake of our children and grandchildren's generations, we seek to leave a godly legacy.

Foreword

If, according to actress Cameron Diaz, "Marriage is a dying institution," do we really need another marriage book? The answer depends on whom you ask. For you, it may depend on your perspective when you read the following:

"And so the story goes…the hero rescues the damsel in distress, they fall in love, and then get married…and they live happily ever after."

Any way you slice it, that little fairytale phrase highlights the need for this book.

If you believe that every marriage results in living "happily ever after," then, oh boy, you really need this book. You are in for an awakening! All marriages do not simply wind up in the "ever-after" happy state. The fact is most marriages do not. Those that do so only get there by working hard at developing the specific skills needed, perseverance, sacrifice, understanding, and a lot of prayer.

If you think living "happily ever after" is a good idea—great! God's plan *is* for our marriages to be exciting, fulfilling, and filled with joy—and this book is just the ticket to get you there.

On the other hand, if you don't believe there is a "happily ever after," then perhaps you're a pessimist, the by-product of a cynical culture. You probably agree with Cameron Diaz that marriage is dead or at least obsolete, so why bother having a book like this? Right? If so, please read on.

Marriage is not dead. In fact, it better not be, because the future of our society depends on strong marriages. As physicians, we would be remiss if we did not point out that marriage is actually a very healthy institution. Believe it or not, scientific studies have shown that happily married people live longer, are healthier, and report less stress than their unmarried counterparts. They suffer less depression and have fewer debilitating illnesses. Researchers also state that married couples have more frequent—and more satisfying—sex.

i

As certified parenting instructors, we would also be remiss if we didn't point out that strong marriages are very healthy for children. Studies show that children of intact marriages suffer less psychological illnesses, run into trouble with the law less frequently, and achieve higher levels of education.

You may argue that there have been great leaders who have come from single-parent homes and even orphanages—and you would be correct. There are even fairytale stories about children being raised by wolves—but no parent would ever really desire such a thing for their children. This isn't about possibility. This is about what is best for the future of your children. Marriage gives your children the best possible future.

This book that you hold in your hands is a rare treasure that will bring conviction, healing, and passion into your own marriage. It will also provide you with the tools you need to share this treasure with other couples. Directed to those interested in maximizing their investment in the lives of others through marriage mentoring, this book is packed with knowledge, wisdom, and insight that will move a marriage from the routine or even the disastrous, to the exhilarating. *The Solution for Marriages* directs both mentors and mentees to seek the Holy Spirit's power in order to succeed in a society pressuring us to fail.

The Solution for Marriages is ultimately a practical reference book, putting within easy reach all the tools and techniques you need while doing so in simple and understandable terms. Over the years, working as trained marriage mentors, we have agonized with couples whose marriages eventually failed. Right now, reading through this book, we repeatedly asked each other, "Why didn't we have this book when we needed it?"

Chuck and Jeff are great men of God. These two teams, Chuck and Mae Dettman and Jeff and Glynis Murphy, are anointed in this ministry of marriage mentoring. They possess tremendous knowledge and decades of experience in this field, and they are passionate about sharing that information with others.

Chuck and Jeff have worked tirelessly to bring this teaching to print. Time and again they have demonstrated their willingness to "die to themselves" and surrender to God's perfect plan and timing in order to bring forth this book that God has so inspired and ordained. They are living examples of what they teach in *The Solution for Marriages*.

The Solution for Marriages is a biblically sound reference manual—a must-have for all who desire to be part of God's work in healing and strengthening marriages and families. Although initially targeted for pastors, counselors and lay marriage mentors, it will speak to every couple who is married or preparing for marriage. It will equip you with the necessary tools and godly frame of reference to prepare yourself or your mentees to live—you guessed it—"happily ever after!"

> **Celeste Li, M.D.**
> INCAF Certified Parenting Instructor, Marriage Mentor
> Author of *Triumph Over Suffering: A Spiritual Guide to Conquering Adversity*
>
> **John Li, M.D.**
> INCAF Certified Parenting Instructor, Marriage Mentor

Contents

Foreword   i

Authors' Note   vii

Acknowledgements   ix

Part 1: Introduction to Mentoring
1. The Art of Marriage Mentoring   1

Part 2: Preparing to Mentor
2. The First Meeting with Your Mentees   13

Part 3: Using a Relationship Assessment
3. Potential Background Issues to Discuss   27
4. Managing and Coping With Stress - The Personal Stress Profile   33
5. Emotional Stability   41

Part 4: Marriage Skills & Responsibilities
6. Communication   49
7. Conflict Resolution   67
8. Granting Forgiveness - What It Is, What It Isn't, and How to Do It Well   81
9. Dealing With Your Partner's Unique Traits - Partner Styles and Habits   89
10. Financial Management   95
11. Finding Common Ground - Leisure Activities   103
12. Developing Sexual Fulfillment and Intimacy in Marriage (Discussed with the Couple Together)   109
13. Developing Sexual Fulfillment and Intimacy in Marriage - Preparation for Sex and Sexual Expectations (The Men's Session)   127
14. Developing Sexual Fulfillment and Intimacy in Marriage - Preparation for Sex and Sexual Expectations (The Men's Session)   135
15. The Dangers of Pornography   143
16. Breaking Free from Pornography - A Five-Step Process for Victory   157
17. Testing Before Marriage (STDs /STIs)   163

Part 5 Family and Friends

18. Family of Origin   169
19. Boundaries and Your Couple and Family Map   181
20. Handling Cultural Differences   187
21. Managing Wedding Planning Boundaries   195
22. Surviving the Holidays as a New Couple   199
23. Protecting Your Relationship - The Internet, Social Media, and
    Friends   203

Part 6 Relationship Dynamics

24. The Biblical Roles of Husbands and Wives   211
25. Decision Making In Marriage   227
26. Spiritual Beliefs and Developing a Personal Relationship with
    Christ   235
27. Developing Spiritual Intimacy in Marriage   241
28. Marriage Expectations   249
29. Relationship Outlook   259
30. Building Trust in Your Relationship   267

Part 7 Remarriage and Stepfamilies

31. Remarriage   273
32. Stepfamilies   277

Part 8 Supplemental Materials for Mentors

Mentors' Letter to the Parents   283
The 3-6 Month Post-Marriage Follow-up   285
Premarital Couple's Evaluation of Mentoring Experience   288
How Relationships Are Impacted by Cohabitation   290
Additional Information on Pornography for Mentors   299
State Marriage Handbooks (USA)   303
Certificate of Completion   305

Notes   306
About the Authors   318

Updates, additional information, and downloadable
tables and forms are available in the Resources section of:
TheSolutionForMarriages.com

Authors' Note

The power of mentoring has been proven throughout the ages. The ancient Chinese used the principles of mentoring to train students in mastering the martial arts. Jesus mentored his twelve disciples for three years before sending them off on their new mission, the Great Commission (Matthew 28:19). While the "tools of the trade" are best passed from generation to generation by mentoring, today's culture of broken homes has allowed fewer young adults to go into their own marriage having experienced a great marriage as modeled by their parents.

While the vast majority of weddings take place in churches, fewer than 5% of churches utilize lay marriage mentors and only about one third require couples to take a relationship assessment as part of their marriage preparation. That's a tragic, lost opportunity to provide engaged couples with the skills they will need for a successful marriage.

In this practical guide, *The Solution for Marriages,* we show you how to successfully apply the best practices for marriage mentoring with timeless, biblical principles that, together, provide the solution to the global divorce crisis and the destruction of families. When writing this book, we drew from a combined 50+ years of marriage ministry experience and more than 75 years of successful marriage.

Couples new to marriage mentoring and those with many years of experience will benefit greatly from using this manual. Our goal in writing *The Solution for Marriages* is to provide you with the tools and topical information you need to confidently coach couples through their marriage journey and to enhance your effectiveness as a marriage mentor.

There are several relationship assessment programs available, such as PREPARE/ENRICH (Life Innovations), FOCCUS© and REFOCCUS© (FOCCUS Inc.), PAIRS (PAIRS Foundation), Start Smart (LivetheLife.org), Before "I Do" (K. Jason Krafsky), and Couple Communication™ (Interpersonal Communication Programs, Inc.).

These offer excellent relationship assessments and skill development tools that can benefit couples at any stage: dating, engaged, newlywed, married, cohabiting, remarried, or on the brink of divorce.

The Solution for Marriages is designed to complement any of the marriage and relationship programs available. It provides the "second mile" elements for marriage mentoring, filling the gap between the report that a couple assessment provides and what a mentor needs to know in order to make a positive, lasting impact. Simply select and review the area you plan to discuss with your couple, use this book to prepare for your mentoring session, and have FUN!

The mentoring process, even when dealing with sensitive topics, can be exciting, practical and fun. *The Solution for Marriages* will help you consistently accomplish those objectives. As you work with couples and continue developing your own mentoring and marriage skills, you'll be surprised how fulfilling marriage mentoring can be and how much your own relationship is enhanced as you serve others.

Many communities are experiencing dramatic, positive results by simply providing marriage mentoring to pre-marital couples, married couples in need of enrichment, and even those ready to "call it quits." You too can have a profound impact one mentoring session at a time, one couple at a time, and one community at a time.

Thank you for being willing to share your passion for building healthy marriages with others. Welcome to the world of marriage mentoring!

Jeff Murphy   Chuck Dettman

PS - This guide is presented through the eyes of Christian authors. However, the timeless values and principles included in this book are applicable to both Christian and non-Christian audiences.

Acknowledgements

We are deeply grateful to those who have helped us throughout our combined 50⁺ years of marriage ministry and 20⁺ years of marriage mentoring.

First, to our wives who have stood by our sides for 42 years (Mae Dettman) and 33 years (Glynis Murphy) and provided their input during the development of this book. Through your patience, love, wise counsel, and biblical role modeling, you have inspired us and enabled us to become the men and husbands that we are today.

Secondly, thank you to the pastors we have been able to learn from and serve under. You have provided opportunities for us to mentor couples and lead marriage ministries in your churches, affirmed us by your feedback and encouragement, and invested in our development as mentors and leaders.

Third, a special thanks to our publisher, Today's Promise; our editor, Gregory S. Baker; our medical advisors, Celeste Li, M.D. and John Li, M.D.; technical advisor, Steven Murphy; page formatters, Mike and Kay McCoy; and, photographer, Jamice Ivie. We are also thankful for Heather Khadij, Charbel Khadij, Judy Mayer, Jim Mayer, those who previewed and endorsed this book and our friends and family who provided suggestions and encouragement. You have all been exceptional partners in making our vision for this book a reality.

May marriages be blessed for generations to come as a result of the impact each of you have had on our lives.

Part 1

INTRODUCTION TO MENTORING

Chapter 1

The Art of Marriage Mentoring

Introduction
Throughout history, the primary way of passing knowledge from one generation to the next has been through mentoring. Examples of mentoring are found throughout the Bible with Jesus and His disciples (Matthew 4:19), Paul and Barnabas (Acts 13-15:35), Naomi and Ruth (Ruth 1:11-18), Eli and Samuel (1 Samuel 3:1), and the instruction given in Titus 2:2-5.

Today, as more people grow up in broken homes within a culture that increasingly devalues marriage, couples preparing to get married need mentors who can model what a strong, lasting marriage looks like and to teach them the skills of successful relationships. Unfortunately, marriage mentors are in short supply. You could play a vital role in changing that reality for couples in your area.

The purpose of marriage mentoring is for a mature, successfully married couple to intentionally invest in the preparation, enrichment, and/or restoration of another couple's relationship. By walking alongside those couples with love, compassion, and transparency, mentors are instrumental in reducing the number of divorces and fractured families.

Potential mentors are often unaware of their latent ability to have a profound impact on other couples by investing even a small amount of time with those contemplating marriage. Mentors may think their marriage isn't "perfect enough," be fearful due to their own lack of knowledge or mentoring experience, or feel incompetent to instruct others. These concerns are often unfounded.

The following are some questions that potential marriage mentors often ask. Reviewing these will be helpful in determining if mentoring is right for you at this time.

Common Questions Asked by Mentors

1) What are successful mentors like?

Common characteristics of successful Christian marriage mentors include:

- Experienced and fulfilled in their marriage.
- Motivated to help others and make a difference in their lives.
- Knowledgeable of biblical principles for marriage and committed to applying them in their own marriage (e.g. Ephesians 5:22-33).
- Emotionally and relationally transparent and self-aware (able to share their own life/marriage story).
- Flexible, respectful, and accepting of differences (perspectives, values, backgrounds, etc.).
- Active listeners with strong communication skills and a sense of humor.
- Available to meet several times with their mentees.

Marriage mentors also need to recognize their limitations and not attempt to diagnose and treat psychological problems in which they have neither the experience nor the expertise. Individuals or couples with addictions, infidelity, clinical depression, psychological disorders, uncontrollable anger, or abuse should be referred to a licensed Christian therapist or counselor specializing in these areas.

2) What resources should marriage mentors use?

There are three key ingredients necessary for successful mentoring:

- Your life experience individually and as a couple.
- A Couple Assessment tool which is available from organizations such as Life Innovations (PREPARE/ENRICH Assessment or Couple Checkup), FOCCUS, Inc., USA (FOCCUS© Pre-marriage Inventory), PAIRS Foundation (PAIRS), or other like organizations. A validated assessment provides you with a detailed report on the couple's relationship skills and guidance for developing your mentoring plan.
- This book which provides you with a wealth of information on how to address the topics evaluated in these assessments as well as other topics you may encounter when working with couples.

Some of the organizations providing couple assessment services require that you be trained and certified in the use of their assessment tools.

3) What are the goals of marriage mentoring?

Some of the goals of marriage mentoring are to:

- Help couples understand the challenges that all couples face and encourage them to succeed.
- Strengthen the couple's relationship and help them prepare for a more successful marriage.
- Teach them key marriage skills such as communication, conflict resolution, and managing their finances.
- Help reduce a couple's excess anxiety about getting married.

4) *What are a marriage mentor's responsibilities?*

The responsibilities of the mentors are to:

- Commit the time and energy necessary to properly mentor (typically 6-8 meetings of 1½ - 2 hours duration).
- Prepare for each session and customize the meeting agenda based on the couple's needs.
- Provide an engaging learning environment with engaging dialogue (*not* a monologue or lecture).
- Be friendly, positive, transparent, and approachable role models.
- Help the mentees see God's design and vision for their marriage.
- Provide resources that will help the couple prepare for a successful, long-lasting marriage.
- Be both learners and doers by staying current with new marriage resources and applying what you teach to your own marriage.
- Balance the need for confidentiality with accountability to church leadership and/or the person planning to perform the wedding ceremony.

5) *Is marriage mentoring a short-term or long-term commitment?*

- The duration of the commitment is determined by the mentor couple. You should commit to meeting with the couple until key skills have been taught (6-8 sessions is common). After the wedding, you may choose to meet occasionally with some couples as "mentor-friends" while for others, you may elect to not do so.
- If you encounter critical issues that you are unable or unwilling to address, feel free to refer them to a licensed Christian counselor.
- You may also want to meet after the wedding to discuss progress and point them to further help if needed.

6) My marriage isn't perfect. Can we still be mentors?

- Actually, recognizing that your marriage isn't "perfect" is a great starting place for all mentors. No one has a "perfect marriage," and being honest about it is important. Your willingness to be transparent with your mentees is a key ingredient to being a successful mentor.

- Often, great mentors come from marriages that have gone through difficulties, recovered, and are now thriving.

- Before you begin mentoring, use this book to improve your own marriage and get Christian counseling if needed. Then, when you both feel you are ready, begin to mentor other couples.

- You should have a solid, healthy marriage. This will enable you to help your mentees learn from your own marriage successes and failures. Mentoring with honesty and integrity also requires that you apply what you are teaching to your own marriage. Realize that you are also likely to encounter spiritual attack in the midst of serving as marriage mentors. Be strong and be on guard.

7) What are the minimum recommended qualifications for being a mentor?

- Mentor couples should be married for at least 10 years for pre-marriage mentoring and at least 15 years for mentoring married couples.

- In some cases, mentors who have been married for a shorter period of time may be developed and called upon. At a minimum, you should be 3-5 years further along in your marriage journey and life experiences than the couple you are mentoring.

- We strongly recommend that mentoring be done by a husband and wife team whenever possible. This provides the optimum role modeling for a successful marriage, provides a comfortable setting for both the male and female mentees, and enables you to do any one-on-one sessions as necessary.

8) *Currently, our pastor does all of the pre-marriage and marriage counseling. Should our church start a lay marriage mentoring ministry?*

Some benefits of a lay marriage mentoring program are:
- Couples are often more open and honest with lay mentors than with their pastor.
- The couples are able to spend more time together during each session than is typically available in a pastor's schedule.
- A pool of mentor couples will have more to offer in dealing with a wide variety of life experiences (remarriage, adoption, addictions, etc.).
- The couple can get both a male and female perspective on marriage issues.
- There is a greater likelihood of establishing an ongoing relationship with the couple.
- Mentor couples are blessed and challenged within their own marriages.
- Pastors can be freed up to focus more on "equipping the saints for the work of the ministry" (Ephesians 4:12) and other areas of their ministry responsibilities.
- Most pastors love the freedom of being able to utilize multiple resources for marriage needs.

9) *Does marriage mentoring really make a difference in a couple's marriage?*

- Absolutely! Nearly every couple we have mentored during the last ten years has reported that they were better prepared for the challenges of marriage.
- Improvement was reported in about 90% of couples studied by Life Innovations, Inc. Others became more aware of the issues they were facing and some (typically 10-15%) broke off their engagement.[1]

- Well established mentoring programs, like the one at South Hills Church of Christ in Abilene, Texas, have mentored over 300 couples and seen divorce rates of only 2% over ten years of tracking.[2]
- As an added benefit to mentors, it has been consistently demonstrated that mentoring on a regular basis helps keep your own marriage fresh and vitalized.[3]

Tips for the Mentor Couple
Before mentoring, read through this book with your spouse and work on areas of your relationship that need improvement. This will establish a strong foundation from which you can mentor others. Then, refer back to the applicable chapters of this book as you prepare for each mentoring session.

It is not necessary to take mentees through every topic in this book or in the couple's assessment report. Pick the top five or six areas that need improvement and focus on those.

1) *Seek to establish trust and rapport with the mentees early on.* This is the first step in starting an effective mentoring experience. Couples can sense if you genuinely care about them. Take your time during this stage, and explore opportunities to make connections which will lead to trust and open, honest discussion. If either party has reservations, real mentoring won't happen. You are better off having them assigned to another mentor couple or counselor.

2) *Discuss confidentiality and potential limits on it.* Usually, you will be able to maintain full confidentiality. We recommend that you inform the couple that there may be situations where it is necessary to share concerns with their pastor or the person planning to marry them. Let them know that you will discuss any significant concerns with the couple *first*. Then let them know if further discussion outside the four of you is necessary.

   Remember, absolute confidentiality in the midst of significant sin issues or concern for their plans for marriage is *not* a biblical principle. For example, in cases where abuse or addictions are

7

ongoing, this should be brought to the attention of the pastor or marriage ministry leader.

3) *Discuss the level of interest and commitment the couple has in the mentoring process the first time you meet.* We use the couple's level of commitment to guide how much we invest as well. Otherwise, you are likely to burn out. Discuss and share expectations with each other up front. As a general principle, don't work harder or invest more than the couple is investing in the mentoring process.

4) *After your first mentoring session, ask the couple what worked and what didn't work for them and why.* Ask them what they learned and what they would like to do differently during your future sessions.

5) *Listen to what your mentees say and to what they don't say.* Watch their body language too. Great mentors understand the nuances of nonverbal communication. Lack of eye contact, nervousness, or rolling of eyes may indicate that something significant is happening at that moment.

6) *Don't try to fix their problems for them or to give them all the answers.* That's the couple's responsibility and the work of the Holy Spirit. Your role is to be a guide who points them in the right direction by sharing biblical truth, the hard lessons that you learned in your marriage, modeling good marriage skills, and encouraging them in their journey.

7) *If you don't know the answer to an issue, take the time to discover the answer.* If a situation or question arises where you don't have a good answer, don't make one up. Take the time to investigate the problem or seek guidance from someone with more experience or expertise before getting back to your couple.

8) *Be a learner.* All great mentors continually invest in their own learning and development. Make it your practice to attend seminars, dialogue with other mentors, and read good books. See the Recommended Resources below and at the end of the other chapters in this book.

9) *Be realistic in your expectations.* Relationship areas needing help didn't develop overnight, and it will take time for them to be addressed and improved on. Seeing progress with married couples will often take longer than with engaged couples.

10) *If you are struggling in your own marriage, use this book to work on your marriage first before seeking to formally mentor other couples.* Symptoms to look for may include disunity, frequent bickering and miscommunication, unresolved issues with abuse, lust or pornography, drugs or alcohol, workaholicism, family conflict, or other areas of chronic sin.

Continuously Improving Your Mentoring Skills

Mastering the skill of marriage mentoring will take time as you try different approaches and develop your knowledge base. We recommend that, as you prepare to mentor each new couple, you focus on further developing one area of your mentoring capabilities (e.g. communication, finances, etc.). Give particular attention to one chapter of *The Solution for Marriages* to refine your own skills and expand your own knowledge base with each couple you mentor.

Tips for the Leader of a Marriage Mentoring Program

1) *Plan on investing time in the development of your mentors.* This book is a great place to start.

2) *Help couples with strong marriages become certified in the use of a couple's assessment tool.* Depending on the number of couples needing mentoring in your church, help some couples with strong marriages to get certified in the use of one of the couple assessment tools available from organizations like Life Innovations. Plan to have one trained and certified couple for every 2-4 couples that will need pre-marriage and marriage enrichment mentoring in a typical year.

3) *If you are administering a marriage mentoring program, match the following mentor-mentee characteristics to maximize effectiveness and success:*
   - The mentee's needs with the mentor's experience.
   - Backgrounds (spiritual, ethnicity).

9

- Life experiences (divorce, blended family) and the mentee couple's development needs.
- Couple type (based on the assessment) and the mentor's level of skill and experience.
- Mentor's schedule and availability before the wedding date.

4) *Track your results for impact on couples before getting married, after their marriage, and to improve your program.* Marriage expert Mike McManus says that if less than 5% of the couples you work with decide not to marry, "your church's program is ineffectual. A rigorous marriage prep program will spark 10 to 20% to break up, most of whom will avoid a bad marriage before it begins."[4]

In the end, Christian marriage mentoring is about being a trusted advisor to another couple and sharing God's Truth about marriage and life in a way that will encourage, admonish, comfort, and help them. Your words should be firmly rooted in Scripture, a personal, living faith in Jesus Christ, and a loving, caring marriage relationship of your own.

Recommended Resources

Olson, David H. L., and Amy K. Olson. *Empowering Couples: Building on Your Strengths*. Minneapolis, MN: Life Innovations, 2000.

Stoop, David A., and Jan Stoop. *The Complete Marriage Book: Collected Wisdom from Leading Marriage Experts*. Grand Rapids, MI: F.H. Revell, 2002.

Part 2

PREPARING TO MENTOR

Chapter 2

The First Meeting with Your Mentees

Introductions and Background Information
The following is an outline of topics typically discussed in the initial "get to know you" meeting with your mentees. During this meeting, you are seeking to learn about each other and identify areas of common interest and background. A successful outcome is achieved when the mentees begin to feel comfortable discussing their relationship with you.

1) *Discuss Confidentiality*
   - Review the "Couple Consent Form for Marriage Mentoring" (at the end of this chapter) with the mentees.
   - Discuss situations where you would be obligated to inform church leadership regarding major concerns.
   - If this becomes necessary, be sure to inform the couple that you will discuss all concerns with them prior to discussing it to the pastor or marriage ministry leader.

2) *Introducing Yourself to Your Mentees*
   Share the following:
   - Your Christian experience and journey.
   - How you met each other.
   - How long you dated, when you got engaged, and when you got married.
   - Ages when you got married.

- The marriage preparation you received, if any, prior to your wedding.
- The condition of your marriage during the early years, when you had children, etc.
- The impact that Jesus Christ has had on your marriage.
- Number of children and their ages.
- Your careers.
- Other topics that may be relevant to your mentees (see the couple assessment report to identify other areas of commonality).

3) *Questions to Ask About the Mentees*
- How did you meet?
- Describe your family background?
- What is your church/spiritual background (growing up and now)?
- What do you do/plan to do professionally?
- Have you had any prior marriage preparation (formal or informal)?
- How was your experience with the couple assessment?
  - What new areas for discussion did it open up for you?
  - Any problems, issues or discussion points raised?
  - Did you discuss any of it before our meeting?
- What does an "ideal marriage" look like to you? What's important to you?
- What are your greatest fears regarding marriage? Possible responses or concerns are usually:
  - 43-50% of marriages end in divorce.
  - Of intact marriages, about half are "unhappy" and only half are "satisfied."
  - A far smaller percentage is "very satisfied."

- What would you like us to know about your life, your past relationships, and your current relationship that would be helpful for us to know?

4) *Explain What Mentoring/Coaching Is and Is Not*
   - Mentoring is about openly sharing experiences, highlighting biblical truths, and providing tips and suggestions for the mentees to consider.
   - Mentoring is *not* counseling! Mentors don't diagnose or treat any psychological or emotional conditions. They focus their time on where the couple's relationship is now and where they would like to be in the future. They don't look very deeply into a couple's past.

5) *Explain the Benefits of Mentoring*
   - Research has shown that even a small amount of mentoring (4 sessions for a total of 6 hours) can have a detectable, positive impact on a couple's level of marital satisfaction. [1]
   - Some mentors have a marriage mentoring "success rate" of greater than 90% of marriages staying intact over a 10 year period of time.[2]
   - Share your own results if you have mentored a sufficient number of couples.

6) *Discuss Their Commitment to the Mentoring Process*
   - What is their level of interest and availability? Discuss how they can get the most out of the mentoring experience.
   - Match your level of commitment to the mentoring process to their level of commitment.
   - Discuss their expectations regarding openness and honesty during your discussions.
   - Ask if they have any questions or concerns about the mentoring process.

7) *Miscellaneous Topics of Discussion*
   - What are the mentees preferred learning styles? How can you adapt your approach for them?

        o   Visual (seeing, reading)?

        o   Auditory (listening)?

        o   Kinesthetic (doing, practicing)?

- What's the best way to stay in touch (e-mail, phone)?

    Him: _____   _____

    Her: _____   _____

- Schedule for the next one or two meeting dates.
- Provide the couple with the cost for the mentoring assessment, mentoring charges (if any), and any other expenses involved (books, printing, etc.).

8) *Topics For Engaged Couples to be Married for the First Time*
Inform your mentees that you will be sending them the "Emotional Spiritual Physical Relational Questionnaire" (found at the end of this chapter and in the Resources section of TheSolutionForMarriages.com). Request they complete and return it before the next meeting. This will help you address any areas of special need.

The following information is necessary if you plan on sending the mentees' parents a letter, brief questionnaire (see an example in Part 8) and request for their prayer support. We have found this to be helpful to parents as they work through the process of "letting go."

- His mother's e-mail address: _____
- His father's e-mail address: _____
- Her mother's e-mail address: _____
- Her father's e-mail address: _____

9) *Discuss Wedding Attendance and Gifts*
During this meeting or during the early sessions with your mentees, consider mentioning how you handle wedding invitations and gifts for the couples you mentor. Some mentors purchase a meaningful and unique custom-made gift that they give each couple they mentor. Mentors should discuss:

- If they will attend wedding ceremonies.
- If they will attend wedding receptions.
- If they give a wedding gift to their mentee couples.

Congratulations! You have made it through your first meeting with your mentees!

The Couple Consent Form

In order to ensure that the couple understands the extent and limitations of your mentoring services and to protect you from any legal action based on your skills and approach, consent for mentoring should be obtained prior to working with a couple. An example of a consent form is shown on page 19.

Emotional, Spiritual, Physical & Relational Health Questionnaire

This questionnaire provides the mentors with additional background information to help determine if mentoring is appropriate for the couple (vs. counseling) and to further identify areas to discuss during your mentoring sessions. The questionnaire is shown on pages 20-23.

Both of these files are also available in the Resources section of TheSolutionForMarriages.com.

Couple Consent Form for Marriage Mentoring
(To be completed at the start of the first meeting.)

We understand that we are voluntarily entering into a relationship with a marriage mentor couple in order to build our relational skills, learn from the experiences and insights of our mentors, and strengthen our relationship as a couple.

We recognize that our marriage mentors are not professionals, licensed counselors, or psychologists. Their contributions to the mentoring process are *not* based on professional training, but rather by valuable experience as a happily married couple. Marriage education is *not* therapy; it is *education*. It does not involve any diagnosis or "treatment," and mentors do not give marital, financial, or legal advice. Couples being mentored are solely responsible for all decisions that they make as a result of the mentoring process.

We understand that the results of our Couple Inventory and any information discussed during the mentoring process will be kept confidential by the marriage mentors. We hereby authorize the marriage mentors to share the Couple Inventory results and other information divulged during our mentoring sessions with a member of the clergy and/or the marriage mentoring supervisor and with any other parties as required by law if they feel it is appropriate.

We understand that at any time we may terminate the marriage mentoring process or request a new marriage mentor couple to be assigned to us if we are unhappy with how the process is going.

Please sign below to indicate that you have read and understand the information above.

Signatures of Couple Being Mentored:

Partner 1: _____ Date: _____

Partner 2: _____ Date: _____

Signatures of Mentor Couple:

Mentor 1: _____ Date: _____

Mentor 2: _____ Date: _____

19

Emotional, Spiritual, Physical and Relational Health Questionnaire
(Confidential)

Please complete the following information, and return it to your mentors prior to the next session.

This information will only be used to help us tailor your future mentoring sessions, and it will not be shared outside this mentoring relationship as stated in the Couple Consent for Marriage mentoring form.

A) Your Emotional and Mental Health
(Questions in this section may indicate a need for professional assistance and are not intended as a diagnosis, prognosis, or mental health evaluation.)

1) Do you or have you ever suffered from depression, anxiety, or any other mental health issue?
   Yes ☐ No ☐ If yes, when?

2) Is or was this condition treated medically or professionally?
   Yes ☐ No ☐ Taking medication? Yes ☐ No ☐

3) Do you have any phobias? (e.g. excessive fear of the dark, dying, loss of a parent, etc.) If yes, please explain.

4) Have you discussed your emotional health in detail with your fiancé? Yes ☐ No ☐

5) Have either of you ever been physically, verbally, or sexually abused (including rape)? Yes ☐ No ☐ If yes, have you discussed this with a professional? Yes ☐ No ☐ With each other? Yes ☐ No ☐

6) Have you had or been associated with an abortion? Yes ☐ No
   If yes, have you discussed this with a counselor? Yes ☐ No ☐
   With each other? Yes ☐ No ☐

B) Your Spiritual Condition and Health

Please complete the following statements regarding your spiritual life without the assistance of your fiancé.

1) Is Jesus the Lord of your life? Yes ☐ No ☐ Unsure ☐ Please elaborate:

2) Do you have a personal, saving relationship with Jesus Christ? Please describe it:

3) When do you read your Bible and for what reasons?

4) Describe your personal commitment to attending a church (How often? For what reasons?):

5) Describe your prayer life and devotional time (Where? When? Why?):

6) My definition of sin is…

7) Describe how you deal with sin:

8) Explain any recent changes or problems you are having with your spiritual walk:

9) What change(s) would you like to make in your spiritual life?

10) Have you ever been involved in a cult, the occult, astrology, fortune tellers, etc.? Yes ☐ No ☐   If yes, please describe your involvement (Dates, duration, and extent):

C) Your Physical Health and Sexual Boundaries

1) Are there any physical health issues that you have not yet fully discussed with your fiancé?

2) Have you had a recent physical exam with a gynecologist (her) or physician (him)?

3) Have you discussed plans for children, family planning and contraception with each other? Yes ☐ No ☐ With your doctor? Yes ☐ No ☐ N/A ☐

4) As the process of premarital mentoring begins, it is important to consider your sexual boundaries prior to marriage. Many couples have not taken the time to discuss boundaries with each other.

   The following exercise, to be completed individually, will challenge you to identify where your sexual boundaries are. Consequently, you will know when you are approaching the limit you have set for yourself and your fiancé.

   Below is an example of a possible physical progression of intimacy in a relationship:
   A. Holding hands
   B. Arm around shoulder/waist
   C. Embracing
   D. Kissing
   E. French kissing
   F. Arousing physical contact (clothed)
   G. Fondling sexual areas (clothed or unclothed)
   H. Oral sex
   I. Sexual intercourse

5) As an engaged couple, have you specifically discussed your physical boundaries and how to establish a foundation of purity and pursue holiness in your relationship? Yes ☐ No ☐

6) What step(s) in the progression listed above in question #4 are off limits for you?

   A☐ B☐ C☐ D☐ E☐ F☐ G☐ H☐ I☐
   Unsure ☐ None ☐

7) Write out your physical boundaries as you and your fiancé interpret them.

8) What specific things are you both doing to protect those boundaries? Has that been consistently effective for you? Yes ☐ No ☐

9) How do you feel about the decisions you made in this area? What brought you to this conclusion?

10) Do you have an accountability partner who regularly checks in with you about maintaining these boundaries? Yes ☐ No ☐

11) If no, would you like one of us, as your mentors, to do this for you? Yes ☐ No ☐ Unsure ☐

D) Relational Health

1) Do you have any broken relationships with your parents or siblings? Yes ☐ No ☐ If yes, please describe:

2) Are you still in contact with or have emotional ties with any previous boy/girlfriends? Yes ☐ No ☐ If yes, please describe involvement (dates, frequency and extent):

3) Do any boy/girlfriends still have contact or emotional ties with you? Yes ☐ No ☐ If yes, please describe involvement (dates, frequency, and extent):

4) Do you have any remaining legal or financial ties from previous relationships? Yes ☐ No ☐ If yes, please describe involvement (duration and extent):

Part 3

USING A RELATIONSHIP ASSESSMENT

Chapter 3

Potential Background Issues to Discuss

Introduction

After the couple takes the assessment, a Mentor's (or Facilitator's) Report is generated. This forms the primary basis for determining the topics that will be discussed with the couple in future sessions. Results from the assessment may include brief comparisons between the individual's backgrounds which provide the initial clues for mentors on areas they might want to discuss further.

The contents of this book align well with the PREPARE/ENRICH program from Life Innovations as well as assessment programs from other sources.

In this chapter, we will focus on the common elements found in couple's assessments—similar to the Background Information section of the PREPARE/ENRICH Facilitator Report. This sheet is included in the Facilitator Report only, and should not be given to the couple as it may be overwhelming and/or confusing.

Develop and Incorporate Your Own Story

When discussing the couple's background, look for areas where there are natural connection points to your own background and briefly mention those that might help build rapport with the couple. Don't fear speaking about your own marriage mistakes. Couples can learn more from your mistakes than from only hearing a sanitized version of what marriage should look like.

Tips on Discussing Background Issues

As you review each category, look for potential strong points as well as possible areas of concern. Also consider interrelationships between different categories in the assessment (e.g. idealistic distortion and passivity).

Item[1]	Considerations for Possible Discussion
Age	If either is very young or they have a large age difference, ask about their relationship with their parents; review family of origin issues; check Idealistic Distortion scores.
Ethnic Background	If different, review the chapter on Handling Cultural Differences.
Education Completed	If different, discuss what the less educated person does or can do to continue growing intellectually.
Religious Affiliation	If different, consider reviewing the chapters on Spiritual Beliefs and Developing Spiritual Intimacy, expectations each has of the other, how they will raise children, and handling of holiday celebrations.
Area of Employment	Discuss if there will be differences in hours or shifts worked, work related travel, stability of employment, and how they plan to deal with any issues.
Role at Work	Are there different levels of stress or frustrations from work? Are there any changes anticipated?
Employment Status	Discuss stress related to any unemployment and contingency plans.
Individual Yearly Income	If large differences, how will finances be managed? Will they depend on one income at some point? What is their debt and expense load?

Item[1]	Considerations for Possible Discussion
Birth Position in Family	Birth order can influence people in a variety of ways. For more information see the Birth Order section in the chapter on Family of Origin.
Number of Children in Your Family	Check for differences across this item, the number of children wanted, and when. Is there agreement?
What is your current living arrangement?*	If one or both partners have been living on their own for several years, discuss the need for flexibility in adjusting to married life.
Where do you live?	Does this impact their preferences on where to live in the future? Are they in agreement?
Length of relationship?	Less than 6-12 months? If so, is there a reason for the rush to get married? How much time did they spend together/apart during that time? If several years, was there a reason for hesitation? How was that resolved?
Length of engagement?	Less than 3-6 months? If so, is there a reason for the rush to get married?
Months Until Marriage	Will there be sufficient time for mentoring sessions to address growth areas?
How long have you and your partner been living together?*	Plan to discuss the information provided on How Relationships Are Impacted by Cohabitation, in the supplemental material section.
Friends Feelings About Your Marriage Plans	If not supportive, why? Has the couple honestly considered this? What role will these friends play in your lives after the wedding?

Item[1]	Considerations for Possible Discussion
Family's Feelings About Your Marriage Plans	If not supportive, why? Has the couple honestly considered this? Is there a parental problem with "letting go?" Recommend that this be discussed directly between the individual and his or her parents (not between future in-laws).
Number of Children You Currently Have	Review information in the chapters on Stepfamilies and Remarriage.
How many children do you want to have?	Is there a need for compromise? What if one person changes his or her mind? How will you handle it if you are unable to conceive? Discuss views and options regarding contraception. See section on Family Planning and Contraception in Chapter 12. Discuss how the new parent will deal with their partner's children (parental roles, discipline, etc.).
When do you want children?	Discuss views and options regarding contraception. Is there a need for compromise?
Is the woman pregnant?	If yes, how will they compensate for missing the "honeymoon phase" of marriage?
Number of Times Broken Up	How many times this couple has broken up with each other while dating or engaged? Discuss this if there has been a breakup (e.g. lessons learned, feelings, forgiveness, etc.).
Number of Previous Marriages (if applicable)?	Discuss questions before considering remarriage. Is there a biblical basis for doing so? Have they considered the increased risk they face due to a previous divorce? How will they be more proactive in this marriage?

Item[1]	Considerations for Possible Discussion
Parents Marital Status	What type of role models did they see growing up? What do they want to keep for their marriage or discard? Have they considered the increased risk they face due to a parent's divorce?
Raised By	Discuss the quality of their parent's marriage, parenting style, and how are they like or unlike their parents.

* Depending on the couple's current living arrangements, this question may or may not appear in your report.

Couple Exercises

There are no specific exercises associated with this background information since this is for the mentor's reference only. Preliminary indications should be confirmed by other portions of the assessment when making a determination of how to handle them.

Recommended Resources

David H. Olson, Ph.D. Amy K. Olson-Sigg, *Empowering Couples: Building on Your Strengths*, Life Innovations, Inc. Minneapolis, Minnesota, 2000.

David H. Olson, Ph.D., Amy K. Olson-Sigg, Peter J. Larson, Ph.D., *The Couple Checkup* ™, Thomas Nelson, 2008.

Chapter 4

Managing and Coping With Stress - The Personal Stress Profile

Introduction
Stress tests are a useful starting place for anyone seeking to combat stress. These tests provide an opportunity for mentors to objectively look at a mentee's circumstances and determine how stress is affecting his or her life.

Since stress affects individuals in different ways, there is no universal remedy for stress relief. Reducing sources of stress when possible and learning effective methods for coping with stress can both play an important part in dealing with it.

What Experts Say About Stress
We've all experienced stress in our lives, but what exactly is it, and where does it come from? Stress experts offer the following definitions:

> "...a state of tension experienced by individuals facing
> extraordinary demands, constraints, or opportunities."[1]

Stress is what we *experience* in response to *stressors* in our lives. Stressors, which include people, events, situations, unreasonable expectations, and our environment, can be real or perceived.

No one can dump a pile of *stress* on you, but they can cause you to feel a lot of stress by bringing a lot of *stressors* your way! Stress is an emotional, cognitive, and physiological *response,* that simultaneously affects your *feelings*, your *thinking,* and your *body*.

This mentoring session is designed to help mentees:

1) Identify stressors for each person, and how often they are affected by them.
2) Understand the stressors in their lives.
3) Develop effective responses to major or chronic stress.

Common Stressors
Common stressors encountered during a couple's life include:

1) *Stressful Situations and Life Events*
   - Wedding planning
   - Major life changes
   - Holidays
   - Bereavement
   - Chronic or acute health issues

2) *Family Stress*
   - Becoming a parent for the first time
   - Caring for an elderly or ill parent or relative
   - Intrusive or high-conflict extended family issues
   - Last child leaves home ("empty nest")

3) *Relationship Problems*
   - Marriage breakdowns
   - Violence in the home
   - Infidelity

4) *Stress at Work*
   - Threat of job loss
   - Unrealistic demands

Develop and Incorporate Your Own Story
Share a major stress experience you encountered as a couple, how you constructively handled it, and how that experience benefitted or enriched your relationship with your spouse.

Tips on Discussing Stress

Healthy Ways of Dealing with Controllable Stressors

1) Identify ways that you can avoid last minute crisis by improving your planning and being more proactive.
2) Learn to say "No" more often. Focus on those things that are most important to you and drop the rest.
3) When possible, limit the amount of time you spend with people who stress you out.
4) Use assertive communication skills more often and also look for opportunities to compromise.
5) Ask yourself, "Is the situation really *that* important? Will it matter in five or ten years? In eternity?"
6) Can you find anything positive in the situation? If so, choose to focus on that part of the issue more.
7) Start an exercise and nutrition program, and get more rest.

Ways to Cope with Unchangeable Stressors

1) Realize that you can't control everything, so don't become obsessed with these types of issues. Let go!
2) Share your feelings with a close friend. The emotional release can do you good.
3) Recount the good things that God has done for you.
4) Start an exercise and nutrition program, and get more rest.
5) Treat yourself to something special (a short trip, perhaps) as a way to get away and emotionally regroup.
6) Find something you enjoy, and do it at least once a day. Look forward to that special time each day.
7) Try to maintain your sense of humor.
8) Practice relaxation techniques when you encounter this type of stress.

If the mentee(s) continues having difficulty in this area, consider referring him or her to a professional counselor.

Couple Exercises

Stressors are events that create an emotional and/or physical reaction. Stress can come from positive sources (a wedding, job promotion, new baby) or negative sources (loss of job, car accident, major illness, death of a family member). What is important is to be able to properly deal with the various stressors in a person's life.

Stress is often managed using a prioritization process. Use the list below to identify the important issues you are each facing.

1) For each item on your list, determine which situations can be changed or resolved and which ones are outside of your control.
2) Prioritize the ones you can control and want to work on.
3) Discuss ways that you can better cope with the issues that can't be changed or are beyond your control.

Life Events & Stress [2]

	Stressful Life Events	Able to Change? (Yes/No)	Priority	How to deal with the stressor	How to cope with the unchangeable stressors
High Level Stressors	Death of spouse				
	Divorce				
	Marital separation				
	Death of close family member				
	Personal injury or illness				
	Getting married/ Wedding				
	Loss of Job/Retirement				
	Marital problems				
	Change in work shift				
	Family member health problems				
	Other				

	Stressful Life Events	Able to Change? (Yes/No)	Priority	How to deal with the stressor	How to cope with the unchangeable stressors
Medium Level Stressors	Pregnancy				
	Sexual difficulties				
	Drug/Alcohol abuse				
	Addition of a new family member				
	Significant change in finances				
	Death of close friend				
	Career change				
	Loan for major purchase				
	Foreclosure of mortgage				
	Change in work responsibilities				
	Child leaving home				
	Conflict with in-laws				
	Childcare difficulties				
	Spouse elects to begin or stop work				
	Returning to school				
	Other				
Lower Level Stressors	Disruption in living conditions				
	Trouble with boss				
	Change in work hours				
	Moving				
	Moving to a new school				
	Change in church				
	Sleep difficulty				
	Vacation planning				
	Holidays				
	Minor violations of the law				
	Other				

Discussion Starters

1) What approach do you usually take in dealing with stress from situations you can change or influence? What about situations you can't change?
2) How stressful is your daily life typically—apart from your current wedding preparations?
3) Have you found any ways to help each other cope with the stress you face? What have you tried?

Biblical References

Philippians 4:6-7, *"Don't worry about anything; instead, pray about everything. Tell God what you need, and thank him for all he has done. Then you will experience God's peace, which exceeds anything we can understand. His peace will guard your hearts and minds as you live in Christ Jesus." (NLT)*

Matthew 6:28-30, *"And why worry about your clothing? Look at the lilies of the field and how they grow. They don't work or make their clothing, yet Solomon in all his glory was not dressed as beautifully as they are. And if God cares so wonderfully for wildflowers that are here today and thrown into the fire tomorrow, he will certainly care for you. Why do you have so little faith?" (NLT)*

1 Peter 5:7, *"Cast all your anxiety on him because he cares for you."*

Matthew 11:28-29, *"Come to me, all you who are weary and burdened, and I will give you rest. Take my yoke upon you and learn from me, for I am gentle and humble in heart, and you will find rest for your souls."*

Romans 5:3-5, *"...but we also rejoice in our sufferings, because we know that suffering produces perseverance; perseverance, character; and character, hope. And hope does not disappoint us, because God has poured out his love into our hearts by the Holy Spirit, whom he has given us."*

Recommended Resources

Schermerhorn, John R., Richard Osborn, and James G. Hunt. *Organizational Behavior*. 9th ed. New York: Wiley, 2005.

STRESS Obstacle or Opportunity?, A. Pihulyk. Source: Canadian Manager (Summer 2001): 26.2, p.24.

Chapter 5

Emotional Stability

Introduction

Emotional stability demonstrates our ability to remain relaxed and calm even when we are faced with stress—versus those people whom are more reactive to the stressors in their lives. How we express our emotions (negative and positive communication) reveals much about our level of emotional stability.

Perhaps the most difficult obstacle to overcome in relating well with others is our own emotions. It is exceptionally difficult to love other people when we ourselves are hurting. In John 13:34-36, Jesus instructed His disciples to love one another as He loved them, but Peter was not in the right emotional condition to hear what He had to say. As a result he didn't receive Jesus' message of the need to love one another instead he focused on why he could not go where Jesus was going. Often, we respond the same way.

We often consider being nice or loving someone only when we are feeling okay. But when we are frustrated, we find ourselves being short tempered with our "loved ones" or even being downright mean. This is why emotional management is a skill vital to emotional stability. In order to love others like Christ does, we have to be able to control our feelings rather than be controlled by them.

This mentoring topic is designed to:

1) Help the mentees understand where emotions originate.
2) Help the couple identify emotional control skills they can develop and implement.
3) Provide a series of steps that couples can use to work with one another's emotional differences rather than attempting to change each other.

Common Emotional Issues

Couples tend to score low in the following assessment areas:

1) Core issues such as a person's basic identity, self-worth, and emotional needs.
2) Communicating only on a "logical" level rather than considering the "abstract" needs such as security, love, acceptance, and forgiveness.
3) Communicating without understanding their partner's basic need for significance (importance, meaning, and adequacy).

Unless we address the basic personal needs and the assumptions we have concerning how our needs are met, it is impossible to experience anything but superficial understanding of emotions. This is not to say that there is no overlap in gender specific needs—there is. Men, as well as women, seek and need security, love, acceptance, and forgiveness. Women, as well as men, seek and need significance, importance, meaning, and adequacy. But each gender approaches these differently.

Develop and Incorporate Your Own Story

Share techniques that have worked well for you and how those experiences enriched the emotional state of your life and marriage.

Tips on Discussing Emotional Stability

Psychologist Albert Ellis, Ph.D. proposed what he called the ABC Theory[2] of emotions to help us understand our responsibility for our feelings. He stated that an event (A) does not produce the consequence (C) by itself. In between A and C is B, which stands for *beliefs*. According to his theory, what we believe about ourselves because of event A is the real determinant of our feelings. This puts the responsibility of our emotions on us. No longer are we able to blame others or circumstances for the consequences of our actions, and in taking the responsibility, we find a key to emotional management.

If we accept what Ellis says, we have the ability to control what we feel in any situation by what we chose to believe about ourselves. Emotional management is possible if we understand the important role our self-talk[1] (the silent conversations we have with ourselves) plays in determining how we feel in any given situation.

Managing our emotional responses, however, does not mean that we are able to avoid emotional pain! Without this emotional management, we will allow our pain to drive us into destructive and sinful emotional responses that strip from us any degree of control. It is important to work through negative feelings in order to maintain a degree of divine love for those who make us angry, to endure real agony with "an inexpressible and glorious joy" (1 Peter 1:8), and to face our fears with the "peace of God that passes all understanding" (Philippians 4:7).

Since our beliefs determine the quality of our emotions, it is important to understand what we need to believe about ourselves in order to manage our own emotions. For instance, despite the example of Jesus Himself, most people still believe that we can avoid suffering and pain by what we do or don't do to please God. We hold to a belief that if we are good, then God is good to us.

If we are bad, then God is bad to us. This belief then stimulates negative emotional responses to negative circumstances—particularly if we believe we are suffering unjustly. If, however, our belief about our suffering is more in line with Jesus who endured the cross for the joy set before Him, we too will endure suffering for the joy we believe to be set before us.

Share the following truths with your couple:

1) In order to understand this, we need to consider where our emotions come from. Emotions do not simply fall out of the sky and neither are they produced solely by the things that

happen to us. Our feelings are also the result of what we tell ourselves (our beliefs) in light of what has happened to us. Emotional responses stem from our belief about the core issues of identity and personal needs, whereas our emotional expression is too often about superficial issues related to current circumstances. We need to dig beneath the superficial issues to recognize and discuss the core issues. Questions such as, "How are you feeling about yourself?" or "What do you think about yourself?" begin to probe beneath the surface and explore our core beliefs.

2) While it is important to listen to the superficial issues being discussed, effective communication goes beyond to discuss the underlying issues of identity and personal needs. Listening to people vent their feelings of frustration due to certain circumstances is useful, but the assurance and comfort they really need will only come from addressing the underlying core issues.

3) In addition, it is important to be honest with our family members and others around us about our motivation if we are going to redirect our emotional responses. The only difference between ministry and manipulation is motive. All too often, we seek to manipulate our spouse, children, or parents under the guise of "doing what is best for them." Despite our best efforts to cover such selfish motivation, our family members frequently discern our manipulation tactics. Honesty in this area will allow us to redirect our emotional responses to achieve reconciliation and stronger emotional stability.

4) Emotional redirection requires recognizing the true nature of our motivations. The Bible contrasts a life falsely motivated by fear, guilt, and pride with one motivated by faith, hope, and love. A healthy lifestyle of grace is referred to as "walking in the light" or "walking in the Spirit." This lifestyle is in stark contrast with the legalistic or religious lifestyle the Bible describes as "walking in the vanity of our minds" or "walking after the flesh." The personal skill of emotional redirection is the ability to change our motivation from fear, guilt, and pride (a lifestyle of law) to faith, hope and love (a lifestyle of grace).

Couple Exercises

Here are two exercises that you can do with your mentees.

Exercise 1:

Describe a recent situation in which your feelings were hurt by what someone said or did. What were you feeling at the time (anger, hurt, fear)? Do you have a natural tendency to blame the other person for the way you were feeling to justify or rationalize your response to them? Try to identify the false assumptions you may have been telling yourself after you were offended. Note how much easier it is to blame others rather than identifying our own false assumptions and addressing them.

Exercise 2:

List three to five important issues or topics you would like to discuss with people in your life (at home, on the job, or in the community). Compare those issues to the definition of "core issues," and note how many of our "important issues" in life are really superficial, rather than core issues. *Core issues* are those having to do with a person's basic identity, self-worth, and needs. Regardless of how important the other issues may be, compared to the core issues of a healthy identity and a genuine sense of personal worth, such issues are *superficial*.

Discussion Starters

1) What are some sensitive areas that can be easily hurtful to you? Have you shared these with your spouse?
2) How much time have you spent discussing your "feelings" with your spouse?

Biblical References

1 Peter 4:12, *"Dear friends, do not be surprised at the painful trial you are suffering, as though something strange were happening to you."*

Romans 5:3-5, *"Not only so, but we also rejoice in our sufferings, because we know that suffering produces perseverance; perseverance, character; and character, hope. And hope does not disappoint us,* *because God has poured out his love into our hearts by the Holy Spirit, whom he has given us."*

Romans 8:28, *"And we know that in all things God works for the good of those who love him, who have been called according to his purpose."*

Recommended Resources

Smalley, Gary, and John Trent. *The Blessing*. Nashville, TN: Thomas Nelson, 1986.

Selye, Hans. *The Stress of Life*. New York: McGraw-Hill, 1978.

McMillen, S. I., and David E. Stern. *None of These Diseases: the Bible's Health Secrets for the 21st Century*. Grand Rapids, MI: F.H. Revell, 2000.

Glenn, John. *The Alpha Series: the Gift of Recovery*. Bloomington, IN: AuthorHouse, 2006.

Part 4

MARRIAGE SKILLS & RESPONSIBILITIES

Chapter 6

Communication

Introduction

Communication is the one crucial ingredient that defines a relationship. Communication is essential because it is the link to every aspect of your relationship. The outcome of discussions and decisions about finances, children, careers, religion, and even the expression of feelings and desires will all depend on the communication styles, patterns, and skills you've developed together.

This mentoring session is designed to:

1) Help each person identify the communication style they typically use during times of stress.
2) Teach couples what assertive communication is, and why that style leads to the most vitalized relationships.
3) Teach couples how to actively listen and practice effective communication using the Imago Dialogue.

Common Communication Issues

Couples tend to need improvement in the following assessment areas:

1) Not believing everything their partner says.
2) Making comments that belittle or degrade each other.
3) Having difficulty conveying needs and desires with each other.
4) Having difficulty sharing negative feelings with each other.
5) Not listening to each other well.

6) Getting defensive every time someone disagrees with them.
7) Being more interested in proving who is to blame rather than looking for solutions.

Couples typically resist discussing *negative feelings* because they do not want to create problems or start arguments. Unfortunately, this only facilitates the creation of additional problems and leaves all of them unsolved. As with an untended garden, ignored feelings have a weed-like way of taking over. Eventually, they lead to resentment, disinterest, and a lack of desire to repair the relationship. Spouses who wait too long to discuss what is bothering them gradually become apathetic toward each other.

Develop and Incorporate Your Own Story
Share a few communication techniques that you have learned and how that has benefitted your marriage.

Couple Exercises in Communication
The following two exercises are designed to teach the couple new communication skills.

There are four major communication styles: passive, aggressive, passive-aggressive, and assertive. While the assertive style is usually the most effective of the four, many couples do not use this style as often as they could, resulting in interactions that are frustrating and unsatisfying.

Have the mentees separately complete the following assessment of their individual communication style. Then discuss the results with them.

Exercise 1 - Communications Style Assessment
In the midst of conflict with my partner, I tend to:

Communication Style (Weights)	Always (9)	Often (6)	Sometimes (3)	Rarely (1)	Never (0)
Section 1					
Remain mostly quiet and don't say what I truly feel.					
Look for ways to avoid the other person.					
Be quick to offer an apology.					
Be reluctant to fight for my opposing viewpoint.					
Speak softly and patiently wait for my turn to speak.					
Not make eye contact, or turn away from the other person.					
Feel that the other person's wants or demands are much more important than mine.					
See myself as the cause of the conflict.					
Feel helpless, disrespected, or resentful.					
Fear that I will be rejected.					

Communication Style (Weights)	Always (9)	Often (6)	Sometimes (3)	Rarely (1)	Never (0)
Try to please the other person regardless of how it might impact me personally.					
				TOTAL 1	

Communication Style (Weights)	Always (9)	Often (6)	Sometimes (3)	Rarely (1)	Never (0)
Section 2					
Strongly state my position, feeling that it is typically superior.					
Insult the other person or their opposing point of view.					
Feel competitive and see myself as victorious when I win the argument.					
"Stare down" or look down at the other person.					
Raise my voice with the other person in order to get my point across.					
View my perspective as the best there is.					
Sometimes feel remorse or guilt over the tactics I used to win.					

Communication Style (Weights)	Always (9)	Often (6)	Sometimes (3)	Rarely (1)	Never (0)
View the other person's perspective as silly, ignorant, or unfounded.					
Ignore the other person's desires.					
Take control of the direction the discussion takes.					
Defend my own rights while seeking to win at any cost.					
				TOTAL 2	

Communication Style (Weights)	Always (9)	Often (6)	Sometimes (3)	Rarely (1)	Never (0)
Section 3					
Fail to meet my commitments due to circumstances beyond my control.					
Find it difficult to accept responsibility for disappointing others.					
Feel entitled to get my own way, even if it conflicts with "commitments" I have made to others.					

Communication Style (Weights)	Always (9)	Often (6)	Sometimes (3)	Rarely (1)	Never (0)
Not feel fully responsible for the actions that I take.					
Fear that I would be rejected if I was more assertive.					
Fear confrontation with others.					
Want to get my own way, without having to take too much responsibility.					
Feel resentful over what others expect from me.					
Give in to others quickly, just so I don't have to deal with the issue anymore.					
Indirectly resist their demands by procrastinating or giving a vague or ambiguous response.					
Blame others (or circumstances) for the problem in order to justify my behavior.					
				TOTAL 3	

Communication Style (Weights)	Always (9)	Often (6)	Sometimes (3)	Rarely (1)	Never (0)
Section 4					
Be able to express my wants and feelings confidently, directly, and thoroughly.					
Be open to the other person's perspective, recognizing that they may have insights I haven't yet considered.					
Feel comfortable agreeing to disagree with their perspective.					
Stay relaxed.					
Recognize that the other person's viewpoint can be validly held by them, even if I don't fully agree with it.					
Make eye contact and appropriately maintain it.					
Believe that we both have something valuable to contribute to the discussion, so I give and take.					

Communication Style (Weights)	Always (9)	Often (6)	Sometimes (3)	Rarely (1)	Never (0)
Accept responsibility for what I say and how I say it.					
Feel positive about how I treat others.					
Don't feel I have to "win" the argument all the time.					
Control how I behave, but not try to control my partner's behaviors or feelings.					
				TOTAL **4**	

Total the scores in each section and note the highest score. This is likely to be the person's primary communication style. Discuss the descriptions below with the mentees in order to validate the results.

Total 1 = Passive Style Score
This communication style is characterized by an inability to override the demands of others. The person fails to see the options available to them and instead gives control to others. They avoid giving opinions on both major and minor issues and typically wait for others to give their opinions first. This person may simply agree or change opinions just to suit the other person, but often end up feeling helpless.

Total 2 = Aggressive Style Score
This style is characterized by attempting to get the other person to submit to them through verbal manipulation. They downplay the other's opinion as stupid or wrong. They are critical of the other's point of view and attempt to change others' opinions through intimidation, sarcasm or heated arguments. This style may seemingly

be effective in the short term but often results in resentment and the loss of affection and loyalty from others.

Total 3 = Passive Aggressive Style
This communication style combines elements of both Passive (fear) and Aggressive (anger) styles, *at the same time**. Feeling angry, this person wants to retaliate but fear holds them back from doing it directly. The result is "disguised aggression." They resort to ways of attacking that enable them to not get caught, thus avoiding an open and candid discussion.
* Not to be confused with the person who alternates between passive and aggressive communication styles. The main problem for these people is usually being too passive initially but building up to an explosion of intense anger before reverting back to the passive again.

Total 4 = Assertive Style Score
Assertiveness is a very valuable communication skill. In successful, vitalized couples, both individuals tend to be assertive. Assertive people don't assume their partner can read their minds. They ask specifically and directly for what they want.

> Assertiveness is the ability to ask for what you want and need and express your true feelings.

The goal of the Assertive Style is having relationships that don't deny others or us. It is not a strategy for getting our own way. Being assertive puts you on equal footing with others.

Assertive communication enables people to express themselves in a healthy, non-defensive, and non-insistent manner. It involves asking clearly and directly for what one wants and being positive and respectful in one's communication. Assertive individuals take responsibility for their messages by using "I" statements. They avoid statements beginning with "You." When one partner speaks assertively, it encourages the other person to also respond positively and assertively. When a person is heard and understood, it increases intimacy.

An "I" statement is a fact about your feelings. "I" messages are important because they communicate facts without placing blame and are not likely to promote defensiveness in the receiver. Since "I" messages do not communicate blame, they are more likely to be understood. In contrast, "You" messages create defensiveness because they sound accusatory. For example, think about how you would respond to the following "I" and "You" statements:

"You" statements:

1) "You are so inconsiderate to me in front of your friends!"
2) "You said that you would get the car tuned up and you didn't. You never do what you say you're going to do."

"I" statements:

1) "I feel hurt when I'm put down in front of your friends."
2) "I'm disappointed that the car didn't get tuned up before our trip. I am really worried about the tires, and the oil needs changing. Do you have time to take it to the shop this morning?"

Assertive people express respect for the feelings and opinions of others without necessarily adopting their opinions or doing what they expect or demand.

Assertiveness doesn't mean that you become inconsiderate of the wishes of others, but rather you listen to their wishes and expectations and then decide whether or not to go along with them.

Be aware, however, that it is not necessary to be assertive all the time!

The Active Listening Process
By restating both the content and feelings communicated, the active listening process lets the speaker know whether or not the message sent was clearly understood. Active listeners avoid judgment and criticism and instead listen curiously with the hope of understanding

their partner. Instead of thinking about what they will say next, the active listener tunes into what is being said while remembering they'll have their turn to be the speaker soon enough.

> *Active listening involves listening attentively without interruption and restating (mirroring) what you hear until the speaker is satisfied that they have been heard and understood.*

Although this approach to giving feedback slows down communication, it minimizes misunderstanding and conflict. It also allows the speaker to feel understood and appreciated.

Review the communication styles your mentees use most during times of conflict. Then ask the following questions: Is this different from how you respond when you are not having a difficult conversation? How are you and your partner alike? How are you different?

Exercise 2 - Three Steps to Better Communication – The Imago Dialogue[1]
The Imago Dialogue, or Dialogue as it is also known, was developed by Harville Hendrix, Ph.D. and Helen LaKelly Hunt, Ph.D. It is a three-step process for connection: *Mirroring, Validation, and Empathy.*

In this exercise, mentees practice using the three steps in the Imago Dialogue by sharing a few concerns or issues from their wish list with their partner. See below.

Mirroring
Using "I" language, one person (the Sender) makes a statement that conveys his or her thoughts, feelings, or experiences to the other person (the Receiver) such as: *"I feel," "I love," or "I need."* They are to avoid shaming, blaming, or criticizing their partner, and talk about themselves instead.

In response, the Receiver echoes the Sender's message—by paraphrasing—using a lead-in sentence like, "Let me see if I understood you. What I heard you say is..."

If the receiver correctly restated what the Sender said, the Receiver asks, "Is there more?" After this question is asked, the Receiver should wait for a response to show his sincerity and desire to hear more. Often their partner might say, "Well no...er...let me see...maybe there is." Given more time, they will often go deeper and share more. That sharing can be the most fascinating part of the conversation as deeper feelings are revealed.

The Receiver may want to encourage this by saying, "Wow, that's interesting. Is there more?" The more the Receiver can reassure his partner that he is truly interested in what is being said, the more he can connect with the Sender—even if he finds the subject area challenging or unfamiliar.

When the Sender says, "No, that's all," then the Receiver can re-summarize with, "So, in summary I heard you say..." It is important for the Receiver to check to make sure he understood it all.

When the Receiver mirrors his partner well, the Sender will feel satisfied that her point of view has been received and validated.

Validation

Validation can be challenging, especially if one's partner has a very different perspective on things. To connect as a couple, it's important that your mentees realize and acknowledge that what each has to say makes sense to each other. In this part of the dialogue, creating that connection is paramount. Who is right or wrong is secondary. As many marriage mentors have said, *"You can be right, or you can be married!"* With the Imago process, your mentees might find a solution where it doesn't matter whether either of them are right or wrong on the issue, because the underlying pain is uncovered and can now be addressed.

After the mentee has summarized for his or her partner, they can provide validation by simply saying, *"That makes sense to me."* or *"I understand how you feel."* They don't have to agree, but they should show respect for the other person's reality. Encourage them to use phrases like, *"That makes sense to me because…"*

Empathy
In the empathy step, you want your mentees to imagine what the other may be feeling, such as anger, sadness, loneliness, fear, joy, and so on.

One might ask their partner, *"I imagine you might be feeling afraid and perhaps a little sad too. Is that what you are feeling?"* Then if he or she shares additional emotions, the empathizer should mirror what was said, *"Ah, a little excited too."*

Provide Mentor Feedback
As the mentee couple practices this skill, check for the following.

Did they both:

1) Have a confident posture?
2) Use clear and concise statements?
3) Include a positive point and then get to the point?
4) Discuss one issue at a time?
5) Make good eye contact and use appropriate facial expressions and body language?
6) Use a consistent, relaxed vocal tone?
7) Make good use of "I" statements?
8) Not blame ("You make me feel…") or use absolutes ("You never…")?
9) Wait through periods of silence?

After you try this exercise with your mentees, provide them with feedback on how well they used assertive communication (including good body language), mirroring (active listening skills), validation, and empathy.

How did the mentees feel during this exercise? Did it help them understand each other more and bring them closer?

NOTE: *If you find that your mentees are having a bit of difficulty during this exercise, there may be unresolved resentments that are "leaking out." Explore this with the couple.*

Tips on Discussing Communication
The mentees efforts in developing these skills are worthwhile because they offer many benefits such as:

1) Allowing you to relate to others with less conflict, anxiety and resentment.
2) Allowing you to be more relaxed with others.
3) Helping you focus on the present, rather than allowing your communication to be contaminated by old resentments from the past.
4) Allowing you to retain your self-respect without trampling that of others.
5) Increasing self-confidence by reducing your attempts to live up to unrealistic standards set by others and reducing the need for their approval.
6) Acknowledging the right for others to live their own lives.
7) Giving you more control of your own life. By reducing feelings of helplessness, assertiveness may also diminish feelings of anxiety and depression.

Assertiveness is the only strategy that allows us to fully *be* in the relationship. Unless we intentionally use this skill, our natural response to stressful situations can lead to non-assertive communication. See the chart on page 63.

> *"Assertiveness means that you let others know your thoughts, feelings, or desires about a situation. This is nothing more than being honest with that person but doing so in a way that is not a threat to them or apologizing for making your desires known."*
> ~ Charles Cerling ~

Anxiety and Unassertive Behavior[2]

Encounter Danger

⬇

Response to Perceived Threat

Flee	Fight	Fight by Avoiding	Confront With Poise
⬇	⬇	⬇	⬇
Avoid Conflict at Any Cost	Win at Any Cost	Win by Avoidance	Find Best Solution for All
⬇	⬇	⬇	⬇
Passive Behavior	Aggressive Behavior	Passive-Aggressive Behavior	Assertive Behavior

Tips for Healthy Communication
Share the following tips with your mentees:

1) Give your marriage attention on a daily basis. Give it at least 15 minutes of meaningful dialogue. The focus of this daily dialogue should be on your feelings about each other and your life together.
2) Be a student of your mate. Give your relationship the same priority and attention you gave it when you were first dating—ask lots of questions.
3) Be willing to *self-disclose.*[3] Share your innermost thoughts and most private experiences.
4) Seek counsel if communication problems persist. Don't allow them to become more serious.

More Tips from Observing Great Communicators

1) *Don't jump to conclusions.* A key part of active listening is not drawing premature conclusions about the person or what they are saying.

2) *Don't interrupt.* Talking doesn't help you understand the other person's perspective. You'll learn more if you don't keep interjecting your own ideas.

3) *Seek to know more.* If you ask questions about what you heard, you'll get more complete information. Draw the other person out. Asking questions demonstrates that you care and are carefully listening.

4) *Choose to listen carefully.* It's natural for your mind to wander, but whenever you notice that happening reconnect and resume listening. With practice, you can train yourself to get back "in the moment."

5) *Recognize gender differences.* Body language usually differs by gender. Men tend to stare as they listen and nod to signify they understand. Women may nod to encourage the speaker to keep talking when they don't yet understand.

The Impact of Communication on Intimacy

The following table shows how the different communication styles impact intimacy in a marriage.

Communication Styles and Levels of Intimacy[4]				
Communication Style				
Person A	**Person B**	**Relationship**	**Who wins?**	**Level of Intimacy**
Passive	Passive	Devitalized	Both lose	Low
Passive	Aggressive	Dominating	I win, you lose	Low
Aggressive	Aggressive	Conflicted	Both lose	Low
Assertive	Passive	Frustrated	Both lose	Low
Assertive	Aggressive	Confrontational	Both lose	Low
Assertive	Assertive	Vitalized/ Growing	Both WIN	HIGH

SOURCE: Life Innovations

Discussion Starters

1) Has your partner been a very good listener and been able to easily express his or her feelings about sensitive issues?
2) If it has been difficult to share your feelings with your partner, what are some things you could do to improve communication?
3) What could your partner do (or not do) to enable you to feel heard? What prevents you from finding good resolutions to your differences?
4) Do you typically feel understood while discussing problems?
5) Is it usually easy for you to ask others for what you want?

Biblical References

Colossians 4:6a, *"Let your conversation be always full of grace..."*

Matthew 12:35-37, *"The good man brings good things out of the good stored up in him, and the evil man brings evil things out of the evil stored up in him. But I tell you that men will have to give account on the Day of Judgment for every careless word they have spoken."*

Ephesians 4:29, *"Do not let any unwholesome talk come out of your mouths, but only what is helpful for building others up according to their needs, that it may benefit those who listen."*

Proverbs 18:13, *"He, who answers before listening— that is his folly and his shame."*

Proverbs 10:19, *"When words are many, sin is not absent, but he who holds his tongue is wise."*

Proverbs 17:27, *"A truly wise person uses few words; a person with understanding is even-tempered." (NLT)*

James 3:10, *"And so blessing and cursing come pouring out of the same mouth. Surely, my brothers and sisters, this is not right!" (NLT)*

Recommended Resources

Burke, H. Dale. *Different by Design: God's Master Plan for Harmony between Men and Women in Marriage*. Chicago: Moody, 2000.

McNulty, James K., and Benjamin R. Karney. "Positive Expectations in the Early Years of Marriage: Should Couples Expect the Best or Brace for the Worst?" *Journal of Personality and Social Psychology* 86.5 (2004): 729-43.

Parrott, Les, and Leslie L. Parrott. *Saving Your Marriage before It Starts: Seven Questions to Ask Before--and After-- You Marry*, Grand Rapids. MI: Zondervan, 2006.

Stanley, Scott. *A Lasting Promise: a Christian Guide to Fighting for Your Marriage*. San Francisco: Jossey-Bass, 1998.

Townsend, John Sims. *Who's Pushing Your Buttons?: Handling the Difficult People in Your Life*. Nashville, TN: Integrity, 2004.

Wright, H. Norman. *Communication: Key to Your Marriage: a Practical Guide to Creating a Happy, Fulfilling Relationship*. Ventura, CA: Regal, 2000.

Chapter 7

Conflict Resolution[1]

Introduction
It's not the absence of conflict that defines a good marriage, but rather how conflict is handled and resolved. This chapter looks at the couple's ability to discuss and resolve differences. It also measures how effectively they are able to communicate opinions, ideas, and feelings with their partner—even during times of stress or conflict.

This mentoring session is designed to:

1) Help the couple understand the value that conflict can bring to a relationship, if it is handled constructively.
2) Help the couple identify conflicts that need to be discussed and resolved.
3) Provide a series of steps that they can use in working towards solutions of major or chronic issues.

Common Issues Regarding Conflict Resolution
Couples tend to need improvement in the following assessment areas:

1) One partner not taking disagreements seriously.
2) Having major disputes over unimportant issues.
3) Some differences never getting resolved.
4) One person tending to give in too quickly just to end arguments.
5) Partners disagreeing on the best way to resolve differences.

Develop and Incorporate Your Own Story

Share a (major) conflict that you experienced in your marriage, how you constructively handled it, and how that experience strengthened your marriage commitment.

Tips to Assist in Topic Discussing Conflict Resolution

Share the following truths about conflict with your couple:

1) Conflict is natural in all human relationships, including marriage. Occasional conflict in marriage is both normal and inevitable. Since we all have a sin nature, expect it. How a couple handles conflict (submitting to the flesh or the Spirit) determines whether it harms their relationship or helps it to grow.

2) Most marital conflict is not dealt with constructively, because most people haven't been taught *how* to effectively deal with conflict.

3) Unresolved conflict may go "underground," but it will grow and show up elsewhere in the relationship. The more people try to avoid or hide from conflict, the bigger the problem becomes.

4) Unresolved conflict in areas of major importance to one or both partners results in a less satisfying marriage.

5) How a couple responds to conflict will determine if it helps produce deeper intimacy or becomes a bigger problem.

6) If a couple wants conflict to play a constructive role in their marriage, developing strong conflict resolution skills must be a priority for both partners. Couples who learn conflict resolution skills before marriage reduce the risk of divorce by up to 50%.[2]

7) Forgiveness is essential. The ongoing practice of seeking forgiveness and being forgiving is essential to a healthy, Christ-centered marriage.

8) In the early years of marriage, it takes courage to take the risk of engaging in constructive conflict in order to establish and develop trust with each other.

The approach a couple takes to resolve conflict will affect the outcome. The more constructive the approach they take, the greater the probability of success.

Conflict Resolution Tactics

Share the following tactics with your mentees:

1) Separate yourself from the situation and take time to think through your anger. Then you will be able to discuss the issue with more clarity. Thinking through anger is very different from suppressing anger. Clarify your own thoughts, feelings and, preferences. Ask, "What's the real issue here?" and, "What do I want to see changed?"

2) Focus on what you desire from the relationship and how that can be achieved. In the "Win-Win" situation, needs are met on both sides. It doesn't necessarily mean compromising. Sometimes compromising creates a quick-fix solution where no one is pleased with the outcome. Furthermore, important issues may be overlooked.

3) Don't negotiate in moments of anger, fatigue, hunger, low blood sugar, etc.

4) Focus solely on the current and relevant issue.

5) Deal with the root issues, rather than just the event that took place. To get to the root issue, ask a few times, "Why do you feel that way?"

6) Be intentional about identifying the source of your feelings and then discuss it calmly and confidently with your spouse.

7) Just as with a physical illness or mechanical problem, the sooner you treat the problem, the easier it will be to fix it. While problems rarely go away with time (they often get worse), timing is everything. Don't ignore the early warning signs that your relationship needs attention.

8) Recognize and acknowledge that problems are rarely the fault of only one person.

9) Share both negative and positive feelings.

10) Be approachable. Help the other person feel understood when they raise an issue. Behave in a way that encourages sharing of feelings and opinions during disagreements.

11) Work towards finding common ground while also accepting that you will not agree on everything. Forbearance (restraint with patience) is an act of love.

12) Take disagreements seriously and give them the attention they deserve.

13) Speak the truth in a loving manner. Working through conflict successfully takes honest and truthful communication done in a loving manner. Remember to examine your motives. Would you be able to receive it if someone came to you in this manner? Love is a very considerate awareness of the other person's emotions and identity.

14) Deal with anger and hurt proactively. Don't deny it, suppress it, or let it turn to bitterness.

We strongly suggest that you end each fight with asking for and granting forgiveness and doing some act of love together.

Steps for Resolving Couple Conflict

When you have an issue that isn't solved through communication alone, go through the steps below. For minor issues, you can move through the steps fairly quickly. However, for emotionally-charged, difficult issues, you should move through the steps slowly and deliberately.

1) Pick a good time and place to have the discussion.
2) Pray about the situation.
3) Define the problem or issue of disagreement.
4) Discuss how each of you contributes to the problem.
5) Brainstorm several possible ways to resolve the conflict.
6) Discuss and evaluate the pros and cons for each of these possible solutions.
7) Summarize, compromise, prioritize, and then agree upon a plan of action to try.
8) Discuss and agree on how you both will work towards making this solution work.
9) Set a date and time to evaluate how well the selected solution has worked. Revise your approach if necessary.
10) Reward each other as you each contribute to resolving the problem.

NOTE: *If you continue to have difficulty or cannot find a way to solve the issues on your own, seek counsel from an elder, minister, mentor, godly friend, or Christian counselor.*

Understanding the Good in Conflict
Is a relationship better without conflict? Not at all! While couples prefer to have minimal conflict, occasional confrontation, when handled well, affords an opportunity to grow closer by working together, learning from one another, and building a stronger love for each other. A relationship without conflict may indicate the couple is avoiding important issues needing discussion. Having a goal to minimize conflict is healthy with the understanding that when conflict does arise, you can develop methods to work through it to strengthen your relationship.

Be Quick to Hear
As you work through differences, keep in mind your partner desires to be heard and understood as much as you do. Most quarrels will have positive results simply by using assertive communication and active listening skills. Listening and trying to understand your partner is a practical way to show love and honor, and gives credence to the conversation.

Be Slow to Speak
Words spoken in haste during a dispute can wound one's feelings very easily. Later, we may regret the cruel words. Unfortunately, they cannot be retracted once said. Keep in mind, once you say something hurtful, you also damage yourself. Our desire to express our angry feelings with angry words is not a proper method to handle frustration. Words spoken in anger and haste are neither of God nor are they beneficial.

Rate Your Level of Anger/Tension from 1 to 10
Please see the scale below. As our tension level goes up, our ability to think clearly and solve problems effectively *goes down*. Many couples try to work through their most difficult problems when they are in the High Conflict Zone! These types of conversations often fail to produce the desired results.

71

If your level of hostility is in the Elevated Conflict Zone (8-10), don't try to resolve the problems at that point in time. Attempt to calm down by praying and seeking God's peace and direction, walking or exercising, journaling your feelings, and taking deep breaths. If you think you are in the Modest Encounter Zone (4-7), be aware that you may rapidly transition into the Elevated Conflict Zone. Proceed with extreme caution. In an ideal world, we would communicate to each other from the Tranquil/Passive Zone (1-3) with prayer and our partner's forgiveness in mind.

0 1 2 3	Tranquil/Passive Zone
4 5 6 7	Modest Encounter Zone
8 9 10	Elevated Conflict Zone

SOURCE: Adapted from Apostolic Christian Counseling and Family Services

Slow to Wrath
When disagreements occur, take the time to pray! Seek God's wisdom in rendering your feelings correctly. Try to sympathize with your spouse when revealing your feelings.

Anger is often called a "secondary emotion" because it is the result of another issue. When you are perturbed by something, try to recognize which of the following classifications ignited the annoyance:

1) Expressive harm (e.g. humiliation, feeling of refusal, disgrace)
2) Aggravation
3) Terror
4) Bodily pain
5) Unfairness or wrongdoing (e.g. virtuous irritation)

When you notice any of the above affecting your reactions, try to find ways to resolve the conflict in a Christ-honoring manner. Calming down, taking time to pray, and talking through conflict can usually resolve it. However, if you continue having difficulty working through the conflict on your own, don't hesitate to seek support and guidance from an elder, minister, mentor, counselor, or godly friend.

Avoid the Extremes!

Some individuals are "conflict avoidant" in their relationship. While they may avoid conflicts, they may also shun discussion of important topics that affect the spiritual, emotional, and relationship issues. Conversely, those partners who are "conflicted/argumentative" usually initiate arguments using harsh and unkind words.

Jesus provided us with a perfect example for dealing with conflict. Sometimes He was silent or said few words, while other times, He spoke quite firmly and directly. A great example is in John 8:7 when the Pharisees brought in a woman caught in adultery. *"... When they kept on questioning him, he straightened up and said to them, 'If any one of you is without sin, let him be the first to throw a stone at her.'"* Additional examples of Jesus' approach to conflict resolution can be found in John 8 and in other portions of Scripture.

Examples of Destructive Behaviors During Conflict

There are several types of conflict that you should be aware of and avoid. One researcher calls them the *"Four Horsemen of the Apocalypse."*[3]

1) *Criticism or Escalation* – occurs when spouses verbally spar with negative comments, slurs, and hostile words about character or personality. As the hostile conversation continues, so does the anger and frustration.

2) *Contempt or Invalidation* – occurs when one partner directly or indirectly puts down the thoughts, feelings, integrity, or personality of the other. These are words or gestures that show your spouse you are aghast and distraught with him or her. Examples of this would include: scorn, cynicism, mockery, name-calling, sarcasm, rolling your eyes, and so forth.

3) *Defensiveness or Negative interpretations* – occurs when one partner believes the other person is harboring hidden motivations inconsistent with their words. Instead of using active listening and assertive communication skills, defensiveness involves blaming your spouse and criticizing his or her behavior, opinions, and so on.

4) *Stonewalling or Withdrawal and avoidance* – occurs when one or both of the spouses refuse to continue the conversation. Withdrawing involves "retreating" and trying to get out of a conversation, whereas avoidance is preventing the discussion from starting._Stonewalling includes not saying anything or giving your spouse the "silent treatment."

When to Seek Outside Help

If unsuccessful attempts have been made to solve a conflict, or if negotiations have significantly broken down, or if partners are exhausted from the physical and emotional strain of their differences, then it might be time to enlist the help of a person to intercede and help bring resolution and reconciliation between partners. Other reasons to seek outside help include:

1) Feeling physically unsafe.
2) Feeling verbally assaulted or emotionally betrayed.
3) Fighting repeatedly about the same issue.
4) Either of you are taking your anger out on the children.
5) Either of you are using your children for emotional support.
6) Frequent threats of abandonment or divorce.
7) Feeling you want out of the marriage or considering cheating on your spouse.
8) Being sexually disinterested for a prolonged period.

"Verbal and physical abuse are never acceptable and should not be tolerated in a marriage. These types of abuse are sinful and by striking at the very heart of the marriage, they provide Satan with an opportunity to destroy the marriage. While physical abuse causes visible bruises, emotional abuse crushes the spirit. Examples of emotional abuse include a chronic pattern of using hurtful words, anger outbursts, silence, isolation, threats, etc. to control and manipulate another person. If emotional and/or physical abuses occur in your relationship, seek professional help immediately." [4,5]

Couple Exercises

Review the following information. Then do the couple exercises that follow.

Avoiding the Petitioner-Disengager Cycle

Couples often have dissimilar opinions as to what is the most effective method to resolve conflict. Many times the wife wants to discuss problems right away, while the husband wants time to think about it and talk later. This often leads to the petitioner-disengager cycle.

For example, a wife wants to talk about why the husband has been out of town on business so much. She says, "Why does your job require you to be out of town so much? You never have time to help me around here." He says he wants to talk about it later and goes into another room. This causes the wife to become more irritated and anxious. She follows him, bombarding him with a barrage of additional questions. He has a negative response to the continued questions as he may now see it as criticism or an attack. The husband feels challenged, becomes angry, and shouts, "I work hard all day and this is all the thanks I get!" He then leaves the room.

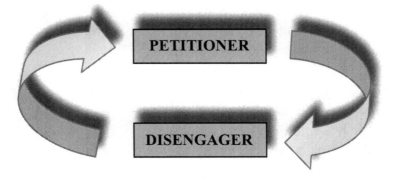

Who "causes" the petitioner-disengager cycle? The petitioner or the disengager? In reality, both do. When the petitioner puts pressure on the disengager to talk when he or she is not ready, the disengager withdraws. Because the husband, in this case, didn't attempt to address the problem right away, the wife became worried that either the problem was in actuality much more serious than she thought or he simply didn't care about her problems.

To avoid this cycle, the couple needs to be respectful of each other by doing the following:

1) Be careful not to be aggressive. If you tend to be a petitioner, be sensitive to your partners' need to be "disengaged" for the moment. Instead of pressing with questions, try to set a time and place you both agree upon to discuss the issue. Then use brainstorming techniques to identify approaches that may help resolve the concern.

2) Be careful not to withdraw without offering your spouse a time when you will be open to discuss the issue. If you tend to be a disengager, you need to let your partner know that you are interested in what he or she wants to say, but now isn't a good time. *However*, negotiate a time in the near future (after dinner, before bedtime, tomorrow, etc.) when both of you can talk out and address the issue.

Exercise 1: Conflict Resolution Styles
Couples often fall into patterns of dealing with conflict that do not change regardless of what they argue about.

1) *Petitioners* – seek to create connections so they can become more intimate and close. They tend to feel rejected if their partner wants more space which leads them to pursue closeness more intensely.

2) *Disengagers* – tend to be emotionally distant and have difficulty showing vulnerability and dependency. They manage stress by retreating into their own world and may terminate a relationship when things become too intense. Disengagers are less likely to open up emotionally when they feel they are being pursued.

How do you see yourself and your partner regarding the two conflict resolution styles just mentioned?

Self: _____   Spouse: _____

How does that manifest itself during times of conflict?

76

Exercise 2: Sensitive Communications

When conflict occurs, be careful how and when you talk to each other. Research shows conversation outcomes are predictable nearly 96% of the time during the first three minutes.[6] Using unkind words at the outset of the discussion can be catastrophic and ruin any conflict resolution. You can avoid this dilemma by simply following the example in James 1:19-20 example, *"My dear brothers, take note of this: Everyone should be quick to listen, slow to speak and slow to become angry, for man's anger does not bring about the righteous life that God desires."*

Think about how you are likely to respond to the situations listed below and discuss your feelings with each other. Is your response likely to be destructive or constructive in deepening a sense of oneness in your relationship?

1) You have just arrived home from work. You are recounting a conversation that you had with your boss that left you very upset. Right in the middle of it, your spouse asks, "Did you bring in the mail?"

2) You are mowing the yard. Your spouse asks you to go to the store for some milk when you really just want to finish mowing.

3) You had another heated discussion about your difficult financial situation and the high level of debt that you have together. Soon after, you find that your spouse has purchased a non-budgeted item again.

4) You notice that whenever you have something important or confrontational to discuss, your spouse yawns, is easily distracted and seems disinterested.

5) It seems that your spouse has difficulty picking up and putting away his or her things. You wonder if they notice the things left on the floor beside the bed.

Discussion Starters

1) When you were growing up, how was conflict handled by your parents? Do you agree with the approach they took? Why or why not?

2) What approach do you typically use for resolving disagreements with your partner?

3) When you discuss differences, are you able to clearly see the underlying heart issues involved?

4) Do you see yourself as more of a *"Petitioner"* or a *"Disengager?"* Does your partner agree?

5) When you are upset, are you more likely to want to solve the problem right away, or do you need extra time to think about it?

6) Do you prefer to keep quiet in order to avoid hurting each other?

7) When you argue, do you usually end up feeling responsible for the problem?

8) How does it make you feel to leave your differences unresolved?

9) How do you think Ephesians 4:26 (*"In your anger do not sin. Do not let the sun go down while you are still angry,"*) applies to you as a couple?

10) What topics do you avoid because you fear causing further conflict or hurt feelings? What needs to be done in order to resolve these lingering issues in a healthy manner?

11) What types of things get your anger or tension level into the High Conflict Zone? What can you do to calm down? How will you each stay aware of what zone you are in?

12) As the spiritual leader of the home, what responsibility do husbands have in making sure that marital conflicts and problems are properly addressed? What is the wife's responsibility in this?

Biblical References
1 Corinthians 7:28, *"...those who marry will face many troubles in this life..."*

Ephesians 4:26, *"In your anger do not sin": Do not let the sun go down while you are still angry..." NOTE: The timing for resolving conflict is given as guidance; this is not a legalistic requirement!*

Ephesians 4:29, *"Do not let any unwholesome talk come out of your mouths, but only what is helpful for building others up according to their needs, that it may benefit those who listen.."*

Proverbs 12:18, *"Reckless words pierce like a sword, but the tongue of the wise brings healing."*

Proverbs 15:1, *"A gentle answer turns away wrath, but a harsh word stirs up anger..."*

Chapter 8

Granting Forgiveness - What It Is, What It Isn't, and How to Do It Well[1]

Introduction

Some have said that the three most important phrases spoken in life are: "I love you," "I'm sorry," and "I forgive you." While forgiveness is a central concept in Christianity and all successful human relationships, many people find it to be a confusing and difficult process.

Many assume that if they forgive someone they are letting the other person "off the hook," even while continuing to suffer the consequences of their uncaring actions.

Common Issues Regarding Forgiveness

1) Individuals being haunted by bitterness from past offenses against them.
2) Individuals being unable to forgive themselves for past sins or actions.
3) Unwillingness to address past issues that continue to hinder intimacy in the couple's relationship.

Develop and Incorporate Your Own Story

How has forgiveness been a part of your marriage or life? Select a challenging situation that you faced in your marriage or family. Share how you were able to get to a point of forgiveness and restoration with your mentees.

Tips for Discussing Forgiveness

Common Misperceptions About Forgiveness[2]

Some people believe forgiveness must be requested before it can be granted. Actually, forgiveness can be given to someone who is no longer living, to someone who doesn't acknowledge any harm was done, or to someone who only acknowledges a portion of the severity of the transgression. *Forgiveness* only requires one person while *reconciliation* requires two cooperating parties.

By forgiving someone, you are not simply "getting over it." Some of the transgressions you may have experienced are very serious and cannot be simply overlooked.

Some people *incorrectly* believe that forgiveness:

1) Denies the seriousness of the sinful offense.
2) Lets people "off the hook" too easily.
3) Places too much responsibility on the victim.
4) Automatically heals the pain.

However, *true* forgiveness:[3]

1) Acknowledges that a wrong has occurred.
2) Recognizes that the wrong has created an obligation for repayment from the offender.
3) Recognizes that sometimes the offender can't provide adequate compensation for the hurt.
4) Realizes that revenge—although a natural desire—isn't a godly or healthy solution.
5) Releases the debt of the offender as an act of obedience to God.

Forgiveness Is Not:

1) *Forgetting.* One does not completely forget an offense when forgiving. Christ-like forgiveness means that we will not hold anger, bitterness, or hostility "over the person's head." Instead of literally trying to forget an offense, the goal is to be released from the unhealthy emotional grip that it has on you.

2) *Pardoning.* Pardoning is a legal term that means to release from punishment or to not punish for some crime or offense.

3) *Reconciling.* Reconciling is the process whereby two people take steps to rebuild a relationship that has been damaged or injured. Reconciliation is the work that both people, the offender and the offended, do to restore a broken relationship.

4) *Excusing the offense.* Forgiveness does not give the offender the right to offend again. Healthy boundaries are important so that we do not simply allow another person's hurtful or sinful actions to continue.

5) *Trusting.* Trust isn't a prerequisite for forgiveness. Trust is earned over time, and the person who committed the offense must accept that regaining trust will not always be immediate.

6) *A feeling.* Forgiveness isn't based on a feeling. You can't wait until you feel better or you feel the other person is truly sorry. Rather, forgiveness is an act of obedience through which God can guide us.

7) *Dependent on time.* A phrase that is sometimes quoted about relationship hurts is, "Time heals all wounds." This just isn't true! We should more accurately say, "Time plus forgiveness leads to the healing of wounds."

Forgiveness Is:

1) *Extended with grace.* God demonstrated the ultimate grace-giving act when He initiated the forgiveness and reconciliation process with us (Romans 5:6; Ephesians 2:4-5). Forgiveness is what one person can choose to give to another. Granting forgiveness may *feel* unfair because those that need to be forgiven don't necessarily "deserve" forgiveness. The one who offended may not have the repentance and remorse necessary to *receive* the forgiveness, but that fact does not preclude the *granting* of forgiveness.

2) *An intentional decision and a process.* We must make a choice to commit to the process of forgiveness. This process is empowered by the Holy Spirit and takes time to work through.

Both parts, making a choice to forgive and committing to the forgiveness process over time, are necessary.

3) *Hard work and multifaceted.* Forgiveness has emotional, relational, spiritual, and physiological components. It involves changing our attitudes, behaviors, feelings, and beliefs. Forgiveness allows us to experience the "emotion" of release when we think of the transgression.

4) *A releasing of a debt.* Forgiveness is often the only way to settle a debt. We choose to release the debtor from his or her debt. This choice also releases us from holding on to bitterness, resentment, or anger. Any of which could hinder our walk with the Lord (Hebrews 12:1-2).

Steps to Forgiveness[5]

1) *Recall the hurt.* The first step to forgiveness involves acknowledging the hurt or wrong. The goal of this step is to accept that you have been wronged, because only then can you begin the process of moving forward. To either deny the pain or to obsessively replay the event in your head will create an emotional barrier that you cannot move past.

2) *Empathize.* In this step, negative feelings such as anger are replaced with empathy. Here, one tries to see the scenario from the other person's perspective. Try to imagine how the other person may have been thinking or feeling. You're not trying to make excuses for them or condone their behavior in any way. Understand that the more horrific the transgression was, the more difficult it is to show empathy. When empathy is too difficult, first try sympathy. For example, you can think, "How horrible it must be to have a conscience so seared that he could have done..."[6]

Although empathy and sympathy are often used interchangeably there is a subtle difference. To empathize is responding to another person's perceived emotional state by experiencing similar feelings. Sympathy is simply a concern for the other person.

---

3) *Commit to forgive.* Make a heroic commitment to forgive and set an "Ebenezer" to remember it by. An Ebenezer is a marker or memorial as described in 1 Samuel 7:12. It reminds us that God has helped us to get to this point. This is most effective if you tell someone else (e.g. the person who wronged you, your spouse, a friend, a minister, etc.) about your commitment to forgive. You need to be able to revisit your commitment when painful memories from the past come up again. Consider writing out the offense on a piece of paper, crumpling it up, and throwing it away.

4) *Stick with the process.* You may need to forgive and repent from your judgment many times each day before forgiveness is complete. You will know forgiveness is complete when you think of that person without bitterness and with unconditional love.

5) *Repent from judging the individual.* The root behind unforgiveness is judgment, and if we don't repent of it, our forgiveness will be superficial and incomplete.

6) *Bless the person you are working to forgive.* Pray blessings over them as the Holy Spirit guides you. It will become hard to hold on to unforgiveness when you are praying this way.

The High Cost of Unforgiveness and Bitterness

The benefits of forgiveness are clear. By following God's example and command, you are provided hope and healing. Conversely, unforgiveness has many detrimental effects. Bitterness is a common result of a refusal to forgive. Holding on to past hurts and refusing to forgive causes damage to oneself. In addition, bitterness can damage the people closest to us.

1) *Spiritual consequences of not forgiving* – Bitterness is the most common spiritual result of being unforgiving. The Bible warns against bitterness (Job 10) and the spiritual damage that results when we harbor bitterness in our lives. Hindering our walk with God is often the most obvious result.

2) *Emotional and relational consequences of not forgiving* – Unforgiveness is like drinking poison and expecting the other

person to die. Bitterness eats away like a cancer in the person who holds it. When we refuse to forgive, we spread the poison to other relationships as well—even those unassociated with the one who wronged us.

Steps to Reconciliation[7]

Reconciliation testifies of God's power and of the power of unity in the Body of Christ. Restoring a relationship after an offense takes two cooperating parties. It can only occur when the two parties agree on each of the steps towards reconciliation. Reconciliation involves restoring a relationship to the degree that it can be. Below are some of the ingredients necessary for rebuilding trust that allows reconciliation to occur.

1) *Repentance.* The first step is repentance. The offender must be willing to confess the transgression and acknowledge the pain it caused the offended. In addition, he or she must have a sincere desire to turn from the circumstances that led to the offense. Genuine repentance is evidenced by a change in behavior.

2) *Restitution.* When the one who did the wrong attempts to make the wrong as right as possible, it validates the sincerity of his or her repentance. When the one wronged participates in the restitution process, not for vengeance but for justice, it allows reconciliation to take place.

3) *Rehabilitation.* Rehabilitation may be necessary in order for the individual who did the wrong to return to a better way of life. This is especially true if he or she has fallen into a pattern of unhealthy and ungodly living. This step helps to provide us with assurance that the offender has truly changed.

Learning to Forgive Yourself

At times, individuals struggle most with forgiving themselves. Even after they have confessed, repented, and asked for forgiveness from God, they may know intellectually that God has forgiven them, but may still *feel* unforgiven and condemned due to shame and guilt. Some condemn themselves believing God could not or would not forgive them.

Satan is the accuser of God's people (Revelation 12:10). Satan's attempts at accusation should not be mistaken for the Holy Spirit's conviction (e.g. true guilt). Don't underestimate the extent of God's love and forgiveness. Walking through the steps below may help you with self-forgiveness.

1) *Trust the Word of God more than your emotions.* Read through Scriptures about God's forgiveness, and by faith, believe they are true even when your feelings don't confirm it. For example, 1 John 1:9 says, *"If we confess our sins, he is faithful and just and will forgive us our sins and purify us from all unrighteousness..."* Choose to believe it is true, even if you don't immediately feel like it is.

2) *Don't fight alone.* Talk to a family member, friend, mentor, or Christian counselor who understands forgiveness and who can help support and pray for you as you work through this.

3) *Accept that you are imperfect and that you will make mistakes during your life on earth.*[8] While each of us desires to live a life that is free from errors and offenses, we don't always do it. Thankfully, we can remember that God understands. The words of Psalm 103:13-14 can bring us comfort: *"As a father has compassion on his children, so the LORD has compassion on those who fear him; for he knows how we are formed, he remembers that we are dust."*

4) *Don't delay getting help.* At times, clinical depression, perfectionism, or other emotional issues result in self-condemnation and an inability to move on. Seeking advice from a minister or Christian counselor will help you discover barriers to self-forgiveness and tools to overcome them.

Couple Exercises to Facilitate Forgiveness

Identify one area where you recently offended your partner and where you haven't yet asked for or granted forgiveness. Apply the steps of asking for and granting forgiveness.

Discussion Starters

1) How easy or difficult is it for you to forgive an offense by your partner?
2) What does it take in order for you to be willing to forgive someone?
3) Are you currently holding any grudges between each other? With other people?

Biblical References

Luke 17:3-4, *"If your brother sins, rebuke him, and if he repents, forgive him. If he sins against you seven times in a day, and seven times comes back to you and says, 'I repent,' forgive him."*

Luke 23:34a, *"Jesus said, "Father, forgive them, for they do not know what they are doing."*

Colossians 3:13, *"Bear with each other and forgive whatever grievances you may have against one another. Forgive as the Lord forgave you."*

Daniel 9:9, *"The Lord our God is merciful and forgiving, even though we have rebelled against him."*

Matthew 18:21-22, *"Then Peter came to Jesus and asked, 'Lord, how many times shall I forgive my brother when he sins against me? Up to seven times?' Jesus answered, 'I tell you, not seven times, but seventy-seven times.'"*

Recommended Resources

Kendall, Jackie. *Free Yourself to Love: the Liberating Power of Forgiveness*. New York: Faith Words, 2009

Shriver, Gary, and Shriver, Mona, *Unfaithful: Rebuilding Trust After Infidelity*, David C. Cook Publishing, 2005.

Chapter 9

Dealing With Your Partner's Unique Traits - Partner Styles and Habits

Introduction

Many couples in marriage therapy complain about their partners strange and annoying habits. We all have a few peculiar traits and behaviors that may be hard for our partners to tolerate. Our partners have their own unique idiosyncrasies that often leave us puzzled. There is a Russian expression that says, *"Everyone goes crazy in his own way."* So what are these peculiar, crazy ways that perplex us, and how can we deal with them lovingly?

Personality theorist, Carl Rodgers, offers some insight on the importance of how we see ourselves *(self-image)*.[1] While our self-image may differ from the way others see us *(other's image)*, both may be different from the way we really are *(real-image)*. Rodgers suggested that the inner turmoil and conflict that leads to personal and relational dysfunction is a result of our self image being different from that of others or who we really are (see Figure 1).

Images

Figure 1²

This mentoring session is designed to:

1) Help us understand where habits and personal styles originate.
2) Look at each person's style and habits as expressed in their behavior.
3) Provide a series of steps that can be used to help mentees understand their partners' habits and style.

Common Issues Regarding Partner Styles and Habits

Couples tend to need improvement in the following areas:

1) Criticizing each other for their individual style and habits.
2) Becoming impatient with each other's habits and trying to change the other person.
3) Having difficulty conveying respect for their partner.
4) Feeling that "If you are unlike me, then there is something wrong with you."

Develop and Incorporate Your Own Story

What were some of the funny (and also annoying) habits that you discovered after you got married? How did you deal with them?

Tips on Discussing Personal Styles and Habits

Some individuals joyfully proclaim, "I am married to my best friend," and rightfully so. A bonded, supportive, and loving friendship in which we are valued, respected, desired, liked, and loved helps us live up to our potential and cope more effectively with life's challenges. Yet, once we develop true intimacy, we may begin to take it for granted and risk losing its benefits.

Research on social connectedness confirms that people who have friends fare better both emotionally and physically and live longer than those who do not have close friendships.

One study done by Erin York Cornwell and Linda J. Waite confirms, *"Social disconnectedness is associated with worse physical health, regardless of whether it prompts feelings of loneliness or a perceived lack of social support."*[3]

One of the essential elements in a good relationship is true friendship in which both parties are accepted and honored for who they are (thoughts, feelings, and actions). Acceptance of a mate requires recognizing your differences and choosing to still cherish them. This creates safety for ones partner to thrive and the freedom to reciprocate.

As couples get to know each other better, they sometimes begin to feel, "If you are unlike me, then there is something wrong with you." When we hold fast to the belief that the way we are, feel, and act is the "only" acceptable way, we are prone to criticize and disparage our partner. Negative judgments and disapproval distance us from empathy and love for our mate.

Acceptance is an essential ingredient of every friendship. It is propelled by curiosity and fascination with the other's being. Acceptance holds another person as precious, even when he or she is feeling, thinking, or acting differently than we do. Acceptance views a person's occasional errors as normal occurrences rather than signs of a character flaw.

Being accepting requires solid loyalty to ones mate, even when he or she has just disappointed you. An accepting attitude minimizes their embarrassing, clumsy, or annoying ways and highlights and affirms the good and beauty in the other person.

It's important to respond to your partner's disappointments, hurts, and insecurities as you would wish them to respond to yours during your weaker moments. Respond with kindness, compassion, and unwavering appreciation and support.

Couple Exercises
Discuss the following with your mentee couple:

Exercise 1:

1) What kind of things or people do you identify with to describe who you are?
2) What is it about your self image that is so important?
3) What is the purpose of each characteristic?

Exercise 2:
Read Ecclesiastes Chapters 1 and 2. Summarize what King Solomon did to achieve satisfaction (The "Solomon Syndrome").[4]

1) What was his conclusion?
2) What are false assumptions?
3) Describe self-centered behavior?
4) Why is a false goal false?
5) To what extent is the "Solomon Syndrome" present in your life?

Discussion Starters

1) What habits do you find most annoying in your partner?
2) If those habits never change, would you be okay with it?
3) Is your partner your "best friend?" If so, why?

Biblical References
Matthew 7:12, *"So in everything, do to others what you would have them do to you, for this sums up the Law and the Prophets."*

Galatians 5:22-23, *"But the fruit of the Spirit is love, joy, peace, forbearance, kindness, goodness, faithfulness, gentleness and self-control. Against such things there is no law."*

Luke 6:31, *"Do to others as you would have them do to you."*

Ecclesiastes Chapters 1, 2 also provide insights into habits.

Recommended Resources
Glenn, John. *The Alpha Series: the Gift of Recovery.* Bloomington, IN: Author House, 2006.

Lewis, C. S., *Mere Christianity: a Revised and Amplified Edition, with a New Introduction, of the Three Books, Broadcast Talks, Christian Behavior, and Beyond Personality.* New York: HarperCollins, 2001.

Chapter 10

Financial Management

"There is nothing wrong with men possessing riches. The wrong comes when riches possess men."
~ Billy Graham ~

Introduction

Money is important! It is spoken about over 2,300 times in the Bible and Jesus spoke about money more often than Heaven and Hell combined. We spend 80% of our waking hours earning, spending, and thinking about money.

This section discusses the couple's opinions about savings, debt, handling money, and making short and long term financial decisions.

Money can provide some security, be used to help others in need, be invested in spreading the Gospel, and be invested wisely. It can also be addictive, become a destructive wedge between a husband and wife, be handled foolishly, be wasted, and provide a false sense of security.

As Winston Churchill wisely said, *"We make a living by what we get, but we make a life by what we give."*

Differing views regarding finances and poor financial management are some of the most frequently cited areas that cause marital problems. A Gallup Poll found that *"56% of all divorces are the result of financial pressure."[1]* In addition, the outcome of discussions and decisions about finances affect many other areas of the marriage relationship.

> *"To some people, money means power; to others, love. For some, the topic is boorish, in bad taste. For others, it's more private than sex. Add family dynamics to the mix, and for many you have the subject from hell."*
> ~ Karen S. Peterson[2] ~

This mentoring session is designed to:

1) Review income and expenses and help the mentees design a workable budget.
2) Help couples identify and develop basic financial management principles and skills.
3) Provide a series of steps mentees can use in working towards solutions to major or chronic financial mismanagement.

Common Issues Regarding Finances
Couples tend to have significant differences in the following assessment areas:

1) Feeling that their partner's spending habits are different than theirs.
2) Disagreement over the amount of money they should save.
3) Concerns about having sufficient income.
4) Not having a specific plan (budget) on how to spend their money or get out of debt.

Develop and Incorporate Your Own Story
Share what your financial journey was like during your early years of marriage, how you integrated your finances as a young couple and how you have seen God provide for your needs as you honored Him with your finances.

Tips to Assist Couples with Managing Their Finances Wisely
Share the following truths with your couple:

Unfortunately in our culture, we tend to define success in financial terms alone. As a result, many people are engaged in the endless pursuit of accumulating more money and falsely assuming that this will bring them happiness or fulfillment.

You can't serve God with all of your heart until you learn to put money in its proper place within your life. Jesus makes it clear that money should not be the goal of your life. It is not a source of ultimate security. It is not a factor in determining an individual's worth or success as a person.

No couple is immune from problems related to money. No matter how much money some families have, they always seem to need more. It's been said that spending always rises to meet (or exceed) income. Compulsive spenders love to spend money on themselves or on others, while compulsive savers feel anxious about spending money or worry that there won't be enough in the future. Chronic arguments about money indicate that a couple has not yet developed an open and well-organized approach to handling their finances.

With the trend of marriages taking place at older ages, there may be more adjusting to do when it comes to merging your finances with your partner's.

Arguments over money can involve:

1) Issues of power and control.
2) Different styles of spending and saving (often related to one's family of origin).
3) Problems deciding what is more important to purchase (e.g. furniture vs. a car).
4) Major debts or level of overall debt.
5) Different views about what money can and cannot do.
6) Personal feelings that money invokes in each individual.

Twelve Biblical Principles of Wise Financial Management

1) Since God has given us the ability to produce wealth, everything we have is a gift from Him (Deuteronomy 8:17-18, 1 Corinthians 4:7).

2) The main purpose of earthly wealth is to provide for our family (1 Timothy 5:8), to help those in need (Proverbs 11:25), and to invest in eternal things (Matthew 6:19-20).

3) Tithing is God's gift to help us manage our thirst for riches and is the process through which He chooses to bless us (Proverbs 3:10, Malachi 3:10). Giving God the first fruits of our labor on a regular basis is our first priority (Proverbs 3:9, 1 Corinthians 16:2). If giving is a new or "tough-to-swallow" concept for you or if it's an undeveloped habit, start out small. Give a little and see what happens. Challenge yourself to increase your giving percentage every few months or annually until you reach the level you feel the Lord is directing you to give.

4) We should work diligently with excellence (Colossians 3:23) and spend less than we earn (Proverbs 21:20).

5) Develop a workable budget. Budgeting gives couples control over their money rather than having their bills and spending control their lives. Budgeting doesn't just mean cutting back on things we really want; rather, it is a way to proactively decide what we will do with our money. It's a conscious, systematic balancing of income and expenses. It's our own way of telling our money where to go instead of wondering where it all went. *A budget worksheet is available in the Resources section of TheSolutionForMarriages.com*

6) Avoid the use of debt (Proverbs 22:7). Only borrow (carefully) to purchase things that are likely to appreciate in value over time.

7) Be honest in all financial affairs (including your taxes) (Proverbs 13:11, Romans 13:7a, Matthew 22:21b).

8) Be content with what God provides (Ecclesiastes 5:10, 1 Timothy 6:6, Philippians 4:12-13, Hebrews 13:5).

9) Set aside funds for emergencies (Proverbs 6:6-8). Consider how long is it likely to take you to find a new job in a bad economy and use that as a guide in determining the number of months and amount of spending your emergency fund must be able to cover.

10) Be generous, understanding that true generosity always involves sacrifice (2 Samuel 24:24a, 2 Corinthians 8:1-4, Luke 21:1-4).

11) Get wise counsel from qualified, independent financial advisors (Proverbs 11:14, 15:22).

12) Take a day of rest each week (Exodus 23:12a).

> *"If I had not tithed the first dollar I made, I would not have tithed the first million dollars I made."*
> ~ John D. Rockefeller[3] ~

Couple Exercises

Here are two couple exercises that mentors can do with their mentee couple.

1) *Important Topics for Discussion - Pick a few.*
   - Make a list of the things God has provided for you. Ask God to make you a more thankful person.
   - Pray that you will arrive at a place where you can say from your heart, *"I have enough."*
   - Individually, what are your short term and long-term financial goals? Compare and decide how you can reach these goals together.
   - What do you value most in life? How does your use of money relate to your values?
   - What debt do you have in your life? How soon do you plan to pay it off? How will you make that a reality?

- How does your willingness to give to God's work and others reflect how much you trust Him?
- What does money mean to you? Does it make you feel powerful, anxious, guilty, loved, responsible, or secure?
- What assumptions and values about money did you develop while you were growing up?

2) *Scenario Communication*
   Want an eye-opener? Take 30-minutes and read the book of Ecclesiastes in one sitting. Written by King Solomon, Ecclesiastes documents one man's exhaustive search for meaning and happiness. Discuss Solomon's conclusions about temporal things.

When to Seek Outside Help

If after unsuccessful attempts have been made to effectively manage your finances together or when financial conversations have significantly broken down, enlist the help of a qualified person who will intercede and help bring about better management of your resources.

Discussion Starters

1) Do you and your partner often disagree on spending priorities? What factors (personal wants or needs) influence how you make spending decisions?
2) Have each of you shared the details of your current and expected income, expenditures, and financial goals?
3) Have you given sufficient thought to your future expenses such as housing, insurance, taxes, food, clothing, and so forth?
4) Will each of you regularly discuss an itemized account of your debts or bills?
5) Do you need help in developing a budget or a plan for handling your finances?
6) What are your greatest concerns about your future financial situation?

Biblical References

Hebrews 13:5, *"Keep your lives free from the love of money and be content with what you have, because God has said, "Never will I leave you; never will I forsake you."*

Luke 16:13, *"No one can serve two masters. Either you will hate the one and love the other, or you will be devoted to the one and despise the other. You cannot serve both God and money."*

Proverbs 13:11, *"Dishonest money dwindles away, but he who gathers money little by little makes it grow."*

Proverbs 22:7, *"The rich rule over the poor, and the borrower is servant to the lender."*

Luke 21:1-4, *"As he looked up, Jesus saw the rich putting their gifts into the temple treasury. He also saw a poor widow put in two very small copper coins. "Truly I tell you," he said, "this poor widow has put in more than all the others. All these people gave their gifts out of their wealth; but she out of her poverty put in all she had to live on."*

Recommended Resources

Blue, Ron, and Jeremy White. *Faith-based Family Finances*. Carol Stream, IL: Tyndale House, 2008.

Chapter 11

Finding Common Ground - Leisure Activities

Introduction

Couples are usually drawn together by physical, emotional, and/or spiritual attraction. For the initial months or even years of marriage, this attraction may be enough to sustain the relationship. Eventually, however, couples will need to find areas of mutual interest in order for their marriage to thrive. The more areas of common interest couples can engage in the better off they are likely to be.

Sharon Jaynes, author of *Becoming the Woman of His Dreams*, says that intimacy in marriage comes from couples developing "a thousand sharings"[1] that enable the bond of marriage to become strong. Having several interests, both individually and as couples, makes their lives more interesting. It's an important part of building a fulfilling marriage.

Familiarity in any relationship can lead to taking one another for granted and to drifting apart. Developing a genuine interest in some things that your spouse enjoys will help couples maintain passion and excitement in your marriage. The specific activities couples choose to do together are less important than actually making the time to do them regularly. Encourage your mentees to show a genuine interest in their partner's hobbies and activities now and throughout their lives together.

The average American couple spends only about 15-20 minutes of quality time together daily. When you compare that to the 8-10 hours spent with co-workers each work day, it's easy to see how married couples can become relative strangers in the absence of shared interests. Finishing life together successfully involves choosing to give up some of your own agenda—just like you probably both did when you were dating.

This mentoring session is designed to:

1) Look at the couple's level of satisfaction with the quantity and quality of leisure time they spend together.
2) Look at similarities in interests and their satisfaction with the balance of time spent together and apart.
3) Help couples identify activities that they can do together.

Common Issues Regarding Finding Common Ground
Couples tend to need improvement in the following assessment areas:

1) Finding time for activities after having children.
2) One person's activities leaving the other person feeling alone.
3) Differing energy levels, physical or mental abilities, amounts of time available, and/or interests between partners.
4) Differing preferences for doing individual activities vs. group or social activities.
5) Careers pulling partners in opposite directions or having differing schedules.

Develop and Incorporate Your Own Story
Share what new activities you now engage in that you didn't both do before or early in your marriage. Discuss a common cause or ministry that you both passionately support. Explain to the couple how doing marriage mentoring has helped your own marriage since it has become a common interest you do with your spouse.

Tips on Discussing Leisure Activities

1) Interests and the availability of time and money change throughout our lives. Strong couples consistently look for and try new things they can do together. The interests they choose don't have to be extreme, expensive, or things they will do forever.

2) This is an area for servanthood and compromise. Sometimes do what he likes and other times do what she likes. This will maintain and deepen the bonds of friendship. This is especially important when children come along.

3) A couple's children won't always be there to provide a common interest, so couples need to find some activities for just the two of them so their relationship grows. If not, 20 years later, when the kids are gone, they will be strangers to each other. The early parenting and post-parenting stages of marriage have high divorce rates!

4) Plan regularly scheduled date nights and weekend activities. If a getaway is not immediately possible, have the couple set it as a goal to work towards.

5) Ignore the "quality time" vs. "quantity time" myth. Healthy marriages need lots of both!

6) It is not necessary that they have the exact same interests. By sharing, couples learn from each other and grow.

7) Take an interest in your spouse's work—in and out of the home. It's a big part of life, so having a basic understanding of it will enable them to intelligently discuss things. This will benefit the couple greatly.

8) Common and separate interests are both important. Make time for both, and support each other in pursuit of personal interests.

For the couple struggling in this area:

1) Every married couple faces occasional dryness in their marriage. That's part of being human. Couples need to guard against letting dryness continue for an extended period of time and get help if necessary.

2) Instead of looking backwards at what was missed along the way, encourage the couple to look forward to what can be accomplished in the years ahead. These can be the best years of anyone's life!

3) Recognize that a strong marriage can still be built, even when there are limited common interests. Doing so, however, will take more effort from both partners.

4) Self-sacrifice is counter-cultural and must be taken seriously. Seek to compromise by sacrificing some of your own rights and wishes for the ultimate good of your marriage.

Couple Exercises

1) This exercise is designed for the couple to do together while they are relaxed or spending time out. Have them identify interests they currently do together and ones that appeal to both for the future. Circle all activities you or your spouse currently do individually—even if only occasionally.

Competitive Activities	
Indoor	**Outdoor**
▪ Swimming	▪ Biking
▪ Playing Cards	▪ Golf
▪ Board/Video Games	▪ Tennis
▪ Bowling	▪ Softball
Non-competitive Activities	
Indoor	**Outdoor**
▪ Painting/Sketching	▪ Photography
▪ Shopping	▪ Scuba Diving/Snorkeling
▪ Theatre/Concerts/Movies	▪ Walking/Running/Rollerblading
▪ Sporting Events	▪ NASCAR
▪ Collecting	▪ Motorcycling
▪ Cooking	▪ Boating
▪ Working out	▪ Hiking/ Walking
▪ Dancing	▪ Hunting/ Fishing
▪ Museums/Art Shows	▪ Snowmobiling
▪ Eating out	▪ Gardening
▪ Reading to Each Other	▪ Bird Watching
▪ Volunteering	▪ Skiing (Snow or Water)
▪ Ministry Together	▪ Camping

2) Which of these activities could you do together and/or more frequently? Pick a couple activities that you don't currently do but would be willing to try. That's a great way to add new life a marriage!

Discussion Starters

1) What are some favorite activities that you enjoy doing together?
2) Do you both feel there is the right balance in the amount of time you spend together and apart?

3) Are there any times when you feel pressured by your partner to participate?
4) How much do you agree with each other about what constitutes a "good time?" Have you discussed these activities with your partner? How has he or she responded?
5) Do these interests compliment or cause conflict in your relationship?
6) Do you have difficulty planning things to do together? Who typically initiates doing something fun and exciting?

Biblical References

John 15:13, *"Greater love has no one than this, than to lay down his life for his friends."*

Recommended Resources

Jaynes, Sharon. *Becoming the Woman of His Dreams: Seven Qualities Every Man Longs For*. Eugene, OR: Harvest House, 2005.

Arp, David, and Claudia Arp. "Dating Exercise." PREPARE/ENRICH, Couple's Workbook. Grand Rapids, MI: Zondervan Pub. House, 1997.

Chapter 12

Developing Sexual Fulfillment and Intimacy in Marriage

(Discussed with the Couple Together)

Introduction

With our culture becoming more sex saturated each year, one might expect couples to be educated and prepared for a satisfying sexual relationship in marriage. Nothing could be further from the truth! While they have heard a *lot* about sex, very few view it in a way that honors *both* the creator of sex (God) and those sex was created for (a husband and wife). We have found discussing this chapter and the next two to be extremely helpful for couples interested in understanding and experiencing the sacredness and fullness of sex as God intended for married couples.

Mentors may initially find sex to be one of the more challenging topics to discuss with couples—especially when mentees have pre-existing problems in this area. If not dealt with correctly, these issues can cause feelings of rejection and inadequacy where transparency and vulnerability are so integral to the very act of sex itself.

Sex can also be one of the most controversial topics in the Christian community. While we recommend that mentors include the material from this section along with the material in the next two chapters, mentors will need to consider church policies and regional sensitivies when mentoring engaged couples. That determination to use this material is left up to the individual mentors.

In this chapter, we address common issues or misunderstandings couples face in the area of sex and how you can help them as their mentor. Sexual expectations and the level of affection being expressed by engaged couples should be discussed. When mentoring married couples, discussing the satisfaction of their sexual relationship may be included at the appropriate time and place.

Common Issues Regarding Sexual Fulfillment and Intimacy
Couples tend to need improvement in the following assessment areas:

1) Concerns about previous sexual experiences that either or both parties have had.
2) Past or present sexual abuse, rape or abortion.
3) Use of pornography.
4) Different levels of interest or desire for sex.
5) Discomfort talking about sex due to embarrassment or lack of a mature sexual vocabulary.
6) Feeling disrespected when affection is lacking in their relationship or manipulated when more intimacy is desired.
7) Disagreement on the use of contraception (if, how, who and when).

Develop and Incorporate Your Own Story
Share how God has brought sexual blessing into your marriage and things you have learned about sex, such as:

1) How men and women are different sexually.
2) Appreciation for the way that God has made you different and alike.
3) What you wished you knew when you were preparing for marriage.
4) How you handled the issue of family planning and why you made those choices.

Tips on Discussing Sexual Expectations and Intimacy
This is a topic that may be highly emotional for some couples due to their past experiences. Thoroughly bathe this session in prayer that you might bring God glory in how you handle discussing His wonderful gift of sex.

The attitude you bring to this session should set an example of how a couple can openly and honestly discuss sex with each other. This will have a great impact on the couple you are mentoring. Remember this classic quote from a professor at Dallas Theological Seminary:

> *"We should not be ashamed to discuss, that which God was not ashamed to create."*
> ~ Dr. Howard Hendricks[1] ~

Encourage your mentees to adopt this perspective as well.

This is an important topic to include in your mentoring. Since Satan will do everything he can to push a couple together prematurely before marriage and everything he can to drive them apart after marriage, couples need this instruction in order to develop a proper level of respect and discipline in the sexual area of their marriage. The following points may be helpful as you discuss this topic with your mentees:

Purpose of Sex

1) God created sex for our delight, to reflect more fully His image, to provide us with a language of love that would show us more fully the depth of His love for us, and to enable us to produce a godly heritage (children).

2) Healthy sex is intimate communication that involves our whole being: body, soul, and spirit. For maximum enjoyment of sex, all three areas of the marriage relationship (emotional, spiritual and physical) must be in harmony. Sex, as God intended, is much more than a physical and emotional act. There is a rich theology of spiritual oneness too, and neglecting or violating that component grieves the heart of God.

Distorted Views of Sex[2]

During much of the church age, sex was viewed as distasteful, evil, or only for purposes of procreation. Other cultures and religions have also distorted what God intended for sex. Through the secular influence of Greek culture (e.g. Plato), the early church viewed sex and passion as intrinsically evil. Some examples of this are:

1) Tertullian – An early Christian pastor (AD 160-220) and Ambrose (4th century) preferred the end of the human race to continued sexual activity.
2) Origen (AD 185 – 254) thought sex was so evil that he allegorized the Song of Solomon and castrated himself to assure that he would never experience sexual pleasure.
3) Crisostamin (4th century) said Adam and Eve didn't have any sexual relations until the fall, and that sex is the result of sin.

Later, that view was modified and sex was seen as grudgingly tolerated by God for purposes of procreation.

1) Thomas Aquinas (1225-1274) believed that marriage was acceptable as long as sex was not enjoyed.
2) Martin Luther (1483-1546) said intercourse was never "without sin."

The truth that God intended sex to actually be enjoyed by married couples (e.g. Song of Songs) didn't gain much headway in Christian circles until Dr. Ed Wheat published his classic Christian sex and intimacy guide, *Intended for Pleasure* (1977). Even then, the book was originally published with cellophane wrapping and placed on the top shelf of many Christian bookstores. While Christians had a relationship with the Creator of sex and marriage, many were still very uncomfortable with *what* He created.[3]

Since the 1980's, the view that sex was intended for pleasure has become popularized. Greater understanding of how our bodies function sexually and how that experience can be fully enjoyed has emerged.

If your mentees have received instruction from someone schooled in an earlier or distorted view of sex, be sure to spend sufficient time discussing the sacredness and glory of sex as God intended.

Sexual "Baggage"

We live in a sexually broken world. As a result, many of those you mentor will have backgrounds significantly impacted by sexual abuse or exploitation, misinformation, and pornography. Some of the lies, sins and distortions couples struggle with include:

1) Fornication or premature sexual arousal heavily influenced by a culture that glorifies sex outside of marriage.
2) Memories of past sex partners and the associated comparisons, flashbacks, fears, and insecurities.
3) Use of pornography and masturbation. (See Chapters 15 and 16, on pornography.)
4) Guilt from an abortion involving either partner.

Sacred Sex

Several recent Christian authors (Dillow, Gardner, Leman, LaHaye, Penner, et al.) have provided fresh insights and helpful resources for enjoying sex, as well as understanding the profound theological foundation of sex.

Many Christians now see sex as a blessed opportunity for married couples to explore and experience God's deepest truths about the mysteries of oneness and love. That view enables married couples to enjoy the fullest meaning of sex when approached as a sacred act. We use the term "sacred" to mean something that is dedicated or set apart, entitled to reverence and respect, highly valued, important, and not secular.

Consider how God has applied the characteristics of sacredness:

1) Set apart and cherished (e.g. The Church).
2) Declared to be good and highly regarded (e.g. God's creation).
3) Has a symbolic meaning (e.g. Baptism, a rainbow, and the flood).
4) Told to be celebrated regularly and properly (e.g. Communion).
5) Is often a target of attack and misuse (e.g. God's chosen people, religious holidays).

Now look at how this compares with God's view of the sacredness of sex in marriage.

1) Set apart and cherished (Within marriage only – Genesis 2:24, Hebrews 13:4).
2) Spoken of as good and highly regarded (Like tasting choice fruits – Song of Songs 4:16-5:1).
3) Has symbolic meaning (The mystery of Christ and the Church revealed – Ephesians 5:31-32).
4) To be celebrated regularly as a reminder of the covenant that we entered into on our wedding day. (The only exception being if both agree for a season of prayer, and then resumed – 1 Corinthians 7:5.)
5) Is often a target of attack, misunderstanding, and misuse (e.g. fornication, adultery, sexual perversion, pornography, etc.).

Sex is holy, and it can bring us into a genuine experience of honor and worship of our Creator as we experience the true oneness that He intended sex to provide for a husband and wife.

Married Christian couples have every reason to fully embrace the physical pleasures of their sexuality, knowing that it is a healthy part of our spirituality and helps to develop our personal relationship with God. It is in the "one flesh" intimacy of marital love that a married "man and woman together most fully represent the image of God."[4]

Male and Female Differences
Since men and women often approach sex and intimacy from very different perspectives, it's amazing that this part of their marriage works at all. While there are exceptions to the following chart, it will give you the general tendencies of the differences between the sexual natures of men and women.

Differences in Sexuality[5]

	Men	Women
Perspectives	▪ Physically oriented ▪ One part of the relationship ▪ Physical closeness ▪ Variety ▪ High priority	▪ Relationally oriented ▪ An integral part of the relationship ▪ Emotional closeness ▪ Security and privacy ▪ Other priorities can be higher
Sources of Stimulation	▪ Visually oriented ▪ Her body and scent ▪ Her response to him	▪ Words, actions, emotions and touch ▪ Their relationship
Primary Needs	▪ To be respected and admired by her ▪ Desired by his wife	▪ To feel loved, cherished, and understood by him ▪ Emotionally connected with her husband
Sexual Desire and Response	▪ Consistent ▪ Quick burst of excitement ▪ Goal oriented, focused ▪ Quick and intense ▪ Orgasm needed for satisfaction	▪ Cyclical ▪ Gradual, building excitement ▪ Easily distracted ▪ Longer, deeper, and can be multiple ▪ Satisfaction possible without orgasm

As a result of these profound differences, wives often feel unloved when their emotional needs aren't being met by their husbands. In the same way, husbands often feel ignored or disrespected when their physical needs aren't being met by their wives.

It is very common for couples to have different levels of sexual desire, especially during different stages of married life together. When this happens, couples need to seek to compromise, address any underlying issues that might be interfering with their sex life, and serve one another in this area of their marriage.

Be careful. It is extremely destructive to a marriage for one partner to use sex as a means of manipulation by bartering for something else in return for sexual "favors" or by frequent denial for one's own convenience. That only cheapens the gift of sex in your marriage and violates 1 Corinthians 7:5.

Tips for the Wedding Night

1) Try to be as rested as possible. If you are traveling a long distance to get to your honeymoon, then consider planning a shorter trip for the first night.

2) Relax as much as possible and anticipate the cherishing and possessing of each other. Take time to emotionally and spiritually connect. Verbally express your love and commitment to each other. Pray together.

3) Take time to refresh yourself. Shower, shave, brush your teeth, and use mouthwash.

4) Nervousness can inhibit having an orgasm—especially for her. Some things you can do to reduce nervousness during your first several nights together are:
   - Discuss your expectations for the first night in advance (who will shower first, how the room will be made ready, how you will greet each other, what you each will or will not be wearing, praying together, and so on).
   - Let reasonableness, tenderness, and mutual understanding be your guide. You don't need to live up to any "standard" except for the one you set for yourselves.

5) Things to consider bringing on the honeymoon:
   - Bathrobes for each of you.
   - Scented candle and matches or a night light, for low lighting.
   - Music.

- Massage oil.
- K-Y® personal lubricant or Astroglide®.
- Washcloth nearby for secretions.
- Anything else you both feel will add to your enjoyment together.

The emotional barrier of seeing each other naked is best broken during your first night together.

For a new husband on his wedding night, it is important to take things *slowly*. Take your time with foreplay. Start with kissing and then explore the different areas of each other's bodies. As arousal builds, change pace, pressure, and intensity as she directs you to or as you gage her responses. If she is enjoying something, continue doing it gently.

The wife may not be comfortable or relaxed enough to have an orgasm the first time you have sex—or even the first several times. A virgin bride may also experience some pain with intercourse initially due to the rupture of her hymen. She should gently let he husband know what she is enjoying and what she would like done differently. Use this time to learn how your body responds to different types of stimulation. During this time, it is important for the husband to be understanding and to have a servant's heart without adding to any performance pressure or anxiety over her having or not having an orgasm.

Engaging in sex is natural, but mutual sexual satisfaction is a learned process. The husband and wife need to progressively discover how to provide pleasure for each other. Don't be too hard on yourselves. Learning how to have an orgasm may take time, especially for her since it will be more technique dependant. Most women will not consistently experience orgasm through intercourse alone.[6]

During and After Your Honeymoon

1) We suggest taking a shower together at least once during your honeymoon.
2) Talking about what you like and dislike may feel awkward initially. Be understanding and open with each other, and

don't stop talking about how you are feeling no matter how awkward it seems. Ultimately, you are each responsible for your own orgasm.

3) Make sure your spouse knows what you like or dislike. Just be extremely gentle with each other so that egos and emotions are not hurt and openness and vulnerability hindered.

4) Pay attention to her monthly menstrual cycle. Her sexual interest and response will vary over the course of the month. Make her orgasm the top priority, especially during the one to ten days after her period ends. Discuss how you will deal with sex if she has her menstrual period on her wedding day or during the honeymoon.

5) Over time, experiment with different positions and different ways of stimulating each other. Be creative and sensitive to each other's desires, preferences, and level of comfort.

What Couples Can Do to Deepen Their Sexual Experience

1) Make a commitment to accept your mate's sexuality as God's provision with a spirit of appreciation and forgiveness (if necessary).

2) Commit to making sex a priority in your marriage. During busy times, this might require scheduling time for intimacy even though doing so doesn't feel very romantic. While sex is likely to be more frequent during the early days of marriage, couples in most healthy marriages have sex once or twice a week. If sexual frequency is less than once a month, it may indicate that there are other issues to be addressed in the marriage relationship.

3) Use a variety of techniques (verbal and non-verbal) to communicate affection.

4) Be creative in keeping the sexual relationship dynamic (technique, tenderness, scented candles, lotion, music, massage oil, surprise getaways).

5) Remember that men and women respond differently. God created us that way, so be a student of your spouse in this area and learn to enjoy your differences.

Keeping Sex Alive After Marriage

1) Kiss passionately every day.
2) Talk about your sex life together—what you like, don't like, and desire. If you were raised in a home where sex wasn't discussed, it may take extra effort to discover ways to meet each other's needs.
3) Read good Christian books on sexual fulfillment out loud together. Keep open to new ideas which fit within biblical teaching.
4) Make your sex life a priority—even if it means scheduling it on your calendar.
5) Stay physically fit and well groomed.
6) Keep your eyes, thoughts, and desires focused on home. Satan desires to divert your attention elsewhere, but never reveals the high cost involved until it's too late.
7) Stay positive. Much like learning to play a musical instrument well, learning to have great sex takes time to master.

What's Okay and Not Okay Sexually?

There are some things about sex that are expressly prohibited in the Bible. These include:

1) Fornication (1Corinthians 7:2, 1Thessalonians 4:3).
2) Adultery (Leviticus 21:10).
3) Homosexual relations (Leviticus 18:22; 20:13; Romans 1:27; 1 Corinthians 6:9).
4) Prostitution (Leviticus 19:29, Deuteronomy 23:17, Proverbs 7:4-27).
5) Incest (Leviticus 18:7-18; 20:11-21.
6) Lustful thoughts or passion outside marriage (Matthew 5:28).
7) Use of pornography (Job 31:1).
8) Obscene or crude language (Ephesians 4:29).

There are other areas not directly addressed in the Bible. For these, we suggest prayerfully using five scriptural principles as a guide to seek the Lord's leading in conformance with these principles (e.g. use of a vibrator, or oral stimulation).

1) Is it prohibited in Scripture? If not, it *may* be permissible (1 Corinthians 6:12a).
2) Does it interfere with a healthy, enjoyable sexual relationship? If not, it *may* be permissible (1 Corinthians 6:12b).
3) Is this practice harmful or distasteful to either the husband or wife? If so, it's *not* permissible or beneficial. Balance your "freedom" with your responsibility to your spouse (Philippians 2:3).
4) Does it involve or include anyone other than your spouse or expose you to others? If so, it's *not* permissible (Hebrews 13:4, Romans 14:13).
5) If you are in harmony with each of these four principles, determine if God is giving you both a sense of peace about it.

God is full of wisdom (Daniel 2:20). He promises that He will give it to us if we ask Him (James 1:5). If you are considering trying a sexual practice that is not prohibited in Scripture and that meets these guidelines, try it. If you both like it, consider it morally acceptable for you, and enjoy the new way of providing pleasure and love for each other. If one of you feels uncomfortable or turned off, the initiator shouldn't attempt to force the issue by manipulation or pressure. If possible and it meets the principles above, the reticent partner should seek to prayerfully work towards what their spouse requests.

God has given great freedom in your sexual relationship with your spouse. Remember His words to Solomon and Shulamith: *"Eat, friends; drink and imbibe deeply, O lovers."* (Song of Songs 5:1b)

Family Planning and Contraception
Birth control has been around for about four thousand years, tracing back to ancient Egyptian and Chinese times, although not all methods used were safe or effective. Throughout this time, God's people have wrestled with this issue as they sought His leading in their lives. It is likely that some Christians in all ages have used birth control via medical device, drug or other means.[7]

There are three major issues for a couple to come to consensus on.

1) *Is birth control/family planning methods biblically permissible and wise?*

   The first consideration a couple must address is biblical teaching. Within the couple's biblical understanding, additional considerations may include emotional desires and fears, financial situation, health of the couple, ministry needs, and the couple's ability to parent and provide for additional children.

   Encourage couples to seek God's leading, examine their reasons for considering contraception, study the options available, and to prayerfully make an informed decision.

2) *If so, will we use contraception/family planning?*

   Since this is the couple's personal decision, only they can decide, after praying for God's discernment and direction. There are morally right and wrong reasons for using contraceptives or other family planning methods. For example, it would be contrary to God's will for a couple to selfishly decide that they will never have children just so they can travel more. Another couple might choose to temporarily use contraception so as to not conceive and potentially harm a developing child, while the mother is being treated with chemotherapy. Some couples may find one approach suitable when they first get married (e.g. birth control pills) and alternate methods (e.g. condoms) later in their marriage.

3) *If so, what approach will we take?*

   This is a constantly evolving area with new options being introduced periodically. For the latest, reliable medical information on options available, go to the Mayo Clinic web site[8] or other similar sites and do a search for "birth control." All drugs and devices used for contraceptives have different effectiveness rates and side effects that the couple should carefully consider. Christian couples should *not* use methods that are abortive in their designed mode of action should fertilization take place (e.g. RU-486, some types of IUD's, and birth control pills containing only progesterone).

Tips for Discussing Prior Sexual Experiences

It is very reasonable to ask if a potential mate is a virgin, but one should also carefully consider if they are better or worse off knowing the specific, minute details—especially prior to one becoming a Christian. Will the minute details lead to a greater sense of closeness and security, or will it lead to resentment and insecurity? Will it just provide fuel for future issues such as flashbacks, comparisons, or a vivid imagination?

Many couples find that sharing every intimate detail does little to strengthen the marriage bond they are trying to form. In the end, each couple must decide how to handle this discussion keeping in mind their own good and the good of their relationship.

Encourage couples to:

1) Not keep secrets from their future spouse. If they have had sex, they should be honest about it. Lying or waiting until they're married to tell the truth will only cause bigger problems with trust later on.
2) Get tested for any STDs/STIs that they could potentially have, and discuss the results with each other.
3) Discuss any past abortions, rapes, or sexual abuse that they have experienced or been associated with. Professional Christian counseling is strongly recommended if any of these have been experienced.

As their mentor, your goal is to help spouses and future spouses find, in Christ and each other, true freedom from their past sexual history. Have them read Psalm 51 together to put sexual sins in proper perspective. Determine if they can both see this sexual sin as primarily against God. Find out if one person is holding this sin against the other while conveniently ignoring any other sexual sins of their own.

Even with a demonstrated lifestyle change, including growth and commitment to following Christ, a person can be haunted by past sexual sins. It is essential that the mentor help the couple determine how much a hold these sins may have on the individual and guide them to true healing in Christ. Ultimately, the couple must determine if a sufficient period of time has elapsed to demonstrate that the grip of past experiences has been broken.

Signs of an Unhealthy Sexual Relationship
Instruct your mentees to watch for any of the following after they get married:

1) Lots of physical involvement with little other deep emotional or spiritual interaction.
2) Pressure by one partner to do things the other partner is uncomfortable with.
3) The withholding of sex (by either party) as a weapon or as leverage in the relationship.
4) The use of (or demand for) sex to "atone" for other relational failures.
5) *Any* use of pornography.
6) Repeated mechanical, passionless, "quickie" sex.
7) Indifference by either party in providing the other with sexual pleasure.
8) Selfishness by either party.
9) So called "rough" sex or anything that is intentionally, physically painful.

The quality of the sexual relationship can sometimes act as an emotional barometer for the overall relationship. A good sexual relationship is often the outcome of a good spiritual and emotional relationship.

Couple Exercises

1) Have each person write out their understanding of why God created sex. Have them discuss and compare their thoughts and ideas with each other and with the proper biblical perspectives.
2) Discuss the ways sex brings honor to God and ways it can dishonor God.

Think about it...

"If you don't want to do his laundry, he can take them to the cleaners. If you don't want to cook any more, he can go out to any number of great restaurants. Maybe you have great friends that you enjoy so much, that he doesn't need to be your friend any more. He can decide to spend more time with his coworkers or golf buddy. If he needs to talk about his struggles, he can go see a counselor.

BUT, if your husband isn't getting his sexual needs met at home with you, and he goes anywhere else, God calls it sin. If he sins in this way, he is responsible. But also recognize that a wife plays a powerful role in empowering him to turn away from temptation."

~ Barbra Rainey[9] ~

Discussion Starters

1) How open and comfortable are you with discussing each of your sexual expectations?
2) What do you believe are the basic differences in the way men and women approach sex? Experience sex?
3) What do you believe the boundaries of your sexual expression should be before marriage? After marriage?
4) Regarding your partner's sexual desires or interests, do either of you feel uncomfortable or pressured in any way?
5) What are your expectations regarding sex on your honeymoon?
6) Have you discussed and reached a consensus regarding your plans for using or not using birth control?

Biblical References

1 Corinthians 7:3-5, *"The husband should fulfill his marital duty to his wife, and likewise the wife to her husband. The wife's body does not belong to her alone but also to her husband. In the same way, the husband's body does not belong to him alone but also to his wife. Do not deprive each other except by mutual consent and for a time, so that you may devote yourselves to prayer. Then come together again so that Satan will not tempt you because of your lack of self-control."*

Romans 8:1, *"Therefore, there is now no condemnation for those who are in Christ Jesus,"*

Psalm 103:12, *"...as far as the east is from the west, so far has he removed our transgressions from us."*

A note on abortion – *The Scriptures use the same word, brephos, when mentioning Elizabeth's unborn child, John the Baptist in Luke 1:41, 44, the unborn baby Jesus in Mary's womb in Luke 2:12, and the children brought to Jesus in Luke 18:15. Clearly, God sees the unborn child as fully human.*

Recommended Resources

Dillow, Joseph C. *Solomon on Sex*. New York, NY: Thomas Nelson, 1977.

Gardner, Tim Alan. *Sacred Sex*. Colorado Springs, CO: WaterBrook Press, 2002.

Leman, Kevin. *Sheet Music: Uncovering the Secrets of Sexual Intimacy in Marriage*. Wheaton, IL: Tyndale House, 2003

LaHaye, Tim F., and Beverly LaHaye. *The Act of Marriage: the Beauty of Sexual Love*. Grand Rapids: Zondervan Pub. House, 1976.

Penner, Clifford, and Joyce Penner. *Getting Your Sex Life off to a Great Start: a Guide for Engaged and Newlywed Couples*. Dallas: Word Pub., 1994.

Chapter 13
Developing Sexual Fulfillment and Intimacy in Marriage -
Preparation for Sex and Sexual Expectations
(The Men's Session)

Introduction

There are a couple of goals for this module: First, to build a basic understanding how God created men and woman differently, and secondly, to help him fulfill God's plan for their sex life in a way that honors God, satisfies his wife, and strengthens the physical intimacy intended for their marriage.

Common Issues a Man May Encounter

1) His wife having a different level of interest in sex than he.
2) Her desire for more emotional connection while his desire is more for visual or physical connection.
3) Thinking sex is more about performance or technique than about connecting spiritually and emotionally first.
4) The emotional and/or physical consequences of his or her past sexual relationships.
5) Use of pornography by either partner.
6) Being unfamiliar with the biblical view of sex and how it differs from the Hollywood myth.

Develop and Incorporate Your Own Story
Share your initial discovery of sex, the journey you traveled to learn what God intended for sex, and what you wish you had known about sexual intimacy when you were getting married.

Tips on Discussing Sexual Expectations
The following material is intended for the male mentee who has not had sexual relations or has not had healthy, satisfying sexual relations. It is intended to be discussed in a one-on-one mentoring session with the male mentor. Feel free to discuss these topics in more detail depending on questions that are raised and the specific needs of the mentee.

Understanding Yourself

1) *Don't put unnecessary pressure on yourself or your wife sexually.*
   - There isn't a preset standard or Hollywood ideal you have to strive for—each married couple sets their own.
   - The first night together will be something you will always remember. It does not have to be "the best" sex, so focus on enjoying this new part of your relationship.
   - A fulfilling sex life is something you develop together with practice, communication, tenderness, adjustment, experimenting, variety, and priority.

2) *While most men will not have difficulty performing sexually, some may still encounter problems performing sexually.* Most of these issues can be treated and/or controlled. Don't be ashamed to seek medical help, if your own efforts don't resolve a problem. Possible problems may include:
   - Premature ejaculation.
   - Impotence.

3) *Go very slow, especially on the first night—slower than you think.*
   - Take time for each of you to relax, to pray together, and to thank God for each other and the gift of sex that He has now given to you.

- Begin with non-sexual touch such as kissing, snuggling, and massaging.
- Explore each other's bodies, and begin the process of figuring out what you both enjoy, prefer, and don't prefer. You will find that there are other erogenous zones besides the obvious ones!
- Foreplay prepares your bodies for sex (erection for you, lubrication for her). It prepares you emotionally (enhances the pleasure) and determines the ultimate intensity of your orgasm.
- Use a lubricant to minimize irritation, if necessary. This is a common need due to the vaginal stretching involved during the initial days of sexual intercourse.
- Commit to learning how to please and pleasure your wife throughout your marriage.

4) *Guard your mind and eyes in order to stay pure before God and to protect the sanctity of your sex life.*
- Avoid the use of slang or coarse language related to sex.
- Don't lust after or fantasize about other women. (Matthew 5:27)
- Be aware of the pornography trap and the need for male accountability. See Chapters 15 and 16 for guidance as this is very difficult to defeat on your own.
- Have eyes for your wife exclusively. When you are married, your wife is forever to be your standard of beauty.

Understanding Her

1) *Every woman is different.* Your charge from God is to learn to "live with her in an understanding way" (1 Peter 3:7). This especially applies to the sexual area of marriage.
- The verb translated "live with" is consistently translated in the Old Testament as "have sexual intercourse with." God wants a husband to have intercourse with his wife in a way that is filled with

an understanding of how she has been designed and created.

2) *Focus on the "whole person" needs of your wife.*
    - Spiritual and emotional intimacy comes before maximum physical intimacy.
    - Always provide an environment of total acceptance, security, privacy, and safety.
    - Be a student of your wife's needs and desires.

3) *Sexual fulfillment is likely to be easy for you, but providing sexual fulfillment (including orgasm) for your wife is a learned process.*
    - While intercourse alone will typically provide sufficient physical stimulation for a man to have an orgasm, it is fairly unlikely that this will be enough stimulation for his wife to climax. She may need additional stimulation.
    - Your wife will typically enjoy the pleasure from your careful, manual stimulation of her vaginal area either leading up to or after intercourse. The key areas for careful stimulation are her clitoris and labia.

4) *Achieving Orgasm.*
    - While this is necessary for your sexual satisfaction, it may not always be necessary for her to feel satisfied (that's her call). Follow her lead in how she wants her needs met in this area.
    - Her experience will be enhanced by creating a romantic atmosphere and by verbally expressing your love to her in ways that she will find thrilling.
    - Couples may want to introduce variety over time (location, positions). Doing Kegels (a pelvic exercise) can also enhance sexual enjoyment for both of you.
    - Note that male and female orgasms have similar characteristics (heart rate, breathing, contractions) as well as differences (timing, frequency, duration). While you will climax quicker and with less effort, her orgasm will take longer to begin but will last longer too. God designed it this way so that you could

demonstrate your love through your patience and the attention you give to satisfying her.

5) *Her heart is fragile.* She needs your tender love, support and encouragement. That's a very sexy thing for you to do for her as she prepares to give herself to you. Never criticize her looks, effort, size, or technique. That can harm your marriage for life.

6) *Be careful not to seek sex to the point where your wife begins to feel as if she is nothing but a sex object to you.*
   - If you always respond to your wife's expressions of affection, physical touch, or even just seeing her naked as an invitation to have sex, she may go out of her way to avoid those situations because she feels less loved and more used by you. This will only add frustration to you both.
   - Realize that her sexual desire is more cyclical than yours, so enjoy some of these "little treats" without pressuring her for more.

7) *Your wife will be motivated to be more respectful of your needs in response to your showing her unconditional love (Ephesians 5:33).*

Understanding Each Other

1) *Have fun as you "learn to make music!"* Develop a realistic perspective on the time and patience required to learn about each other's bodies and the complexity of expressing love sexually (just like learning how to play a musical instrument). Mastering these skills takes careful attention, gentle, open and honest communication, creativity, and playful exploration.

2) *Don't fall for the myths of the entertainment world.* The first time will be memorable, but the best times will happen over the course of your lifetime. There is no need to put unnecessary pressure on yourself. Relax, keep talking, and keep learning.

3) *There is no "failure" in how you and your wife develop your sexual relationship.*

4) *God created differences in the sexual response of men and women.* This enables procreation through the man's response while encouraging deeper emotional connection for the couple through the fulfillment of her needs.

5) *Recognize your needs for spiritual connection, emotional connection, and nonsexual physical touch.* All of these contribute to the sexual fulfillment of married couples.

6) *After you are married, periodically discuss the following questions:*
   - "How can I best communicate to you that I'm interested in your sexual needs?"
   - "How often do you desire to have sexual intercourse?"
   - "What thrills you most about our sexual relationship?"
   - "What would you like me to do more often? Less often? Stop doing?"
   - "If I'm not in the mood for sex when you are, how can I tell you in a way that doesn't leave you feeling rejected?"

"Nothing good is going to happen in bed between a husband and wife unless good things have been happening between them before they go into bed. There is no way for a good sexual technique to remedy a poor emotional relationship."
~ Masters and Johnson[1] ~

Individual Exercises
Discuss the following questions:

1) What was the setting like when you heard about sex for the first time? Who told you about sex? How was it handled?
2) What impact did your initial or early awareness of sex have on your perceptions of sex? Did you understand sex to be something special, sacred, and a gift from God?
3) What do you do to keep sexually pure? What areas do you struggle with regarding sexual temptation? Do you have

someone in your life that encourages you and holds you accountable in this area?

4) To what extent have you been exposed to and/or involved with pornography?

5) Have you ever been sexually molested or abused?

Discussion Starters

1) To what extent are you comfortable discussing sex with your partner? If not, why?

2) If you could only get one question about sex answered, what would it be?

Biblical References

See Chapter 12, Developing Sexual Fulfillment and Intimacy in Marriage.

Chapter 14

Developing Sexual Fulfillment and Intimacy in Marriage - Preparation for Sex and Sexual Expectations

(The Women's Session)

By Glynis Murphy

Introduction

There are a couple of goals for this module: First, to build a basic understanding of how God created men and woman differently, and second, to help her fulfill God's plan for their sex life in a way that honors God, satisfies her husband, and strengthens the physical intimacy intended for marriage.

Common Issues a Woman may Encounter

1) Having a different level of interest in sex than her husband.
2) His visual or physical connection versus her desire for a more emotional connection.
3) Not recognizing or understanding her husband's need for sexual release.
4) Her or his past sexual relationships.
5) Use of pornography by either partner.
6) Past sexual abuse or rape.
7) Seeing sex as 'dirty' based on how she was raised.
8) Being unfamiliar with the biblical view of sex
9) Feeling that she doesn't measure up to the Hollywood standard.
10) Hindered desire due to physical exhaustion and distractions.

Develop and Incorporate Your Own Story
Share your initial discovery of sex, the journey you traveled to learn what God intended for sex, and what you wish you had known about sexual intimacy when you were getting married.

Tips on Discussing Sexual Expectations
The following material is intended for the female mentee who has not had sexual relations or has not had healthy, satisfying sexual relations previously. It is intended to be discussed on a one-on-one mentoring session with the female mentor. Feel free to discuss these topics in more detail depending on questions that are raised and the specific needs of the mentee.

Understanding Yourself

1) *Give yourself permission to be sensuous.* God created you to be that way and to enjoy being so with your husband. *"For everything created by God is good, and nothing is to be rejected, if it is received with gratitude."* (1 Timothy 4:4). When God sees a married couple enjoying each other sexually, He blesses them, declaring, *"Eat, friends; drink and imbibe deeply, O lovers"* (Song of Songs 5:1).

2) *Learning what pleases you sexually will take time, and it will vary over the course of your monthly cycle.* Keep learning, and try not to put too much pressure on yourself.

3) *Learn the biblical instructions found in 1 Corinthians 7 and Song of Songs.* God created sex for your pleasure, and He intended it to be a creative expression of passion and love in marriage. Learn to let yourself go!

4) *A woman's mental image of her own body can interfere with sexual enjoyment.* You are most likely fixating on this more than your husband, so either redefine your "ideal" body type or take some reasonable steps to move closer to your ideal. Read Song of Solomon 7:1-9. They didn't let her *"waist as a mound of wheat"* figure (vs. 2) interfere with their passionate lovemaking! There's no need to be enslaved by Hollywood's airbrushed images of "beauty." Through the use of plastic

surgery, airbrushing and software, Hollywood has created artificial images to which no mortal woman can compare and which are also as fake as plastic fruit.

5) *A woman who feels beautiful will be more beautiful to her husband.* Don't forget, he chose *you* to be his wife, not someone else.

6) *If you are feeling inhibited, try taking small steps to move from inhibition to sexual freedom.* Linda Dillow's book, in the Recommended Resources section, may be helpful.

7) *The most common sexual problems for women are difficulty reaching orgasm and a lack of sexual desire.* Most women need more clitoral stimulation than can be achieved through intercourse alone. You will need to learn together how you are stimulated best. If desire is a problem, discuss it together and with your doctor. Common causes of this are taking antidepressants, an overloaded schedule, distractions, and so on. Try to carve out "couple time" even if that means scheduling it on your calendar.

8) *Use anticipation as a tool for stimulating desire.* Early in the day, share something with your spouse that would help create romantic anticipation for sex. Letting those thoughts build during the day can have a positive impact on lovemaking in the evening. Remind yourself that sex is a pleasing gift that God has created for you. Think about ways to make your evening romantic and sensual.

9) *Guide your husband's hand to where you want stimulation.* If you want to reach orgasm, ask him to manually stimulate you so that it will provide you with pleasure. Take your time. A husband will often enjoy seeing his wife gradually aroused to the point of orgasm. Don't view this as a burden for either you or him. The extra time it takes you to be aroused is part of God's design to keep sex from becoming too rushed and mechanical. It can also heighten the intensity of his orgasm.

10) *Many women need a high level of stimulation in order to have an orgasm.* Intercourse alone will not necessarily be enough. In this case, the wife should guide her husband to provide

additional external stimulation. Show your husband what you need and he most likely will be delighted to do whatever it takes to bring you pleasure and help you reach orgasm— not only because he loves you and wants you to experience the same pleasures he is experiencing, but also because your orgasm heightens his.

11) *Learn from the example of Shulamith in Song of Songs.* She was sensuous in her thoughts (5:10-16), uninhibited (2:6), expressive (2:3), adventurous with her husband (7:11-13), and responsive (4:16). She learned to enjoy all that God had created for her, romantically and sexually.

12) *Don't cheat yourself by faking an orgasm.* Doing that just leads to a downward spiral of lowered expectations. For you, satisfaction is possible at times without orgasm, so let him know that. Depending on where you are in your menstrual cycle, seek a balance between "okay" sex and "memorable" sex.

13) *Don't always wait to be "in the mood" before agreeing to have sex.* It is a choice to provide your husband with the physical release he needs. In doing so, you just might be surprised by the pleasure you derive from the experience.

14) *Fantasize only about your spouse (Matthew 5:27).*

15) *Let go of false information you may have heard about sex, such as:*
   - Sex is mostly for your husband and less for you.
   - Great sex requires that you have a great body.
   - Only a few lucky people have great sex lives.
   - Great sex comes naturally. If you have to work at it, something is wrong with you.
   - Men are animals that need to control themselves when it comes to sex.

16) *The reality is, God created sex for you to enjoy together. He intended sex to bring joy to your minds, bodies, and marriage.*

> *"It is as important to be filled with the Spirit in bed with your husband, ministering to him, as it is for you to be filled with the Spirit when you are teaching the Bible or ministering."*
> ~ Vonette Bright[1] ~

Understanding Him

1) *While a woman can express her femininity in a variety of ways (sex, childbirth, nursing a child), your husband's manhood is primarily expressed through sexual intercourse.* His sexual relationship with you is an inseparable part of who he is.

2) *For your husband, sex is a source of connection, enjoyment, love and passion.* It makes him feel wonderfully alive.

3) *Temptation can get a foothold when your husband's sexual needs are unmet.* This includes his need to feel desired by you. That's why *all* of the warnings about sexual temptation in Proverbs are directed at men.

4) *Your husband is stimulated visually, probably more than you are.* God created him that way, so being "visually generous" with him during the day will go a long way towards pleasing him and helping him fight the temptation to lust after other women.

5) *He is most stimulated by sight and smell.*

6) *After your husband connects physically with you, he'll be more likely to open his heart emotionally.* You'll generally want to connect emotionally first and then open up sexually to him. God created us differently so we can complement and serve each other.

7) *While it's important to affirm your husband in all areas of his life (e.g. provider, lover, friend, father) there is probably nothing that makes your husband feel better about himself than when you initiate sex with him.*

8) *While he may be tough on the outside, his ego is fragile.* He needs you in his corner—cheering him on, affirming him, and being respectful. That's a very sexy thing for you to do for him. Never criticize his looks, effort, size, or technique. That can harm your marriage for life.

9) *Your husband will be motivated to be more loving in response to your showing him unconditional respect (Ephesians 5:33).*

10) *Your husband's sex drive is one of his strongest drives, especially if unmet.*

11) *Make a conscious choice to thank God for how He designed your husband and the role He has given you to complete your husband.* Otherwise, you will get lost in a pit of second-guessing God.

> *"Your husband will never be the man God created him to be if you don't validate his maleness and understand and satisfy his need for sexual intimacy. You are God's primary instrument of love and affirmation if he is to become God's man. You have the power to make him or break him because men are not born, they are made."*
> ~ Barbara Rainey[2] ~

Understanding Each Other

1) *Mutual sexual enjoyment will be achieved when you each take responsibility for it.* This involves learning how your body responds to stimulation and then communicating it to your husband in a loving way. Recognize your need for spiritual connection, emotional connection, and nonsexual physical touch in order to be ready to give your body to your husband sexually.

2) *Be willing to give and receive suggestions gently.* Rejection of a particular form of love play must be seen as a rejection of the action, not of your spouse.

3) *It will take you a while to learn what is pleasurable for you, even longer to communicate this to your husband, and even longer for him to understand and respond appropriately.* Be patient with yourself and your husband.

4) *If your love life is unfulfilling, see if there are other underlying or unresolved issues in your marriage (anger, conflict, stress, fatigue, medications, illness, etc.).*

5) *After you are married, discuss the following together periodically:*
   - "How can I best communicate to you that I'm interested in your sexual needs?"
   - "How often do you feel a need for sexual intercourse?"
   - "What thrills you most about our sexual relationship?"
   - "What would you like me to do more often? Less often? Stop doing?"
   - "If I'm not in the mood for sex when you are, how can I tell you in a way that doesn't leave you feeling rejected?"

6) *You can both enjoy sex more if you make your bedroom a special space by decorating with pictures, candles, and so forth.* Have a lock on the door when children come along, and teach them to respect your privacy.

Individual Exercises
Discuss the following questions:

1) What was the setting like when you heard about sex for the first time? Who told you about sex? How was it handled?
2) What impact did your initial or early awareness of sex have on your perceptions of sex? Did you understand it to be something special, sacred, and a gift from God?
3) What do you do to keep sexually pure? What areas do you struggle with regarding sexual temptation?
4) Have you ever been sexually molested or abused, raped or had an abortion? If so, what counseling have you received?

Discussion Starters

1) Are you comfortable discussing sex with your partner? Why or Why not?
2) If you could only get one question about sex answered, what would it be?

Biblical References
See Chapter 12, Developing Sexual Fulfillment and Intimacy in Marriage.

Recommended Resources
Dillow, Linda, and Lorraine Pintus. *Intimate Issues: 21 Questions Christian Women Ask about Sex.* Colorado Springs, CO:
WaterBrook, 2009.

Chapter 15

The Dangers of Pornography

Introduction

A person is first exposed to pornography at the average age of eight. Perhaps your mentee was impacted by exposure to porn or sexual abuse at a young age, and that exposure set off a series of encounters with pornography during different periods of his or her life. This will lead to a growing problem for them and those they love.

What is pornography? Why is it so addictive?

The Supreme Court of the United States struggled with a legal definition of pornography (*Jacobellis v. Ohio,* 1964). But if a person is going to be victorious over this trap in their life, they will need a practical, working definition of pornography.

> Pornography is *any* entertainment that uses immodest or indecent images to stimulate the participant's sexual thoughts or feelings.[1]

By this definition, even a mainstream television program, magazine, or advertisement may contain pornographic content. While challenging to do, if these images trigger sexual feelings, they need to be avoided.

With pornography, there is no such thing as "just looking." Looking is the problem. One can easily get hooked on those pleasurable feelings, especially if they seem to relieve stress or anxiety. Exposure to pornography can begin a cycle of addiction that can become just as strong as an addiction to drugs is.

Pornography has been around throughout recorded history, so what's the big deal?

> *"Although pornography has existed for millennia, never has it been as widely available or used as it has been in recent years... there is evidence that more people - children, adolescents, and adults - are consuming pornography sporadically, inadvertently, or chronically, than ever before."*[2]

Pornography seeks and destroys those who engage with it, and now it has the power and presence to destroy the natural love relationships of entire generations. It's imperative that mentors recognize and understand the fight we are in against pornography, because pornography is both pervasive and aggressive in today's society.

For the first time in human history, the fantasy image of a nude woman has the power and allure to supplant that of a real naked woman. As a result, for some porn-saturated men, a real naked wife ends up being viewed as just "bad porn" in comparison to the images he views.

Evidence of this rapidly growing problem can be found in the extraordinary growth and far-reaching nature of pornography.

1) Hollywood makes about 400 new films a year. In 2005, 13,585 new hardcore pornographic video titles were released in the United States. This was up from 1,300 titles in 1988.[3]

2) Approximately a quarter of all Internet search requests are related to pornography with approximately 116,000 of those searches targeting child pornography each day.

3) Worldwide pornography revenue was estimated to be $100 billion dollars with $13.3 billion of that being generated in the United States.[4]

4) It is estimated that the production and sale of explicit pornography is now the seventh largest industry in America.

5) 66% of Internet using men between the ages of 18 and 34 look at online porn at least once every month.

6) 80% of pornography users felt they were spending so much time on pornographic sites that they were putting their relationships or jobs at risk.[5]

7) 51% of pastors admit that looking at Internet pornography is their biggest temptation. Porn use is an actual problem for 37% of American pastors.[6]

8) 25% of employees in the United States are accessing porn at work despite the risks involved.[7]

9) Approximately 30% of Internet pornography consumers are now female.[8]

One of the problems with pornography is voyeurism. Porn teaches men to view women as objects and supplants the skills necessary to form lasting relationships with women as human beings. Because pornography involves looking at, but not interacting with the woman, it elevates the physical while ignoring or trivializing the other aspects of the woman. A woman is literally reduced to her body parts and sexual behavior.

Most users don't realize the extent to which their thinking is reshaped by pornography until it has a deep-seated grip on their lives. Once you've downloaded it into your mind's hard drive, the harmful images can keep replaying over and over again.

> *"Those who claim pornography is harmless entertainment, benign sexual expression or a marital aid, have clearly never sat in a therapist's office with individuals, couples or families who are reeling from the devastating effects of this material."*
> ~ Dr. Jill Manning, LMFT[9] ~

Pornographic sex is commercialized, lacking true emotion, stripped of real humanity, and ending in a lonely, unfulfilling experience.

"Increasing numbers of clients report that porn has become "the great spoiler" for them sexually by spawning unhealthy interests and reducing their natural responsiveness. One man confided that he could no longer get an erection with a real partner. "I want to go back to how it used to be before I was into porn...How can I get my old sexuality back?" he asked."[10]

Couples struggling with pornography that we have mentored show less intimacy and trust while having greater levels of anxiety, duplicity, isolation, and insecurity.

Pornography is Often Addictive and Progressive

In 2004, before a U. S. Senate Committee examining the Brain Science Behind Pornography, Dr. Judith Reisman described the addictive properties of sexually explicit images. She explained, "We now know that emotionally arousing images imprint and alter the brain triggering an instant, involuntary, but lasting, biochemical memory trail. Once (these) neurochemical pathways are established they are difficult or impossible to delete. Erotic images also commonly trigger ... emotions of fear, shame, anger and hostility. These media erotic fantasies become deeply embedded, commonly coarsening, confusing, motivating and addicting many of those exposed."[11]

For that same hearing, Princeton University's Dr. Jeffrey Satinover identified the "addiction to pornography (as) chemically nearly identical to a heroin addiction...the pornography addict soon forgets about everything and everyone else in favor of an ever more elusive sexual jolt...he will place at risk his career, his friends, his family... will lie to cover his addiction heedless of risk or cost to himself or to others."[12]

Dr. Victor Cline, a clinical psychologist at the University of Utah, has identified a four-stage progression describing the addictive quality of pornography.[13]

Stage 1:

After exposure and repeated viewing, a person enters the beginning stage of addiction. Viewing pornography, typically accompanied by masturbation, triggers the release of testosterone and a powerful cocktail of neurotransmitters—what some refer to as the "erototoxin" of dopamine, oxytocin, and serotonin. These flood the brain and provide a high similar to that produced by heroin and other narcotics.

"Porn begins feeling like interacting with a compliant mistress who promises an exciting, erotic alternative to the realities and challenges of sex with a real partner. Always available, she caters to his every desire without complaint or requiring any attention for herself. She never says no to his requests (unless he runs out of money) and is willing to partake in any type of behavior. For the sex addict, even though he may love his wife and experience satisfying sex with her, his use of porn with masturbation may be perceived as 'the best sex ever.'"[14]

Stage 2:

As the person continues to get hooked, materials that formerly produced a "high" no longer satisfy as the Law of Diminishing Returns takes effect. Greater amounts of pornographic material, longer viewing times, and harder, coarser, more degrading material is sought in order to achieve the same degree of stimulation. This phase is often accompanied by compulsive masturbation.

Stage 3:

This is the desensitization stage of addiction where material which was originally perceived as shocking, taboo-breaking, illegal, repulsive, or immoral is now considered acceptable to the user.

Stage 4:

The final stage involves acting-out what the user has seen in pornographic materials. This could take the form of seeking out prostitutes, engaging in group sex, inflicting pain, compulsive promiscuity, exhibitionism, voyeurism, strip clubs, adultery, rape, bestiality, or child molestation—anything to feed their craving.

Progression rates through these stages can vary and will likely be quicker for someone who watches pornography nightly versus someone who looks at a soft-core pornographic magazine or movie occasionally.

Characteristics of Pornographic Addiction

1) Lack of control over how often they engage in the activity.
2) Obsessive and compulsive sexual behavior regardless of the growing negative consequences for the person or their relationships.
3) Develop a tolerance to it, so that they need higher and higher levels of stimulation for satisfaction.
4) Experience withdrawal if they can't consummate the addictive act.
5) Engage in the behavior instead of having social and personal interactions.

Depending on the motivation of the addict, the skill of the mentor, and the approach taken, success in defeating a pornographic addiction may be achieved for the person engaged in pornography stages one or two. For individuals in stage three or four, professional Christian counseling with someone who specializes in pornography addiction is advised. In such cases, the mentor could possibly serve as an accountability partner. For any couple with abuse in their past, it is strongly advised that you refer them to a qualified professional.

For the porn addict, moderation is impossible. They must avoid pornography completely if they are to break the addictive behaviors. They need to recognize that they will always be vulnerable to pornography addiction and take a multi-faceted approach to guarding and protecting their lives from it. See Chapter 16, "Breaking Free From Pornography – A Five Step Process for Victory."

Millions of people struggle with porn addiction for years in secret without getting caught and continue their behavior even after it begins to have negative consequences in their life (e.g. marriage, family, job, faith).

Most people will be reluctant to bring up or discuss the struggle they are having with porn. This topic might be best handled in one-on-one sessions or referred to a professional, especially if there is a history with abuse. Three out of four sex addicts suffered physical abuse and nearly all have been emotionally abused.

Don't assume Christians are immune from pornography. In Dr. Archibald Hart's book, The Sexual Man, he reports that almost all (94%) of the six hundred 'good men with strong religious leanings' he studied had been exposed to pornography.[15] Clinical Psychologist, Dr. Mitchell Whitman, Ph.D. affirms, "In my experience of working with many Christian men, the use of pornography is a very common problem, particularly among single men."[16]

Like all other addictions, desensitization over time is achieved by more extensive or stronger exposure to pornography in order to produce the same level of arousal. Some claim that porn initially helped them get more excited during sex, but over time it has the exact opposite effect on an individual and couple's relationship.

As a mentor, you will need to establish a foundation of trust, honesty, and transparency with your mentees in order to have an honest discussion of this topic. Due to shame and guilt associated with use, be prepared for the mentee to initially deny a problem or only reveal the true extent of a problem over time and after multiple discussions. It is also likely that there will be periods of relapse as the addict is weaned off porn.

Often, there is an "entitlement factor" involved. Many men minimize this sin because they believe they are overworked, underappreciated, and/or in conflict with their wife, so they rationalize their use of pornography as "no big deal."

Most women have no idea how often their boyfriends or husbands look at pornography. Sometimes the deception is deliberate with many men also denying how often they look at it. Most men simply don't think about quantifying the amount they view. Though men consider trust crucial for a healthy relationship, they seem willing to flout that trust when it comes to their exposure to pornography.

Women and Pornography

Mentors should also consider addressing this topic with women since they comprise 30% of pornography users today. Additionally, an estimated 3% of adult women (and 8% of adult men) will become addicted to pornography at some point in their lives.[17]

> *"In my office, and the offices of many of my colleagues, however, there appears to be increased insecurity, body image issues, sexual anxieties and relationship difficulties for female consumers of pornography. As well, it is not uncommon for a history of sexual abuse or trauma to be entangled in the pornography consumption..."*
> ~ Dr. Jill Manning, LMFT[18] ~

"Today, the pornography industry has convinced women that... learning to pole dance means embracing your sexuality and taking your boyfriend for a lap dance is what every sexy and supportive girlfriend should do. According to a 2004 Internet poll conducted by Cosmopolitan magazine, 43% of women have been to a strip club. In an Elle magazine poll, more than half the respondents...said they weren't bothered if their partner went to strip clubs (52%)."[19]

Attempts to Normalize Pornography

Some men tell women their consumption of pornography is natural and normal, and if a woman doesn't like it, she is controlling, insecure, uptight, or being petty. If the woman demands he stop, she is told she is unreasonable, not supportive, or that she blows everything out of proportion. He doesn't want to give up something he's cherished since boyhood.

An increasing number of women try to write porn off as "a guy thing," but become deeply concerned when they see how pornography is impacting their lives and the lives of their partner. They feel inferior to the unnatural bodies and sexual performance of the women their men watch online, and they often find themselves losing the competition to satisfy their men sexually.

Some of the consequences of pornography use include:

1) Wasted time of increasing duration.

2) Adversely impacting family life, social life, work, and/or studies.

3) Feelings of loneliness, depression, and low self-esteem.

4) Spiritual lethargy as worship, prayer, and ministry seem barren. At the very time they need the work of the Holy Spirit in their lives, they become numb to any connection with God and become spiritually depressed.

5) Less sensitivity to sin. What was once considered sin is now redefined by some as okay in moderation.

6) Increased marital discord. Porn use creates the impression that aberrant sexual practices are more common than they really are and that promiscuous behavior is the norm.

7) Impotence during real sex versus when using pornography.[20]

8) Weakened marriages. Wives frequently feel betrayed by their husband's decision to go online to be sexually satisfied. As one wife described, "It makes me feel fat and ugly, like he'd rather masturbate to those images than have the real thing."[21] In her eyes, their use of Internet pornography implies that she is physically unattractive, sexually undesirable, worthless, and inadequate as a wife.

9) Increased divorce. "An obsessive interest in Internet pornography" was a significant factor in 56% of divorce cases in 2001.[22]

Dr. Dolf Zillman, of the Institute for Communication Research, found that frequent exposure to pornography was associated with the following attitudes and dynamics developing in relationships:[23]

1) Increased callousness toward women.

2) Decreased satisfaction with partner's sexual performance, affection, and appearance.

3) Doubts about the value of marriage.

4) Increased tolerance toward sexually explicit material, thereby requiring more novel or bizarre material to achieve the same level of arousal or interest.

5) Misperceptions about exaggerated sexual activity in the general populace and the prevalence of less common sexual practices (e.g. group sex, bestiality, and sadomasochistic activity).

6) Diminished trust in intimate partners.

7) Decreased desire to achieve sexual exclusivity with a partner and greater acceptance of promiscuity as a normal state of interaction.

8) Perception of sexual inactivity or abstinence as constituting a health risk.

9) Believe marriage is sexually confining.

10) Believe having a family and raising children are unattractive prospects.

11) Increased frequency in lustful thoughts towards others.

12) Decreased interest in one's partner as they avoid true intimacy, become lazy relationally, and feed their addiction.

13) Disconnection from people who once mattered in their life.

Develop and Incorporate Your Own Story
If your mentee struggles with porn, let him or her know that he or she is not alone and that you understand the struggle, because you struggle with your own sins. Maybe you have even struggled with the specific sin of using pornography, and therefore you can share personally what that struggle has been like and how you have achieved victory.

Breaking Free from Pornography
You may feel that this is a difficult topic to discuss, but it is a vital one to include in your mentoring. Many couples are headed for increasing trouble if they don't get godly guidance or professional Christian counseling in this area.

"Satan loves it when we think we can defeat this on our own," says Mark R. Laaser, author of *Healing the Wounds of Sexual Addiction*.

Laaser believes anger is the primary reason Christian men commit sexual sin. He says, "They are angry at God, angry at their spouse, angry at church. They feel abandoned."[24]

Discuss the hope for finding freedom from this addiction with your mentees. For a comprehensive approach that we use with our mentees, see Chapter 16, "Breaking Free from Pornography – A Five-Step Process for Victory."

A one-time "deliverance" from pornography is unusual since breaking this habit involves "renewing the mind" and typically involves incremental, non-linear steps.

Help the pornography user determine what contributing factors are behind the inappropriate behaviors and then determine a way to deal with them in a healthy manner. You may need to address insecurity, loneliness, stress, depression, underlying pain, and/or unresolved grief.

Be patient. Recovering sex addicts' face challenges unknown to some other addicts who can focus on total abstinence from things such as gambling and alcoholism. These last examples can live a healthy, normal life without ever gambling or drinking alcohol. Sex addicts, however, must learn how to have sex with their spouse while maintaining appropriate boundaries and limits.

One role you, as the mentor, may be able to play is to help facilitate a confession and/or discussion between partners, if this problem has been kept hidden.

God's plan for our sex life is that we would wait for and connect sexually with our wife. All other women are biblically referred to as our "sisters." 1 Timothy 5:2 tells us to *treat younger women as sisters, with absolute purity.* Would you want a man looking at your daughter or wife the way you are looking at other women?

It won't be easy or seem natural to treat all women as sisters, daughters, and mothers, but for men struggling with lust, putting this concept into action can turn temptation into pure relationships.

Remember, it is both wrong and dangerous to deliberately view anything that stimulates sexual thoughts outside of your marriage.

Individual or Couple Discussion – Gaining Freedom from Pornography

Discuss some of the consequences of pornography use that the couple has experienced along with future consequences if it is not dealt with victoriously. Help them identify the next step they are willing to take in addressing this problem.

1) At what age were you first exposed to pornography? What were the circumstances? How did you feel after that experience?
2) Many people struggle at times with pornography, attempting to stop it on their own, but periodically falling back into its grip. Does that describe what you have experienced?
3) What impact do you think pornography can have on a marriage relationship?
4) At what times or circumstances in your life are you most vulnerable to the lure of pornography?
5) What stage of pornography addiction are you in?
6) What impact is pornography having on your self-esteem, sense of personal integrity, and marriage?

Biblical References

Ephesians 5:11-13, *"Have nothing to do with the fruitless deeds of darkness, but rather expose them. It is shameful even to mention what the disobedient do in secret. But everything exposed by the light becomes visible—and everything that is illuminated becomes a light."*

Proverbs 5:15, 17-19b, *"Drink water from your **own** cistern, running water from your **own** well. Let them be yours alone, never to be shared with strangers. May your fountain be blessed, and may you rejoice in **the wife of your youth** ... may **her** breasts satisfy you always, may you ever be intoxicated with **her** love." (Emphasis added.)*

Proverbs 4:23, *"Above all else, guard your heart, for it is the wellspring of life."*

1 Thessalonians 4:3-5, *"It is God's will that you should be sanctified: that you should avoid sexual immorality; that each of you should learn to control his own body in a way that is holy and honorable, not in passionate lust like the heathen who do not know God."*

1 Corinthians 10:13, *"No temptation has seized you except what is common to man. And God is faithful; he will not let you be tempted beyond what you can bear. But when you are tempted, he will also provide a way out so that you can stand up under it."*

Recommended Resources[25]

Alcorn, Randy C. *The Purity Principle: God's Safeguards for Life's Dangerous Trails,*. Sisters, OR: Multnomah, 2003.

Arterburn, Stephen, Brenda Stoeker, and Fred Stoeker. *Every Heart Restored: a Wife's Guide to Healing in the Wake of a Husband's Sexual Sin*. Colorado Springs, CO: WaterBrook, 2004.

Carnes, Patrick, and Patrick Carnes. *Out of the Shadows: Understanding Sexual Addiction*. Center City, MN: Hazelden Information & Education, 2001.

Dallas, Joe. *The Game Plan: The Men's 30-Day Strategy for Attaining Sexual Integrity*. Nashville, TN: W Pub. Group, 2005.

Laaser, Mark R. *Healing the Wounds of Sexual Addiction*. Grand Rapids, MI: Zondervan, 2004.

Maltz, Wendy, and Larry Maltz. *The Porn Trap: the Essential Guide to Overcoming Problems Caused by Pornography*. New York: Collins, 2008.

Perkins, Bill. *When Good Men Are Tempted*. Grand Rapids, MI: Zondervan Pub. House, 1997.

Struthers, William M. *Wired for Intimacy: How Pornography Hijacks the Male Brain*. Downers Grove, IL: IVP, 2009

Weiss, Douglas. *The Final Freedom: Pioneering Sexual Addiction Recovery*. Fort Worth, TX: Discovery, 1998.

For Wives
Crosse, Clay, Renee Crosse, and Mark A. Tabb. *I Surrender All: Rebuilding a Marriage Broken by Pornography*. Colorado Springs, CO: NavPress, 2005.

Laaser, Debra. *Shattered Vows: Hope and Healing for Women Who Have Been Sexually Betrayed*. Grand Rapids, MI: Zondervan, 2008.

Means, Marsha. *Living with Your Husband's Secret Wars*. Grand Rapids, MI: F.H. Revell, 1999.

Stoeker, Fred, Stephen Arterburn, Brenda Stoeker, and Mike Yorkey. *Every Heart Restored: a Wife's Guide to Healing in the Wake of a Husband's Sexual Sin*. Colorado Springs, CO: WaterBrook Pr., 2010.

Chapter 16

Breaking Free from Pornography - A Five-Step Process for Victory

Introduction

The need to address any addiction is urgent and critical for a person's spiritual life and for their marriage. In order to do this successfully, your mentees will need to take a multi-pronged approach. The key areas are listed below, along with some specific action steps they can take. Additional steps can be added based on the mentee's specific situation or needs and advice from a Christian counselor.

Most people who experience freedom in this area do so by taking their sin seriously, acting decisively, and involving others to help them make the right choices, and go through the process of repentance and "renewing their mind."

Five-Step Process for Victory

1) *Get Accountability and Godly Counsel*
   - Recruit a team of accountability partners.
   - Tell them about your involvement with pornography and ask them to help.
   - Share with them your desire to be pure. Write our specific goals and the steps you will take to reach them.
   - Update them regularly on your progress and setbacks.
   - Seek their guidance and discuss any corrections necessary.

- Get Christian counseling, especially if you have signs of addiction or have a personal history of abuse.
- Uncover sources of underlying emotional pain and anger and address them.

Why is this important? Satan thrives in darkness and secrecy. When you bring your problem out in the open with your accountability team, it lessens its grip on your life. Don't let your private struggle stay private.

Build a support team to support and hold you accountable. You don't have to face this challenge alone.

> *"I have never met anyone who has experienced sexual-addiction recovery alone."*
> ~ Douglass Weiss[1] ~

2) *Confess and Invest*
- Confess this sin to God and then to your wife.
- Get guidance on how to do this from your counselor or accountability partner.
- Share what you have been doing with pornography and then commit to turning from it.
- Explain to your accountability partner and wife the steps you are committing to taking in order to gain victory over this sinful addiction.
- Be prepared for and accept the response of your mate. Her feelings may be like those she would have if you had an affair.
- Be understanding of her as this is likely to take time. She may also desire spiritual support and a mentor to help her through her feelings of anger and pain.
- Invest in your marriage.
- Work on rebuilding your marriage.
- Attend a marriage class or conference annually.
- Build relationships with couples who affirm marriage.

Why is this important? Your wife needs to know what's been going on in your life as well as your commitment to change. You may not need to go into all the details of your lustful thoughts, but being honest and open is a vital step to victory.

Enlisting her as a "high level" accountability and prayer partner is essential. Don't be surprised if she gets angry or sad. Assure her of your love, and give her time and space. This is your problem and responsibility, not hers.

Share with her the situations that are most tempting for you, and ask her to both encourage you and periodically check in to see how you are doing. However, you may only want to share the gory details of your struggle with your accountability partner or team.

> *"Wash away all my iniquity and cleanse me from my sin."*
> (Psalm 51:2)

3) *Reinforce Your Spiritual and Physical Life*
   - Fill your mind with the superior promises and pleasure of Jesus.
   - Focus on growing to become more like Jesus.
   - Learn to recognize Satan's "addictive voice" (any thought or feeling of continued illicit sexual activity).
   - Quickly confess any failings to your accountability team.
   - Spend daily time in prayer, Bible reading, and worship.
   - Get involved at church and in small, spiritual groups such as a Bible study.
   - Get enough exercise, rest, and nourishment for your body on a daily basis.

Why is this important? Often, men struggling with pornography focus on becoming unlike the devil rather than like Christ.

It is important to "take off" the sinful garment, but it is also important to "put on" the new garment—the virtues of Christ. Work from the inside out. *"Let those who love the Lord, hate evil."* (Psalm 97:10a) and *"When an evil spirit comes out of a man, it goes through arid places seeking rest and does not find it. Then it says, 'I will return to the house I left.' When it arrives, it finds the house unoccupied, swept clean and put in order. Then it goes and takes with it seven other spirits more wicked than itself, and they go in and live there. And the final condition of that man is worse than the first..."* (Matthew 12:43-45).

Ultimately, victory over pornography will be enhanced when a person doesn't just focus on overcoming lust, but on becoming like Christ in all their attitudes and actions.

4) *Remove Sources of Temptation*
    - The goal here is complete abstinence from any illicit sexually related materials. *"...do not think about how to gratify the desires of the sinful nature."* (Romans 13:14b)
    - Get an Internet filter for your computer, and put your computer and TV in plain view.
    - Get rid of cable TV channels like HBO, Pay-per-view, etc.
    - If you're serious about gaining victory, cancel subscriptions to magazines with suggestive content, even the "soft" stuff (e.g. Maxim, Men's Health, and Cosmopolitan).
    - Be proactive with upcoming situations that are likely to put you in the "temptation zone" (e.g. business trips).

Why is this important? A man's inclination to use porn can build from "little" compromises that set him up for a bigger fall.

Personal discipline can be difficult, but remember, *"No discipline seems pleasant at the time, but painful. Later on, however, it produces a harvest of righteousness and peace for those who have been trained by it."* (Hebrews 12:11)

Isn't that what you really want in your life?

5) *Develop the Habit of Personal Removal from Tempting Situations*
   - Learn to recognize the "zone" leading up to temptation.
   - BLAST (Bored, Lonely, Angry, Stressed or Tired). Don't let yourself get "BLASTed." Be especially careful if you are.
   - Other tempting situations include isolation without accountability, poor choices regarding movies, TV, magazines, etc.
   - Apply the "one & one" rule. One look, one second, as you develop the habit of "bouncing" your eyes away from the source of temptation and filling your mind with pure thoughts.[2] The ultimate goal is not looking at anything that can trigger lustful thoughts. This approach has been helpful for many people determined to break the grip of lust.

> *"Be killing sin or it will be killing you."*
> ~ John Owen ~

Why is this important? Create a safety zone for yourself in order to reduce the pull of temptation and provide a way of escape.

Don't wait until it's too late. What you desire to do in a rational, un-aroused state won't easily translate into a sustained behavior change while you are in an excited or aroused state.

If you follow this plan, you will be well on your way to gaining victory over the addictive grip of pornography and sexual sin. There may be some setbacks along the way, but keep connected to God, your wife, and your accountability team. And don't give up!

Chapter 17

Testing Before Marriage (STDs /STIs)[1]

Introduction
In an ideal world, getting tested for sexually transmitted diseases (STDs) or sexually transmitted infections (STIs) before marriage wouldn't be needed. In today's world, with IV drug use, sex before or outside marriage, remarriages, homosexual and bisexual relations, and the occasional contaminated blood transfusions, one can no longer be certain that infection will not be an issue. In an ideal world, none of those situations would be true for you or your future spouse.

Ways to Contract STDs or STIs

1) Any sex before or outside of marriage whether heterosexual or homosexual. This includes vaginal sex, oral sex, anal sex, rape, and some types of sexual abuse.
2) Blood transfusions.
3) IV drug use/Sharing needles.
4) Work-related exposure (needle stick injuries of medical professionals)
5) Infected at birth.

Tips for Discussing Getting Tested Before Marriage
Couples need to determine if either person might be at risk based on the section above. If so, they should get tested. It does not make either him or her safe even if he or she has had "only one" encounter or "only one" previous partner. That "one" partner may have had many

other partners and a person can carry a disease, have no symptoms, and still transmit that disease to their partner.

Getting tested is something you do out of love for each other in order to protect each other. Make it a pre-requisite to marriage. You must decide how the results will affect your decision to get married. If you decide to get married despite bad results, you will need to continue to love your partner, work hard to get through any disappointments together, and plan on the precautions you will take once married.

Requirements for blood testing before a marriage license is issued vary by country or state. Some require tests for some STDs but generally not for all STDs.

Some STDs, such as gonorrhea, are curable; others, such as herpes and HIV/AIDS, are not. Even though some STDs can be cured, they can cause infertility, sterility, pregnancy complications, transmission of diseases to children during pregnancy, permanent damage of some organs, cancer, and even death. Beyond the physical, the emotional scarring may be devastating.

The number of types of STDs and their frequency is climbing at an astronomical rate. In 1960 there were only three known STDs; in 2011 two dozen are listed as incurable. Cases of STDs have tripled since 2001.[2] The World Health Organization reported in 2001 that in North America alone the number of new diagnoses of curable STDs was 14 million.[3] The rate of STD among cohabiting women is six times higher than among married women.[4]

Symptoms of STDs vary. The most common symptoms include genital soreness, unusual lumps, sores or warts, rashes on the genital areas or other parts of the body, itching, pain or burning sensation while urinating or during intercourse, and/or unusual discharge from the genitals. Undiagnosed or left untreated, several STDs can result in serious organ damage and, in some cases, death.

However, not all symptoms of STDs appear right away. Since an STD can be carried without outward symptoms, this could result in a greater risk of passing the disease on to your spouse. For some diseases, there may be a period of time when a person is infected and contagious, but the disease is not yet detected by the medical tests available. This may necessitate repeat testing. Consult your physician to determine if multiple tests are necessary.

There is no single STD test that evaluates for every possible STD. Your physician will determine which STDs to test for depending on your risk profile and your symptoms.

Common STDs /STIs that couples should be aware of include:

1) Chlamydia
2) Gonorrhea
3) Syphilis
4) Mycoplasma genitalium
5) Trichomoniasis
6) Human Papilloma Virus (HPV)
7) HIV/AIDS
8) Herpes (HSV)
9) Hepatitis
10) Pubic Lice (Crabs) and Scabies

Couple Exercises

1) Discuss with your partner any possible exposure to STDs that you may have had. (See "Ways to Contract a STD or STI" above.)
2) Research together the common STDs listed above, their symptoms, and treatment options. For those that are incurable, research the means of protection available to minimize the risk of spreading the disease to your spouse.
3) Decide together if both of you will be tested and how the results will affect your decision to marry.

Discussion Starters

1) Read the ways that a person can be exposed to and STDs (See the Introduction). How many of these apply to your life?
2) What responsibility do you feel you have now for assuring your partner that they will be safe from picking up a STD when you have sex?

Recommended Resources
See reputable medical Internet sites (e.g. WebMD, Mayo Clinic) for more information.

Part 5
FAMILY AND FRIENDS

Chapter 18

Family of Origin[1]

Introduction

When couples marry they each bring their entire families into the new relationship, whether they realize it or not. It can be helpful to review family of origin details with your mentees to help them identify differences in background that are likely to impact their relationship.

Couples may not realize how influential their families can be to their behavior and interpersonal relationships. This chapter presents the couple relationship and how it relates to their "Family of Origin" (the family they grew up in). The goal is to help mentees build on the positive things they have learned and to avoid some of the negative qualities they may have experienced as well.

"In your couple relationship, you either repeat what you learned in your family, or you tend to do the opposite."
~ David H. Olson, Ph.D. ~

Every family is unique in its makeup and function. The fact that families are so diverse can add to the challenge of merging individuals from two different families into a healthy marriage relationship.

The Family Map looks at the parenting style, degree of closeness that each experienced while growing up, and how this affects their perspective on their current relationship. Large differences or unbalanced relationships in their backgrounds can cause problems for couples unless they discuss these differences and reach a consensus on how to forge their own relationship.

Common Issues Regarding Family of Origin

As a result of differences in Family of Origin, couples can experience stress in their relationship in areas such as:

1) Their roles as a husband, wife, and parent.
2) How decisions will be made.
3) The degree of intimacy in their relationship and how love is expressed.
4) Parenting style and methods of discipline they choose.
5) Expectations about 'me' time versus 'we' time.
6) How money is handled and what it represents.
7) The type of church one is comfortable attending.

The degree of difference in their families of origin and how they approach their couple relationship can either enhance the marriage or be a great source of conflict and dissatisfaction.

Individuals from unbalanced homes are likely to have misunderstandings of how healthy families function regarding authority, permanence, sharing, and caring for each other. Healthy views may have been replaced by fears of being dominated, abandoned, or taken advantage of.

Discuss the following questions with your mentees:

1) Who raised you while you grew up?
2) How did you feel about the work demands your parent(s) were under while you were young?
3) Did you or do you fear either of your parents?
4) How was comfort provided during times of loss or grief?
5) Do you wish to do things like your parents did or differently from what you experienced growing up?
6) Do you think your parents were unfair to you?

Develop and Incorporate Your Own Story

Each mentor should briefly describe his or her family of origin and share how it impacted the different phases of your marriage (e.g. adjusting during the early years of marriage, child rearing, etc). Then explain one or two changes that were necessary to make and how you made them in order to improve your marriage.

Tips on Discussing Family of Origin

A person's family of origin still has a powerful influence in his or her life. Your family is very much alive in your relationship. What you saw and experienced growing up shapes many of your perceptions, beliefs, and expectations. Particularly when responsibilities and stress increase, individuals tend to revert to the scripts they learned and followed during their upbringing.

Mentors should look at the Family Map from the perspective of:

1) What are the family scores for each person?
2) What are the couple scores for their relationship?
3) Were the two people raised in similar or under different types of family dynamics?
4) Is the couple in agreement regarding their relationship?
5) How much difference is present between how each person was raised and how they see their relationship with their partner?
6) What direction has each person moved in relation to their family of origin?
7) Was this change intentional or is the individual unaware of that change? Can they explain how and why they changed?
8) Was the change in a healthy or unhealthy direction?
9) Does their partner concur with how each sees their own family?

Look for areas of confirmation or disagreement between the Family Map and results in other areas the couple's assessment report.

There are two things mentors should consider when reviewing the Family and Couples Maps. The first is the difference between the individual's Family Map and their Couple Map. (e.g. The individual was raised in an Inflexible and Disconnected family but shows Flexible and Connected on the Couple Map), We consider it to be a change worth discussing when either mentee shows movement from one region to another or by two boxes or more in any direction.

The second area to discuss is what steps the couple each feel has led to this change. Most couples will naturally either adopt the parenting style that they saw growing up or do the opposite. Which do each plan on doing and why?

Specialized training in the use of the Circumplex Model is included in Life Innovations' PREPARE/ENRICH Facilitator Certification Program.

The Circumplex Model: Couple & Family Map[2]

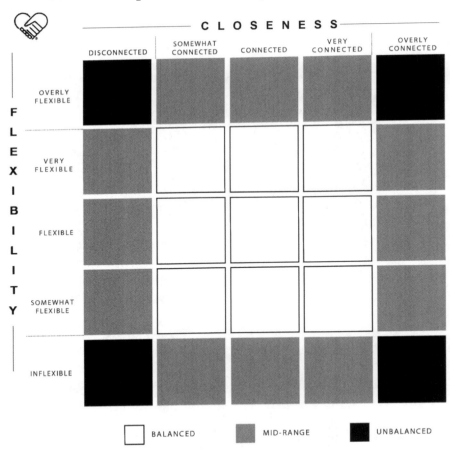

Source: Life Innovations, Used with permission.

172

Couple and Family Closeness

Closeness refers to how emotionally connected one person feels to another. It involves how they balance separateness and togetherness— their private space and their times of close connection.

Although being disconnected (too much *separateness*) or overly connected (too much *togetherness*) might be normal and appropriate during unusual times, relationships that always operate at these extremes are unhealthy.

In healthy, cohesive families, each member develops some dependence on the family and some independence of his or her own. He or she strives for an appropriate amount of sharing, loyalty, intimacy, and independence. They learn how to balance their development as individuals with the growth of the relationship.

In disconnected families, individuals tend to focus more on themselves than on each other. They are highly independent, and they may feel they cannot count on the relationship to give them support and comfort when they need it.

In overly connected families, members can have too much togetherness, demand loyalty, be too dependent on each other, and have little private time or space. In these families, the needs of the relationship often come before the needs of the individual, and it may be difficult for some family members to include or accept others outside of the family in interpersonal relationships.

Couple and Family Flexibility

Flexibility refers to how open to change couples and families are in their relationships.

Since change is inevitable, individual's relationships must be open to it. People also want and need stability; for without it, they will not develop deep intimacy in their relationships.

Relationships that have an appropriate level of flexibility are more structured. Roles are generally well defined and stable, but they can change depending on current needs. Flexibility becomes vital during times of crisis.

When rules and roles change frequently, things don't get done, and the lack of order limits the productivity within the family. These relationships are off balance and chaotic.

Happy couples tend to be creative in handling differences and adjusting when necessary. They are likely to make decisions together and compromise when problems arise.

The application of the Circumplex Model indicates:

1) Couples and families that are balanced types will generally function better than those at the unbalanced extremes.
2) On the Closeness scale, balanced types of couples and families allow members to be both independent from and connected to the family.
3) On the Flexibility scale, balance means maintaining some level of stability in the family system with openness to some change when necessary.

Extreme behaviors on these two dimensions can be appropriate when a family is under stress, but it becomes problematic when families are stuck at these extremes.

"Unbalanced types of couple and family systems are not necessarily dysfunctional, especially if a family belongs to a particular ethnic group (i.e. Hispanic, Southeast Asian) or religious group (i.e. Amish, Mormon) that has normative expectations that support behaviors extreme on these dimensions. Ethnicity is a central trait of families and needs to be seriously considered in assessing family dynamics. What might appear to be an "enmeshed" family of color to a white outsider may be functional for some ethnic groups."
~ David H. Olson, Ph.D.[3] ~

The model is considered dynamic in that it assumes that changes can and do occur in couple and family types over time. Families can move in any direction that the situation or stage of family life cycle requires.

Imago Theory[4]

According to Harville Hendriks, when looking for a mate, each of us seeks someone who can make us whole again, someone who can fill the gaps left by our caretakers early in our lives. He calls the image of this person "the Imago."

"Though we consciously seek only the positive traits, the negative traits of our caretakers are more indelibly imprinted in our Imago picture, because those are the traits which caused the wounds we now seek to heal. Our unconscious need is to have our feelings of aliveness and wholeness restored by someone who reminds us of our caretakers. In other words, we look for someone with the same deficits of care and attention that hurt us in the first place.

"Another powerful component of our Imago is that we also seek the qualities missing in ourselves—both good and bad—that got lost in the shuffle of socialization. If we are shy, we seek someone outgoing; if we're disorganized, we're attracted to someone cool and rational."[5]

Another factor to consider is emotional distancing. It is a way of coping with some childhood pain caused by emotional smothering as one naturally defends themselves against a recurrence of that experience in their marriage.

Birth Order

Birth Order is listed under the couple's Background Information. While there are plenty of exceptions, it may be helpful for mentors to be aware of some *general tendencies* of birth order impact on relationships. While certainly not absolutes, these may provide some understanding of what a mentor sees in other portions of the couple's assessment report.

As a general guide:[6]

1) The highest divorce rates are when an only child marries an only child. Both are used to being the center of attention, making it difficult for them to share the spotlight. They may also have a greater tendency to be bossy.

2) When it comes to dysfunction in the family of origin, the oldest child is usually most impacted by it since they are likely to be the closest emotionally to the dysfunction in the family.

3) The most successful marriages tend to be those where the oldest sister of brothers marries the youngest brother of sisters.

4) Statistically, couples overall with the best chances are those who come from the middle of the pack, but those combinations are not without problems. While generally stable, middle children may struggle with their identity if they were lost in the mix of a multi-child home.

> *"Two people who can go with the flow, sometimes won't tell you how they really feel and that can create a problem in the marriage...people not being honest with each other."*
> ~ Dr. Kevin Leman[7] ~

Since birth order is inexact at best, it certainly shouldn't be a deal breaker.

Working Through Parent Issues
Here are five suggestions for helping your mate work through their past and focus on a successful future.

1) *Work with your spouse to get the problem fully on the table.* Talk about how your parents treated you and ask your mate to share his or her experiences. Be patient. Talking about these things can be very painful. Affirm and strengthen your mate by listening and by expressing your own acceptance.

2) *Help your mate understand his or her parents.* Talk together about them, and put their lives in proper perspective. Remind your mate that his or her parents probably did the best they could.

3) *Give your mate the perspective that God's grace and power is greater than his or her parents' mistakes.* No matter how bad a person's home was, God delights in resurrecting damaged self-images and restoring dignity to broken people. Talk about the overwhelming power of grace, and express your confidence and belief in the greatness of God's love and acceptance.

4) *Encourage your mate to forgive his or her parents completely and to repent of any unjust judgment.* You may need to first talk this out as a couple. A qualified Christian counselor may be needed if you feel you cannot help your mate get on top of this emotionally charged area and forgive his or her parents.

5) *Help your mate determine how he or she will respond to his or her parents.* You have no control over how you were treated as a child, but you do have control over how you will relate to them today. Try to focus on what they did right and how you both are the benefactors. Find ways you can honor your parents.

In some cases, it may take months or years for all the hurt to be brought out in the open. But if you're patient, and if you and your mate are willing to allow Jesus Christ to be Lord of these relationships, healing is possible.

Discuss with each other tangible ways to forgive your parents. Tell God that you are willing to forgive and love your parents.

As a mentor, keep in mind the dynamics of family history, birth order, and socio-economic differences as you review their assessment report. Everything that is in a couple's past can come into play in their marriage and might be indicative of the need for professional counseling.

Couple Exercises

Explain the Family Map to the couple. Refer to the "Guide to the Family Map", in the Resources section of TheSolutionForMarriages. com.

1) Discuss the following:
   - What were the strong points of your family of origin?
   - What things do you wish were done differently when you were growing up?
   - How was your transition from childhood to a young adult handled in terms of closeness, flexibility, and communication?
   - Based on what you experienced growing up and how you each interact in your relationship, what can or do each of you contribute to developing balance in your relationship?

2) Discuss a crisis or stressful time that you have been through as a couple. How did you each respond in terms of closeness and flexibility? Did that differ from how you relate to each other during calmer times?

3) For older couples, map out how your relationship has changed over the years in terms of closeness and flexibility (e.g. Dating, engaged, married, pregnancy, childbirth, parenting, caring for aging parents, and "empty nest"). Discuss those changes.

Discussion Starters

1) When you were growing up, were you free to be a kid or do you feel you had to grow up too fast?

2) Think back to best and worst childhood memories. What specifically did each of your parents do to comfort you? Encourage you?

3) Were your feelings acknowledged and respected when you were growing up? In what specific ways?

4) How do you think the experience of growing up in your family impacts you today?

5) How would you describe your comfort level with verbally expressing your emotions to each other?

Biblical References

Exodus 20:5-6, *"You shall not bow down to them or worship them; for I, the LORD your God, am a jealous God, punishing the children for the sin of the fathers to the third and fourth generation of those who hate me, but showing love to a thousand generations of those who love me and keep my commandments."*

Recommended Resources

Hendrix, Harville. *Getting the Love You Want: a Guide for Couples.* New York: H. Holt and Company, 2008.

Chapter 19

Boundaries and Your Couple and Family Map[1]

Introduction

Boundaries in a relationship are similar to boundaries on your property. Without a boundary of some kind, you are more likely to have arguments or difficulties with your neighbors.

Every relationship needs to develop healthy and balanced boundaries. Without healthy boundaries in a marriage, numerous problems, hurts, and misunderstandings occur. This chapter is intended for couples encountering issues with relational boundaries.

Tips for Discussing Boundaries

Share the following information with your mentees:

Most successful couples establish their boundaries early in their relationship. During the first year of marriage, there may be power struggles as you set boundaries, rules, and responsibilities. While it is still possible, it is more difficult and often quite traumatic to change them later. It is especially hard to make changes without having ever discussed what these specific boundaries are.

Clarifying responsibilities early on enables both partners to decide on a fair distribution of responsibilities in the home. Who will be responsible for what in the relationship? It's important to be assertive about how you feel while doing it in a way that expresses love and commitment to the relationship. Christ-like service is a great way to show love to each other, but it also helps for both of you to know what is expected and what you are doing as an act of service.

Some things are duties and some things are gifts. Problems occur when one person does something as a gift while the other sees it as a duty. For example, the husband may think that the wife should take care of her own car's maintenance. If he fills the gas tank a few times and changes the oil without having discussed expectations in advance, she may feel that he is taking responsibility for maintaining her car. This creates a problem if he feels he is only doing an occasional favor for her. Thus when the car runs out of gas or the oil light goes on, it may lead to a big fight. She may resent his failure to keep the car in order, while he feels that she didn't appreciate his kindness.

Encourage your mentees to stop assuming and get explicit in clarifying their responsibilities. Setting personal and relational boundaries is crucial for a healthy marriage. There is a fine balance needed here. Couples need to love and sacrifice for each other while also taking care of themselves. When both parties love and watch out for each other the way God intended, these principles work together wonderfully. When the relationship is out of balance, problems will arise.

Most people inherit their problems with setting appropriate boundaries from their family of origin.

The following Family Patterns have a distinct impact on a couple's ability to set a healthy balance between closeness and flexibility in their marriage. Examine them closely with your mentees to help them determine appropriate boundaries within their relationships.

Common Patterns Found in Very Distant Families
Characteristics of distant families include:

1) Family members appear to care little for each other, while only caring about themselves.
2) "You live your life, and I'll live mine."

182

3) While the individuals might feel loved, it is rarely expressed verbally or by actions.
4) Members are mostly on their own for getting their needs met.

Later on, people from these families tend to continue distant and disconnected relationships. It causes their marriage to look more like a corporate merger as each pursues their own careers, hobbies, social, and leisure activities.

A possible impact on a marriage often comes right after the honeymoon phase of marriage. Suddenly, one person realizes that the other isn't the "perfect" partner. They resort to the coping behavior that they grew up with and then withdraw emotionally. This worked well when they were growing up as it protected their heart from more pain. But in a marriage, emotional withdrawal only leads to serious consequences. It's important to recognize how and why they are responding that way and help them change.

Common Patterns Found in Very Enmeshed Family Patterns
Characteristics of enmeshed families include:

1) Family members smother each other with love and affection, leading to an unhealthy dependence.
2) Family members have a hard time doing anything on their own.
3) Decision making is difficult because everything needs to be decided together—even irrelevant details.
4) Members may be emotionally punished for doing anything that excludes the whole family.
5) Moving out on your own or going away to college was particularly traumatic.

Imagine a man being depressed due to a work situation. He comes home quiet and reclusive. Being from an enmeshed family, everyone else feels they *must* know what's going on. They can even assume that it is somehow their fault and then press him to tell them everything that is bothering him. This only pushes the man further away, making matters worse.

Some enter marriage thinking that love means enjoying and doing *everything* together. When such partners feel a need to be alone for a while, they experience a deep sense of guilt. It is a concern when one person loses himself or herself in the other person or when one feels guilty for not being totally enmeshed.

In a balanced relationship, the couple enjoys sharing many moments and activities together but will also encourage each other in independent pursuits. Healthy relationships involve interdependent *and* independent activities.

Finding a healthy balance is challenging early in a marriage, if one or both parties did not experience a healthy balance growing up. Change is best approached gradually, especially when patterns are deep rooted. Give your spouse permission to let you know whenever you are responding in unhealthy ways.

Here are some questions to discuss with your mentees:

1) Did you grow up with rigid boundaries or lack of appropriate boundaries? How did it affect you growing up? How does it affect your relationship now?
2) Which way do you tend to lean now: people pleaser or being too harsh?
3) What hobbies or activities infringe on the boundaries of your dating or marriage relationship?

Setting Boundaries with the Opposite Sex after Marriage
A couple being friendly with other couples is fine. It's much more sensitive, though, when you are dealing with one-on-one, opposite sex relationships. There are many people who can be impacted by inappropriate behavior, including the other person, yourself, your spouse, your children, your peers, and so forth. In these cases, extra caution is imperative.

1) Guard your communication. Don't discuss things that are personal or that you aren't fully discussing with your spouse.

2) Set cautious boundaries on your level of intimacy: physical, emotional, spiritual, and verbal.

3) Don't run to this person when you are upset, stressed or struggling in your relationship. If your marriage is struggling in small areas, even a casual friendship with someone of the opposite sex can be fraught with danger.

4) Guard your emotions. If you find yourself thinking about them or looking forward to being together, you are flirting with danger and must back away physically and emotionally. Don't be emotionally unfaithful to your spouse.

5) Guard against your being alone with this person, especially in non-public places. Leave your office door slightly or completely open. Time together should be limited and pure in purpose.

6) Keep your spouse informed before any necessary time alone with someone of the opposite sex. Review the plans in detail, and only proceed if you have your spouse's full consent. If you are lying or misleading your spouse about this person, you have already gone too far.

Discussion Starters

1) Do you feel fully accepted and respected by your partner's family and friends?
2) Do you both feel that you spend the right amount of time with each of your families and friends?
3) Do you anticipate that your family or friends will interfere with your relationship? If so, how?
4) How would you like to see your relationship with your partner's family or friends improved?
5) How do you or could you protect each other from those who would cross your relational boundaries as a couple?

Recommended Resources
Cloud, Henry, and John Townsend. Dr. *Boundaries: When to Say Yes, When to Say No.* Grand Rapids, MI: Zondervan, 1992.

Chapter 20

Handling Cultural Differences[1]

*"Every culture clings to the belief that its own feelings and
drives are the one normal expression of human nature."*
~ Karen Horney[2] ~

Introduction

The history of intercultural marriage and interracial marriage goes
back to at least biblical times. Boaz, a Jew, married the Moabite
Ruth; King Solomon married the gentile Queen of Sheba; and Moses
married an African Cushite woman.[3] Today, as our population becomes
more diverse in ethnicity, culture, and religion and the stigma of
marrying across cultural lines eases, mentors are more likely to have
opportunities to work with more diverse couples.

While the desire for a secure, life-long marriage is universal, the
ways that those needs are addressed are highly influenced by diverse,
cultural norms. This especially holds for first, and to a lesser extent,
second generation immigrants.

Ideally, mentors and mentees would be culturally matched as closely
as possible, but with the increasing combinations of backgrounds,
this is often not possible. To understand the specific cultural issues a
mentee couple is likely to face, the mentor should take into account
such areas as socio-economic status, religion, age, cultural influence,
and value systems. Where a close match is not possible, mentor
flexibility and adaptability are keys for establishing the trust necessary
for a successful mentoring experience.

While there is a heightened level of excitement and enhanced worldview associated with couple diversity, such unions also present greater challenges to building a lasting, fulfilling marriage.

Common Issues Regarding Cultural Differences

All couples need to develop and use effective communication and conflict resolution skills to constructively handle the difficult times when they come.

Common issues that may be encountered include:

1) Communication challenges that are magnified by language differences.
2) Differences in desired levels of cohesion or closeness between partners.
3) Differences in role expectations, including the extended family, and how these issues will be resolved.
4) Extended family involvement and expectations.
5) Birthdays, celebrations, and holidays (which holidays to celebrate—his, hers or both).
6) Food and dietary differences, and what will be served in the home.
7) Choosing what type of neighborhood to live in and encountering and handling discrimination.
8) What social and/or ethnic friendships you will maintain (together and individually).
9) Maintaining your individual cultural identity.

The degree to which these impact a marriage depends on the level of acculturation (the process in which members of one cultural group adopt the beliefs and behaviors of another group—typically in the direction of the dominant cultural group).

"The ability to see the world as one's spouse sees it...and meet it halfway may be the true secret to overcoming the obstacles to a successful intercultural marriage."[4]

Develop and Incorporate Your Own Story

Share cultural differences you have as a couple, how you handled those issues, and how you found solutions and synergies.

Tips for Discussing Cultural Differences

Potential Benefits from Cultural Differences

1) Opportunity for personal growth by wrestling through differences that couples with more similar backgrounds don't encounter.
2) Continuous discovery about yourself and another culture by being exposed to different ways of approaching life and resolving problems.
3) Strengthening through the examination, evaluation, and definition of your own values, ideas, and prejudices.
4) Greater variation and vitality through exposure to different customs, ceremonies, and countries.

Potential Challenges from Cultural Differences

1) When differences are encountered, look at the other person's intentions, not just the surface issue.
2) Don't completely lose your individual identities.
3) Don't let your cultural differences drain your emotional energy. Strive for balance.
4) Be willing to experiment and try new things. You just might like it.
5) Keep and cultivate a sense of humor!
6) Be aware of any tendency to mistrust the other culture during times of conflict. We tend to react defensively when our sense of "rightness" is threatened.

Differences are often based on assumptions, expectations, and convictions that the individuals possess since childhood but didn't realize were there. They are invisible until someone violates them. When people are under stress, they tend to revert to their original cultural programming.

Focus on learning a lot about yourself, not only as an individual but also as a member of your own culture. And then take the time to learn about your partner's culture. Only then can you understand what to do about your differences and make them work for or with you, rather than against you as a couple.

Potential Areas of Cultural Difference and Conflict

1) Value differences (right vs. wrong, important vs. unimportant, and good vs. bad).

2) Husband and wife role expectations (traditional, egalitarian, or flexible; behaviors at home vs. cultural settings; work outside the home; dress standards).

3) Sex practices and expectations. There is the influence of two sets of parents and four sets of grandparents involved!

4) Perceived extended family obligations. You must take into account relationships with parents and in-laws, primary allegiance, handling parental illnesses, privacy issues during visits, financial support vs. self-sufficiency, trips to the homeland, expected demonstrations of loyalty, and conflicting demands of love and traditions.

5) Friendships and what constitutes a "friend." Take into account the social circle for the new couple (mine, yours, ours) and the expectations regarding old opposite-sex friends.

6) Demonstrative behaviors versus more reflective cultural behaviors (how to display culturally appropriate grief, love, anxiety, and how other emotions are handled).

7) Food and drink (what is prepared and how, who serves it, who cleans up, and when the day's main meal is eaten).

8) Raising children. Take into account cultural naming practices, following the dominant culture or a mix in the home, house language used, access to their mixed heritage, education, choice of neighborhood, children's religious instruction and possible resurfacing of your "buried beliefs," and disciplinary style. This can be the most challenging area for intercultural

couples, and it will be a test of how well a couple has learned to handle their differences.

9) Religion to follow, holiday observances, and expectations for each (one, both, or a blend, where holidays are celebrated, conversion to spouse's religion, and place of worship).

10) Concept of time (pace of activity, and being proactive vs. reactive).

11) Death (responsibilities regarding surviving parent and burial practices).

Understanding Individualistic Cultures

These cultures will stress autonomy, self-realization, personal initiative, and decision making. They place a high value on romantic love as the basis for the marriage. People from communal cultures who are exposed to the freedom of the West may suddenly find themselves feeling limited by traditions that previously seemed unquestionable.

Understanding Communal or Collectivistic Cultures

These cultures will stress loyalty to the family group and place high value on the interconnectedness of the family, community, and society. Marriage symbolizes the joining of two families, not just two individuals. The bonds of loyalty and obligation can be intense, while the sense of boundaries between individuals is vague. These cultures stress the nurturance that the group has to offer. Age carries with it respect and power. Westerners who are exposed to these cultures may find their self-sufficiency and individualism very lonely. This culture type is common among Latin American, African, Asian and some European cultures.

Ultimately, the strength of a marriage depends most on the two people involved, not the two cultures.

Cultural Differences Summary

Inter-cultural relationships can present a variety of unique challenges and benefits.

1) Differences can increase disharmony, especially when the differences are numerous, drastic, or the couple is under strains for other reasons.

2) Don't avoid discussing and dealing with tough issues, or the effects will permeate every area of the relationship. Facing the issues will be less risky than avoiding them.

3) Cultural differences can be an easy target. During a crisis, the couple often focuses on and exaggerates their cultural differences. You will need to allow for differences, expect them, and then practice not reacting to them from your own cultural viewpoint.

4) Ask for clarification often before jumping to conclusions.

5) Never criticize the other person's culture or country.

Creating a successful marriage requires constructive conflict as well as caring and compassion. If you are continually having difficulty reaching a harmonious state, seek professional help.

Couple Exercises
There are several things inter-cultural couples can do to strengthen their relationship.

1) If possible, make an extended visit to their country, and/or visit with their parents. (If this is not possible, watch movies made in their country.) Observe the family dynamics that helped shape your partner, and how they act in their native environment. Immerse yourself in the other's culture, and learn how decisions are made, who makes them, how roles, taboos, and responsibilities are defined, how family members relate with each other, to what extent extended family is included, how love and care are expressed, how conflicts and arguments are handled, where and how devotedly they worship, what type of housing and furnishings are typical, what they eat, approaches to cleanliness and hygiene, and how courtesy and respect are displayed.

2) Take an oral history of both of your families. Focus on each of your personal experiences that helped shape who you are

today. As you openly share your personal stories, you both may become more compassionate and understanding.

3) Decide in advance how you will each respond to rude stares, questions, or insensitive behaviors by others. Don't over-protect your children from this as that can make it harder for them to be resilient later in life when they encounter these issues. Don't expose them to too much, too soon either.

4) Maintain positive relationships with both of your families and involve your children in as many of their cultural celebrations as possible. Teach them about both cultural histories.

5) Identify and discuss the level of connectedness for each of your cultures. What are the strengths? Challenges?

6) For couples seeking to forge their own cultural identity as a couple, describe your feelings and perceptions for your family and your partner's family for each of the areas listed below. Complete it separately, and then discuss results. Identify areas that you would like to maintain as well as adapt. Be especially sensitive when you talk about your feelings about his or her heritage.[5]

	His Family		Her Family	
	Strengths/ Benefits	Drawbacks	Strengths/ Benefits	Drawbacks
Spiritual Beliefs				
Family Closeness				
Handling Emotions				
Gender Expectations				
Customs				

Discussion Starters

1) How well do you know, understand, and appreciate your partner's cultural heritage?
2) How do you handle cultural insensitivities by others?
3) What, if anything, intrigues you most about your spouses' culture?

Biblical References

Acts 17:26, *"From one man he made every nation of men, that they should inhabit the whole earth; and he determined the times set for them and the exact places where they should live."*

1 Corinthians 12:12, *"Just as a body, though one, has many parts, but all its many parts form one body, so it is with Christ."*

Galatians 3:28, *"There is neither Jew nor Gentile, neither slave nor free, nor is there male and female, for you are all one in Christ Jesus."*

Revelation 7:9, *"... a great multitude that no one could count, from every nation, tribe, people and language, standing before the throne and before the Lamb. They were wearing white robes and were holding palm branches in their hands."*

Recommended Resources

Crohn, Joel. *Mixed Matches: How to Create Successful Interracial, Interethnic, and Interfaith Relationships.* New York: Fawcett Columbine, 1995.

Romano, Dugan. *Intercultural Marriage: Promise and Pitfalls,.* 3rd ed. Boston & London: Intercultural, a Division of Nicholas Brealy, 2008.

Shelling, Grete, and J. Fraser-Smith. *In Love but Worlds Apart: Insights, Questions, and Tips for the Intercultural Couple.* Bloomington, IN: AuthorHouse, 2008.

Chapter 21

Managing Wedding Planning Boundaries[1]

Introduction
Wedding planning involves two people and two families which often have different values, expectations, and/or priorities. As a result, wedding planning is fraught with potential conflicts. Couples should spend time discussing the values they want to establish in their life together and how they want these values to be reflected in their wedding day plans.

Common Issues Regarding Wedding Planning
Couples tend to have issues in the following areas:

1) Differences in family expectations regarding the wedding.
2) The bride and groom put in the uncomfortable position of mediating between families and friends.
3) Cultural and religious differences and how those will be reflected in the wedding ceremony and reception.

Develop and Incorporate Your Own Story
Share the experience you had (or others you know) planning your wedding. Share how you worked things out, what worked or didn't work well for your wedding, and what is important in the long term.

Tips for Discussing Wedding Planning

Navigating the Wedding Planning "Landmines"
In order to successfully navigate through potential wedding planning "landmines," consider the following:

1) Base your wedding planning decisions on the values and principles that you hold as a couple, not just activities and things.
   - What do you want your plans to say about how you view marriage, family life, religion, tradition, friendship, money, and aesthetics?
   - Let your decisions come from these values, rather than what others are doing or have done.

2) Consider all the parties involved. Yes, it's your day, but it's not only your day. Your family has a lot of hopes, dreams, and prayers invested in you and your future too.

3) Decide on the roles you will each play in the wedding planning. Be clear about the expectations you have for each other, and work as a team. Common wedding planning approaches and decisions include:
   - Co-leaders (make major decisions together with additional defined responsibilities).
   - Leader (bride) plans and supporter (groom) supports.
   - Bride plans it all.
   - Parents work as a team with the couple in the planning and together decide:
     - Who is paying for what.
     - Who will input on what decisions.
     - Who will make the final choices. Be sure to verify expectations and don't make assumptions.

Handling the Relationship Dynamics of Wedding Planning
Today, in most cultures, there is no single standard for wedding etiquette. Focus on helping people feel welcome and respected.

1) Know when you are just thinking out loud and when you have decided something. Be clear to those around you.

2) Focus on the big picture. What relationships are most important? What will really matter ten years from now?

3) When there is conflict between family expectations, understand that "blood always talks to blood." You don't want to create walls between yourself and your in-laws. This applies after the wedding too.

4) Prepare each other and your families for the quirks and odd customs of the other family.

5) Don't let anyone blackmail you with threats to boycott the wedding or withdraw their support; move ahead and let them make their own decisions.

6) Try to keep things in perspective. When everything for the wedding is orchestrated for perfection, how will you cope with the inevitable imperfections that are part of every marriage?

Couple Exercises

1) Evaluate the approach are you currently using and how is it working for you?
2) Talk with your fiancé about the roles you each will have and discuss your expectations.

Discussion Starters

1) What values do you use in determining the decisions to make regarding your wedding and reception?
2) What do you want your wedding day to "say" to others about God?
3) What one memory of your wedding day do you think will be most important to you ten years later?

Biblical References

Ephesians 5:31-32, *"For this reason a man will leave his father and mother and be united to his wife, and the two will become one flesh. This is a profound mystery--but I am talking about Christ and the church."*

Philippians 2:3-4, *"Do nothing out of selfish ambition or vain conceit, but in humility consider others better than yourselves. Each of you should look not only to your own interests, but also to the interests of others."*

Chapter 22

Surviving the Holidays as a New Couple

Introduction
Newlywed couples can encounter a lot of stress around the holidays, due to conflicting expectations of parents, in-laws, siblings, extended families, blended families, employers, and friends. Add in the impact of those who don't recognize or respect the new boundaries of a recently married couple and you have a recipe for disaster.

Common Issues Regarding Holidays
Couples tend to have issues in the following areas:

1) Excessive pressure, manipulation, or hostility from family members.
2) Extended family influence and expectations of holiday traditions.
3) Conflicting family traditions and values.
4) Financial pressure due to expectations and traditions regarding gifts.
5) Differences in the couple's individual priorities regarding holidays.
6) Where and with whom will you spend your holidays.

Develop and Incorporate Your Own Story
Share how holiday expectations impacted you as a newlywed couple and the steps you took to address any conflicts that arose.

Tips on Handling Holidays

1) Address holiday issues quickly, and communicate plans to your families well before the next major holiday. Demonstrate fairness by discussing compromises you are making in order to satisfy the needs of each family.

2) Guard your time with each other during the holidays.

3) Budget for any holiday expenses that you will face together. Be realistic and plan ahead. Don't lose sight of the meaning behind the holiday.

4) Anticipate that some feelings may be hurt, and address these by focusing on how you have tried to be practical and realistic while meeting the needs of all involved as fairly as possible.

5) Take control of the situation and communicate your plans to your extended family individually or together. It would be best if the husband or wife does most of the talking to his or her own family.

6) Stick together. This may be the first threat you face to your oneness as a new couple. Seek to handle these family discussions well, so that you stay united and your marriage grows stronger.

7) Be strong. The first year is the most difficult for you and your families.

8) Balance the desire to please everyone with the practicality of the travel time and/or expenses involved.

9) If necessary, visit the other family the weekend before a major holiday so they don't feel left out of your plans.

10) Focus on making new, pleasant memories for your new family unit.

11) Review how the plan worked after the first year, and make adjustments if you wish. Once you have children, you may also need to reconsider your holiday travel plans.

12) Seek wise counsel from a trusted outside party to provide additional perspective, if necessary.

13) Take special care of yourself and your marriage to counter the stress involved with holidays.

14) Don't let guilt push you to participate in activities that you both don't want to be involved with.

15) Let holiday traditions be your guide, not your personal prison.

16) Don't sweat the small stuff. Holidays will pass.

Couple Exercises

Develop a holiday planning matrix. Do this now, or as soon as possible before the first holiday you will face as a newlywed couple.

1) Make a list of the holidays each of you celebrates.

2) Each prioritizes their own list by ranking each holiday's importance to them individually. Respect any differences.

3) Prayerfully discuss how each of you wishes to spend each of those holidays as a couple. What new family traditions will you make?

4) Note potential conflicts with likely plans and holiday traditions for each of your families.

5) Use the skills learned from the Communication and Conflict Resolution modules to develop your own priorities for the coming years.

6) Wherever feasible, alternate plans for the next year.

7) Communicate the initial plan to each person's own family. Support your decisions as a couple.

8) Continue making your own traditions and sharing in selected family traditions in a balanced way that pleases you as a couple.

Holiday Planning Matrix					
Holiday	**His Priority** (1=Top, 2=Next, etc.)	**Her Priority** (1=Top, 2=Next, etc.)	**Possible Family Conflicts? Who?**	**Year 1 Holiday Plan**	**Year 2 Holiday Plan**
1)					
2)					
3)					
4)					
5)					
6)					

Discussion Starters

1) How important are holiday celebrations to you and to each of your families?
2) What holidays does one of your families celebrate that the other doesn't?
3) How important to your spouse are the holidays that are new or different to you?
4) Are there any holidays that your partner celebrates that you are opposed to participating in? Why?

Biblical References

Colossians 2:16-17, "*Therefore do not let anyone judge you by what you eat or drink, or with regard to a religious festival, a New Moon celebration or a Sabbath day. These are a shadow of the things that were to come; the reality, however, is found in Christ.*"

Chapter 23

Protecting Your Relationship - The Internet, Social Media, and Friends

Introduction

With the ever increasing use of online social networks, text messages, and e-mail, more people are connecting with a much wider circle of "friends" than ever before in history. While these forms of communication enable people to easily stay connected with friends and acquaintances, it also can foster re-connecting with people from our past, including those that we had a previous romantic interest with.

Couples need to discuss and agree on appropriate boundaries to protect the oneness and unity of their marriage. If not, as increasing numbers of couples are finding out, the temptation to emotionally and/ or physically connect with others of the opposite sex becomes a very real problem. Social media also makes it easier for someone who is looking to cheat to do so. The bottom line: Social media will be whatever you allow it to be. Be on your guard. What may feel like love is laced with the poison of sin and shame.

Common Issues Regarding Social Media

Couples tend to need improvement in the following areas:

1) Excessive amounts of time spent on the Internet at the expense of the marriage.
2) Chats with people of the opposite sex about personal, emotional, and intimate details of one's life and marriage (e.g. problems in one's marriage or frustration with one's spouse).

3) Virtual connections leading to in-person meetings with opposite-sex friends without the knowledge of one's spouse.

According to a study conducted in 2010 by the American Academy of Matrimonial Lawyers, more than 80% of the divorce attorneys polled have seen an increase in the number of cases utilizing social networking evidence to justify or force a divorce settlement.[1]

Develop and Incorporate Your Own Story
Share the boundaries and protective measures you have instituted in this area in order to protect your marriage.

Tips on Social Media and Marriage
Suggest to the couple you are mentoring that they focus on how they can provide maximum protection for each other from the potential threat to their marriage. Teach them to avoid looking at such protection as someone checking up on them or "spying" on them.

> *"[Facebook] makes it easier to have anonymous relationships that people think aren't real, but they turn into real relationships."*
> ~ Alan Edmunds, Attorney[2] ~

Consider these potential areas for mentors to discuss with their mentees:

1) Before you get married, review your social media profile and pictures to make sure they properly reflect who you are becoming as a married couple, rather than who you have been individually.

2) There is always a tradeoff with the use of electronic media (time apart, alternate uses of time, etc.). How much time is appropriate for you?

3) Limit computer use to public vs. private areas of the house.

4) Will you have individual or shared e-mail and social media accounts?

5) Share each other's passwords to all devices and accounts including granting each other unlimited, unannounced access to them.

6) Never "friend" people of the opposite sex involving a past or potential romantic interest on their part, your part, or both (e.g. office crushes, the office flirts, old dates, etc.).

7) "Unfriend" or block any social media friends who could possibly be a risk to your marriage. This includes ex-boy/girlfriends and anybody you've had an unshakeable attraction to. If someone has even a remote risk to your marriage, don't have an online association with them. An intense sense of intimacy can quickly develop if that door is opened.

8) Beware that unwanted and unhealthy sexual attraction can flare up due to the mystery and curiosity associated with connecting via social media with people from your past. This risk is heightened if your marriage is going through a stressful or strained period.

9) Social media can easily lead to idealizing another person, wondering about "what might have been" and blurring the line between fantasy and reality.

10) Allow your spouse to read every correspondence you have, if they choose to do so. It's not about your spouse not trusting you. Do this because you have nothing to hide and want to wisely protect your marriage.

11) Make it clear that you are married on your home page. Use pictures of both of you.

12) Have complete respect for your spouse's sense of unease or concern with your connections or friends. If they have concerns, something needs to change.

13) Don't get defensive if your spouse questions any of your activities. See it as an effort to protect your relationship. Help your spouse to realize, by your actions, that your marriage is paramount.

14) In the early stages of marriage (e.g. the honeymoon phase), social media may not seem like much of a threat. When difficult or stressful times come, there will be increasing temptation to misuse social media. Build protective hedges around your relationship now so they will be there when needed.

15) Commit to exhibit honesty, integrity, and full transparency in all areas of your use of social media, texting, e-mail, etc.

If one suspects inappropriate activities by their spouse, investigate the relationship first and social media use second.

Possible Warning Signs

1) One person paying more attention to his or her social media connections than their spouse.
2) Venting to others instead of talking to their spouse about an issue.
3) Having anything to hide regarding your use of social media.
4) Changes or deterioration in one's interest in intimacy as a couple.

If you still suspect something is not right, discuss your concerns with your spouse, and if resolution can't be reached, seek competent guidance or counseling.

Couple Exercises

1) List all of the communication vehicles you use or have access to (e.g. cell phone, text messaging, e-mail, Facebook, Twitter, etc.).
2) Identify boundaries that you each feel are appropriate in using these communication vehicles. Compare lists and discuss how you can help each other be fully accountable and transparent.
3) Make a specific commitment to each other regarding your use of communication vehicles and the protective measures you will take.

Discussion Starters

1) How well do you get along with each other's social media connections (e.g. "friends" and followers)?
2) Do you anticipate that your social media connections will interfere with your relationship? If so, how?
3) What boundaries has your partner established in their relationships with others of the opposite sex at work, socially, on-line, and so forth? How comfortable are you with those boundaries?
4) How would you like to see your comfort level with your partner's social connections improved?

Biblical References

1 Corinthians 15:33, *"Do not be misled: "Bad company corrupts good character."*

Song of Songs 2:15, *"Catch for us the foxes, the little foxes that ruin the vineyards, our vineyards that are in bloom."*

Job 1:8-9, *"Then the LORD said to Satan, "Have you considered my servant Job? There is no one on earth like him; he is blameless and upright, a man who fears God and shuns evil. Does Job fear God for nothing?" Satan replied. "Have you not put a hedge around him and his household and everything he has?"*

Recommended Resources

Jenkins, Jerry B. *Hedges: Loving Your Marriage Enough to Protect It.* Wheaton, IL: Crossway, 2005.

Krafsky, K. Jason., and Kelli Krafsky. *Facebook and Your Marriage.* Maple Valley, WA: Turn the Tide Resource Group, 2010.

Part 6
RELATIONSHIP DYNAMICS

Chapter 24

The Biblical Roles of Husbands and Wives

Introduction

Confusion regarding God ordained roles in marriage have become mainstream along with other distortions of God's design for marriage, sex, church authority, and so forth. Indeed, some evangelicals have also rejected the biblical directives on roles for men and women.

This session provides biblically-based instruction that mentors can share with their mentee couples to help them see a vision for their relationship that will inspire both their minds and their hearts. The goal is to spare them the consequences of applying the cultural misinformation that has put many marriages in harm's way. There is a rich theology behind the God-ordained roles of husband and wife!

Develop and Incorporate Your Own Story

As the mentor, how did you work out applying biblical roles in your own marriage? Was it easy to do? What did you learn about the wisdom of God's Word through the process?

Tips for Discussing Biblical Roles of Husbands and Wives

Most Christians recognize that selfishness, passivity, abuse, and failure to follow the example of Jesus Christ have often distorted the way men and women have historically related to each other. Yet, at its core, marriage is still intended to faithfully portray the love relationship between Christ and His church. This is depicted best with the husband modeling the servant leadership of Christ (Matthew 20:25-26) and the wife modeling the trusting, faithful submission offered by the Church (2 Corinthians 10:5b) in joyful appreciation.

Biblical roles and responsibilities in marriage are also rooted in the order of creation of the man and woman (Genesis 2), in the primary responsibility and accountability for the decisions made by the marriage unit (Genesis 3:9, 17), and in the marital consequence mentioned in Genesis 3:16. God says that Adam sinned in two ways in the garden: he defied God's command when he *"ate from the tree about which I commanded you"* (Genesis 3:17) and by passively failing to exercise his leadership, *"because you listened to your wife* (in conflict with God's command) *and ate..."* (Genesis 3:17). God calls out Adam's disobedience as the pivotal factor in the fall of the human race—not Eve's and not theirs jointly.

As a consequence of the fall, God's curses extended to the primary roles for both husband and wife (Genesis 3:17-19). For him, frustration would accompany his primary responsibility to provide for his family. For her, pain in childbirth and a desire to resist her husband's leadership would mark her primary roles as a wife and a mother.

For both husband and wife, following their call is an act of worship and obedience to the Lord. Failure to follow biblical teaching has resulted in harm to the family, marriage, and the church. The couple is more vulnerable to sin when they neglect the roles and order that God established. God has designed protective coverings over us to protect and build our marriage and family. They are:

Christ ⇨ *Husband* ⇨ *Wife* ⇨ *Children*

When God's people sin or rebel against the authority over them, they subject themselves to additional spiritual attack. (See examples in 1 Corinthians 7:13-15, 11:3, James 5:15-20, 2 Samuel 12:10-11, 1 Samuel 8:6-10, Genesis 3:16.)

Mentors are encouraged to help Christian couples understand a clear, biblically-based picture of what God's Word teaches regarding roles in marriage. The believer's redemption should restore the design of creation with husbands exercising godly leadership and wives exercising godly submission as his helper.

God has made men and women remarkably different, yet each is also an immeasurable representation of the image of God. We are both the amazing handiwork of our loving God! This means that if we were to tabulate the strengths and weakness of the husband, and do the same for the wife, they would both have equal value. If we were to add the two lists together, they would be a synergistic compliment to each other. For example, the brain and the heart perform different roles, but if one fails to function properly, neither can the other. They are not equal in function or duty, but both are equally necessary for the preservation of life and of the body.

The Bible reveals that true masculinity and femininity are defined by God. These timeless, distinct, and complementary roles are rooted in creation—not in cultural conventions. His intent is that a husband and wife would complement and complete each other with the weaknesses of each bringing out the strength of the other.

> *"Our distinct sexual identity defines who we are and why we are here and how God calls us to serve Him."*
> ~ John Piper and Wayne A. Grudem[1] ~

Society's standards for marriage and its roles and responsibilities are ever changing, and they often do not align with Scripture. Since the 1960's, the overwhelming cultural pressure has been to emphasize gender equality by minimizing the unique differences between male and female. The result has been widespread confusion in society and in the church regarding our God-given identity—what it means to be a man or woman. Along with that confusion has been a dramatic rise in promiscuity, sex abuse, delayed adulthood, attempts to redefine marriage, and divorce.

Christians are called to "not conform to this age, but to be transformed by the renewing of their mind" (Romans 12:1-2). Some of these principles may seem antiquated, but they appear that way only because our culture—not God—has labeled them that way. Husbands and wives find favor in the eyes of God when they seek and follow His perfect will. Couples must regularly consult the Scriptures for direction and guidance. The Word reveals God's design for marriage and helps identify and correct unbiblical ways of relating to one another.

Differentiated roles are seen throughout the Bible:

1) See Genesis 2:18-25. God created male and female equally—in spiritual standing and eternal importance. He also establishes His divine order when He made the male the head and the female the helper, modeling the relationship between the Heavenly Father and Christ in 1 Corinthians 15:28.

2) In Proverbs 5:15-19, a husband and wife are to share their bodies exclusively with each other, and the husband is told to rejoice and be captivated by her alone (vs.19).

3) In Proverbs 31:10-31, a godly wife is described in terms of nobility and in ways that fully complement her husband.

4) In Romans 5:12-21, God holds Adam, as the head of Eve, directly responsible for the fall.

5) In 1 Corinthians 11:3-16 (with emphasis on vss. 8, 9 and 14) and 14:33-36, headship of the husband (vs. 3), equal worth (vs. 3), and interdependence (vs. 11) are taught.

6) In Ephesians 5:21-33*, the wife's submission to her husband in obedience to the Lord (vs. 22) and the husband's call to loving, servant leadership in following the example of Jesus (vs.25) are taught.

7) In Colossians 3:18-19*, wives are instructed to submit to their husband in a way that matches their faith in Christ. Husbands are told to love their wife and not to be harsh with them.

8) In 1 Timothy 2:8-15, 3:4, 12, women are told to dress modestly so as to not detract from the beauty of a life filled with good

214

deeds. She is also taught to submit to her husband with a quiet spirit.

9) In Titus 2:4-5*, 6-8, older women (mentors) are told to teach younger women to love their husband and children, be self-controlled, be pure, not neglect the needs of the home, be kind hearted, and be under their husband's authority. The older men (mentors) are to teach the younger men to be self-controlled, model integrity, be diligent, and to use sound speech.

10) In 1 Peter 3:1-7*, husbands are instructed to be considerate, to treat their wife with respect, and to carefully cherish them so that their spiritual life will not be hindered.

While some have tried to find obscure meanings for the Greek word "hupotasso," it is used in each of these verses and widely used throughout Scripture to mean "be subject to," "submit to," or to "place oneself under."

While different secondary roles are characteristic of every culture, there are differentiated primary roles specified in the Bible that refer back to the order of creation in Genesis 2 and the accountability of Adam for sin entering the human race.

His Primary Roles and Responsibilities

John Piper refers to the biblical role of men as "mature masculinity," and defines it as the "benevolent responsibility…to lead, provide for and protect…"[3] Included in the biblical role of a husband is:

1) Growing in his commitment to Jesus Christ as Lord of his life and as the One to whom he is accountable.

2) Practicing the spiritual disciplines (Bible study, prayer, worship, confession, repentance, etc.) so that his walk with Christ is strong, and he is fully able to be led by the Holy Spirit.

3) Providing moral (Genesis 3:9) and spiritual leadership (Ephesians 5:26-27, 29) to his family, teaching them God's Word, helping to cultivate their maturity in Christ, and setting the example for his family through his devotion to Christ.

4) Living righteously so that his family will benefit from his prayers (1 Peter 3:12). Demonstrating integrity in everything, purity in heart, mind, speech and conduct, and accepting responsibility.

5) Guarding his heart from any type of inappropriate attachment with other women (Proverbs 2:16-19, 5:1-8, 6:23-29, 7:25-27, 22:14).

6) Protecting his wife and family from Satan and spiritual attack and leading them in a God-glorifying direction to serve His purposes, not his own.

7) Developing a clear, biblical vision of mature femininity and a deep respect towards it by honoring and treating his wife as a co-heir with Christ (Romans 8:17, 1Peter 3:7) and as his partner in life (Genesis 1:27). Each is to have equal spiritual worth (Galatians 3:28, Luke 13:16).

8) Preparing his bride for Christ. He is called to act *like* Christ in her life and also *for* Christ in her life.

9) Overall responsibility for the management of his family (1 Timothy 3:4-5) and supporting the instruction of his children while not provoking them to anger (Ephesians 6:4, Colossians 3:21)

10) A willingness to lay down his life for his wife and family in any way necessary (e.g. putting their needs ahead of his own per Ephesians 5:25-27) with enduring love (Titus 2:2).

11) Taking responsibility for establishing an environment of active listening and careful consideration of ideas, and not lording his authority over her (2 Corinthians 1:24). He is to do this in a way that honors both husband and wife while leveraging their collective wisdom for married (and family) life.

12) Taking the initiative, having the strength, and making the sacrifice to provide for the good of his wife and children (See Luke 22:26, Ephesians 5:23, 25, 1 Timothy 5:8). As the leader, he is the one who serves. A Christian husband is to follow the example of Jesus by being willing to suffer for his wife, not make her suffer for him.

13) Interacting with his wife with a tender and sensitive heart, respectfully honoring her as the weaker (physical, emotional and/or in authority) partner (1 Peter 3:7, Colossians 3:19), and exhibiting self control (Titus 2:2).

14) Continually learning about and being alert to the deep needs of his wife (emotional, physical, and spiritual), and ministering to her with a combination of strength and tenderness.

15) Conquering pride, fear, laziness, self-pity, and confusion while rejecting passivity in his responsibilities and family activities. Planning ahead in order to shepherd his family through trials that come along.

16) Accepting the burden of responsibility for making the final decision when there are disagreements.

17) Leading in the discipline of his children when both he and his wife are present (Titus 1:6).

18) Utilizing his spiritual gifts to lead and serve the Body of Christ and others in his world.

Authority, for the Christian man, is a responsibility for the good of others without regarding the cost to oneself. In that way, Christ is the authority over the church, and husbands are the authority over their wives in the context of Christian marriage.

Her Primary Roles and Responsibilities
"Mature femininity" is described by Piper as *"a freeing disposition to affirm, receive, and nurture strength and leadership from worthy men..."*[4] It's about what God has designed women to be—not what popular opinion says it should be or what sin has made it to be.

"Submission is the attitude of your heart that says, 'I respect you as my husband and acknowledge the leadership that God has called you to in our marriage. I want to keep myself arranged behind that leadership, to follow your lead and to partner with you as we move along our marriage journey together. I submit to God first, and he has asked me to submit myself to you. I do so willingly and in much the same manner I do this unto Jesus in my spiritual journey.'"[5]

217

Included in the biblical role of a wife is:

1) A growing commitment to Jesus Christ as Lord of her life and her ultimate designer and protector.

2) A clear, biblical vision of mature masculinity in her husband and a deep respect for him (Ephesians 5:33).

3) Affirming the complementary role of submission in the husband-wife relationship (1 Peter 3:1, Ephesians 5:24, Colossians 3:18, Titus 2:5) that God designed from the beginning (Genesis 3:16).

4) Embracing (a matter of action and attitude) her role as a "suitable helper" for her husband, using her gifts to support his leadership within the bounds of obedience to Christ, helping him fulfill his divine calling, and bringing glory to God (Genesis 2:18, Proverbs 12:4, Ephesians 5:25-29).

5) A non-directive approach to influencing and guiding her husband (An example of this approach to influence is found in 1 Samuel 25:23-35, where we see Abigail respectfully appealing to her husband to get him to change his mind).

6) A winsome and affirming spirit towards her husband and recognizing that through her own weakness, her husband's strength is highlighted. This should be characterized by a "gentle and quiet spirit which is of great worth in God's sight" (1 Peter 3:4). Neglecting this approach often leads to passivity or anger on the part of the husband (1 Peter 3:4).

7) Utilizing her spiritual gifts to serve the Body of Christ, teaching younger women (Titus 2:3-5), and serving others (Acts 18:26, Romans 16:1).

8) A disposition to yield to her husband's guidance and a desire to follow his leadership out of reverence to Christ (Ephesians 5:21, Titus 2:5), *"as fitting in the Lord"* (Colossians 3:18), "with respect" (Ephesians 5:33), and "in everything" (Ephesians 5:24).

9) Managing her household well (Proverbs 31, Titus 2:5, 1 Timothy 5:14).

10) Faithfully loving her husband and children (Titus 2:4-5).

11) Providing for the needs of her family in various ways within and outside the home. She is to be faithful to her primary calling of caring for the family (Titus 2:4-5) while also being able to utilize her gifts and talents outside the home during the different stages of her married life (Proverbs 31).

12) A willingness to wait for the rewards of her labor that will become evident in the lives of her children as they grow older and from the Lord in eternity.

Shared Roles of the Husband and Wife

1) Serving one another in love (Galatians 5:13).

2) Not depriving each other sexually (1 Corinthians 7:3-5).

3) Interdependence (1 Corinthians 11:11).

4) Working towards mutually satisfactory decisions after discussion, prayer, and seeking the guidance of God's Word.

5) Teaching their children to respect and obey God (Ephesians 6:4). Proverbs 22:6 says, *"Train a child in the way he should go, and when he is old he will not turn from it."*

6) As members of the church, you are called to submit to one another (Ephesians 5:21), be devoted to each other, and honor one another above yourself (Romans 12:10). This will help keep order and harmony in the church.

"This is the way God meant it to be before there was any sin in the world: sinless man, full of love, in his tender, strong leadership in relation to woman; and sinless woman, full of love in her joyful, responsive support for man's leadership. No belittling from the man, no groveling from the woman. Two intelligent, humble, God-entranced beings, living out, in beautiful harmony, their unique and different responsibilities. Sin has distorted this purpose at every level. We are not sinless any more. But we believe that recovery of mature manhood and womanhood is possible by the power of God's Spirit through faith in his promises and in obedience to his Word. In the home when a

husband leads like Christ and a wife responds like the bride of Christ, there is harmony and mutuality what is more beautiful and satisfying than any pattern of marriage created by man."[6]

May it never be said of Christian couples, *"My people are destroyed for lack of knowledge. Because you have rejected knowledge, I also reject you as my priest; because you have ignored the law of your God, I will also ignore your children."* (Hosea 4:6)

Any successful group has only one person ultimately responsible. There is only one President of a country and one CEO of a corporation. In order to succeed, the primary leader must also have the corresponding authority.

If a wife usurps her husband's responsibility without God-given authority, the husband will tend to become passive in the home and everyone suffers. The desire for a wife to rule over her husband comes from the curse in Genesis 3:16 and is something that wives need to guard against.

> Responsibility Without Authority = Failure, frustration, a passive husband and eventually, emotional and/or physical abandonment.

God has given husbands both responsibility and the corresponding authority for their marriages and homes to succeed.

God has given husbands the authority to lead with the corresponding responsibility, and the husband will have to give an account to God for how he fulfilled that role. If he operates without a deep sense of responsibility before God, he will become an intolerable "monster" in the home. If a husband neglects his relationship with God, everyone suffers.

> Authority Without Responsibility to God = A "monster"

Avoiding Imbalance

God designed these roles to complement one another, and one role is incomplete without the other. Problems can easily arise if the roles are not clearly defined, are too rigid, or if one or both of the spouses isn't being accountable for taking care of his or her responsibilities. For example, if one spouse makes all of the decisions and has complete control, the marriage is unbalanced. Conversely, if one spouse avoids responsibilities, procrastinates, or does not follow through on completing tasks, the marriage is just as unbalanced.

Wives are able to submit to their husbands more easily when husbands love their wives with the self-sacrificing love that Christ exemplified on earth. Likewise, husbands more naturally show love and affection toward their wives when the husbands feel respected and valued.

In order to avoid problems in these areas, remember to "check in" with one's spouse and discuss how each of you feels about the arrangement of responsibilities in the marriage. Clear, proactive communication can help you deal with these issues when they arise.

Dealing with an Unbelieving or Carnal Spouse

For the wife of a man who is living in a sinful state, she can show by her attitude and disposition that she doesn't desire to resist his direction, but prayerfully looks to the day when he will repent from his sin, be freed from its bondage, and lead her like Jesus.

If a wife wants to have the maximum impact on the life of her unsaved husband, she should be a submissive wife in areas that aren't in conflict with God's Word. The gracious, gentle submission of a Christian wife to her unsaved husband is the most powerful evangelistic tool she has. Per 1 Peter 3:1-2, *"Wives, in the same way be submissive to your husbands so that, if any of them do not believe the word, they may be won over without words by the behavior of their wives, when they see the purity and reverence of your lives."* While this can certainly be challenging, cultivating a close walk with the Lord and developing a support system of other mature, godly women can help her persevere in this situation.

What is the responsibility of a Christian husband with an unsaved wife? What should his attitude be? Per 1 Peter 3:7, *"Treat your wife with understanding..."* (NLT). That means to be sensitive to her needs and feelings. Don't be indifferent towards her. Nurture her deepest emotional and physical needs. Be a sensitive, sacrificial leader for her, even when she doesn't want anything to do with Christ. As taught in Ephesians 5, cherish her, protect her, and maintain a deep, tender intimacy with her.

Prevailing Views of Home and Church Roles[7]

1) *Egalitarian (Feministic):* There is no innate distinction between the roles of men and women in the home or the church.

2) *Complementarian (Moderate):* Men and women are partners in every area of life and ministry. While equal in worth, men and women have distinct and complementary gender roles in both the home and church.

3) *Hierarchical (Chauvinistic):* Women are not only commanded to follow male leadership, but are not given a voice with male leaders. Here, women are often chauvinistically kept under thumb as the polar opposite of egalitarian feminism.

After a combined 75 years of marriage, we continue to hold the Complementation view of the husband's and wife's roles in marriage. We encourage mentors to pursue "not what *we* think marriage or family should be, based on our own preconceived notions, preferences, or traditional values, but what we believe *Scripture itself* tells us about these institutions."[8]

Couple Exercises

1) Discuss the following:
   - What are your reactions to the biblical roles and responsibilities referenced above?
   - How have you seen these roles done well? Abused or neglected?

- In what areas are you in agreement regarding roles in marriage? What areas do you still need to resolve?

2) Review Proverbs 31 which describes the actions and responses of a godly couple during the various stages of their married life. Which of these are easy for you? Which are difficult?

The Proverbs 31 Woman
- Is a valued partner (vs. 10).
- Inspires her husband's confidence (vs. 11).
- Speaks well of and does well for her husband (vs. 12).
- Is a hard worker with a good attitude (vs. 13, 17, 18, 24, 27).
- Buys and prepares good food for her family (vs. 14-15).
- Is personable and productive (vs. 15).
- Is a wise, successful investor (vs. 16, 18).
- Is full of energy (vs. 17, 25).
- Is kind and generous to the poor (vs. 20).
- Enables her husband to be a respected leader (vs. 23, 27).
- Courageously prepares for the family's future (vs. 21, 25).
- Is a strong, dignified and wise teacher (vs. 26).
- Manages the affairs of her household (vs. 27).
- Is worthy of praise (vs. 28, 29, 31).
- Isn't preoccupied by outward beauty, but cultivates godly beauty (vs. 30).
- Honors the Lord (vs. 30).
- Is highly regarded (vs. 31).

The Proverbs 31 Man
- Has confidence in his wife (vs. 11).
- Builds a strong marriage (vs. 12).
- Is respected in the community and viewed as wise and fair (vs. 23).
- Sets a good example for their children (vs. 28).
- Encourages his wife with praise (vs. 28).

Discussion Starters

1) How do you plan on handling the work responsibilities inside and outside the home? Before having children? After children arrive?
2) When there are conflicts between your roles and family responsibilities, how do you plan to manage making the final decision?
3) When and how will you adjust roles and responsibilities as your life situation changes?
4) What type of decisions will you each make independently or only after consulting each other?
5) How do you feel about the biblical roles presented in the chapter on Roles in Marriage? Are there areas that you struggle or disagree with?
6) What are household chore roles for the husband and wife?
7) How will you handle headship and submission in your marriage?

Biblical References
Matthew 20:26-27, *"...whoever wants to become great among you must be your servant, and whoever wants to be first must be your slave."*

Proverbs 12:15, *"The way of a fool seems right to him, but the wise man listens to advice."*

Proverbs 19:20, *"Listen to advice and accept instruction, and in the end you will be wise."*

Recommended Resources

For Her
Chervin, Ronda. *Feminine, Free, and Faithful.* San Francisco: Ignatius, 1986.

For Him/Both

Köstenberger, Andreas J., and David W. Jones. *God, Marriage & Family: Rebuilding the Biblical Foundation*. Wheaton, IL: Crossway, 2004.

Piper, John, and Wayne A. Grudem. *Recovering Biblical Manhood and Womanhood: A Response to Evangelical Feminism*. Wheaton, IL: Crossway, 1991.

Chapter 25

Decision Making In Marriage

Introduction

When two young people get married they have often just left home. They are used to living with their parents and are used to either making hard decisions on their own or having their parents do so for them. More experienced couples, especially those whom, for whatever reason, have been single a long time, are very established in their thinking and very used to making decisions solely based on their own individual desires and needs.

For younger couples in marriage, part of "leaving and cleaving" (Genesis 2:24) involves making decisions apart from one's parents. This is a new way of doing things and will require a shift away from the old practice of including parents or roommates in the decision making process. In marriage, decisions are made by considering one's spouse first. You must talk out the decision plan with your spouse and consider the way this decision will make your partner feel and how it will affect him or her.

An example of a difficult decision a couple will face is how to divide holidays and spending time with in-laws. This choice can be even harder when the family members do not live close by. This situation gets harder when one side of the family puts pressure on the couple to come spend time with them. While this type of pressure can be intentional or sometimes unintentional, it puts a couple in a tough position. These types of decisions require compromise and flexibility.

In the end, each couple must decide what to do.

This mentoring session is designed to:

1) Help couples understand God's definition of decision making.
2) Help the couple identify the various areas of responsibility in decision making.
3) Provide a series of steps that they can use in making decisions.

Common Issues in Decision Making

1) *Being proactive about decision making.* Prayer is key to making wise decisions. It demonstrates submissiveness to God's will and the leading of the Holy Spirit. As a couple, you should discuss how you plan to work together to make decisions and how you will manage situations where you do not agree. Here are some questions that you might consider:
   - What type of decisions will require a discussion between the two of you?
   - What types of decisions should you make without consulting each other?
   - What should you do and who will you seek counsel from when the two of you cannot agree on a decision?

   For example, making small purchases for the household may not require a discussion between husband and wife. However, larger purchases such as buying an automobile should definitely be discussed together.

2) *Using common sense, logic, and signs in decision making.* Sometimes making a decision is easy, but other times it is not easy. Study and follow the principles written in God's Word; you can be sure that the Lord will guide you. In decision making, you need to find a balance between supernatural signs and earthly wisdom. Too much of either can hinder a true understanding of God's ways.

3) *Seeking counsel.* You may choose to select different individuals for different areas of decision making. But always remember that it will be best for you to seek out advice from those who

are wise in the Lord and will give you guidance based on biblical principles—even if it is not the easiest thing to hear.

4) *Freedom and responsibility.* We need to remember that God could have written the Bible any way He wanted. That means He could have written it in a different format like a text book for teaching us. He could have put everything in different sections such as parenting, job search, picking a college, or getting new or replacing household appliances. But He did not choose to teach us this way. Instead, in Scripture, God has revealed guidelines and principles to teach us what to do and what not to do. God gave man free will. We were not designed as robots without the ability to make choices, nor were we designed to be morally free agents with no sense of right and wrong. When you choose to walk in God's principles, you can be confident that He will honor the requests that you have made with a contrite and humble heart.

5) *Figuring out what is important:* Preferences, Cultural Norms, Organizational Norms and Absolutes. The figure below helps to outline the different levels of decisions that you will face in your marriage. Some issues will arise that the two will see on different levels of this pyramid. Before you discuss the decision in an effort to come to a mutual conclusion, you need to agree on the level of importance of the decision. If one of you thinks it's very important and the other thinks the decision is not so important, your mutual conversation on agreement in this decision could go badly. If you can agree on the importance level first, it will be beneficial to the outcome.

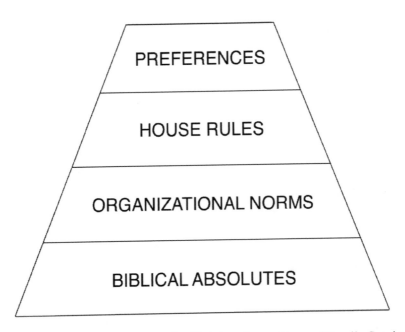

SOURCE: Adapted from Apostolic Christian Counseling and Family Services

Below are descriptions of each level:

Preferences - are personal options, decisions, and choices. Personal preference decisions include things such as which kind of restaurant food you like and what kind and color of car you like. If you disagree on things like this, it doesn't mean that either of you are wrong.

House Rules - are rules of conduct established by couples, families, or groups of closely related people. In a family, the parents have the privilege and right to establish the rules of the house. Other parents may disagree on the rules you have chosen, but each set of parents must decide what they believe is best for their own home and family. For example, one set of parents might set the household curfew at 9:30 p.m. and another set of parents might choose 10:00 p.m. Which one is right or wrong? Neither is right or wrong in comparison.

Organizational norms – are standards of conduct, behavior, dress, and participation or non-participation in activities established by businesses, churches, and social organizations. This level is where many church customs, traditions, and practices are found.

Biblical absolutes – are God's moral laws which are found in His Word as principles and commands. These are true for everybody, everywhere, and every day! In the Ten Commandments for instance, *"You shall not commit adultery,"* (Exodus 20:14) is a biblical absolute. Adultery is a sin in God's eyes—period. This has been a truth ever since it was written, holds true for today, and for as long as the world exists.

Each level of the pyramid above has a different authority. For example, the authority of biblical principles is God's Word, the organization determines organizational norms, and parents determine household rules. In a marriage, the house rules need to be a couple's decision rather than an individual decision.

Each spouse should prayerfully and respectfully consider the other's opinion.

Develop and Incorporate Your Own Story
Share with the couple how your decision making with God has impacted your marriage. What was your most difficult decision? What spiritual decisions did you face together? How did you make them? Is there anything you would have done differently?

Couple Exercises[2]
The following is an example of how to use the pyramid chart above in a decision on how to school your children. Review it with your mentees and then apply the process to a situation that they are facing.

1) *Start with "biblical absolutes."* For example, ask yourselves, "What does the Bible say about the education of children?" A few of the verses that speak to raising children include:

    "Train a child in the way he should go, and when he is old he will not turn from it." (Proverbs 22:6)

"Fathers do not exasperate your children; instead, bring them up in the training and instruction of the Lord."
(Ephesians 6:4)

Clearly, there is a biblical mandate to raise children to know and follow God's ways. However, note that the biblical instruction does not specifically address how children should be taught mathematics or geography or how to teach a child with a learning disability. Therefore, at the biblical absolutes level we have been given a clear teaching about the spiritual nurturance of children; however, it does not provide a command about many other aspects of educating children.

2) *Move up the pyramid to identify organizational norms.*   Ask yourselves, "Has the church given direction on the education of children?"

The church organizational norm has affirmed the biblical absolute. It has given guidance that parents should prayerfully consider and then choose what best fits their family.

3) *Continue to the creation of house rules.* Ask yourselves, "What do we, as a couple, believe about the education of children?"

House rules are accepted and/or created by a couple. Many house rules develop by default without much thought. For example, which chair each person in the family sits in at supper time. Other times, house rules simply develop out of what the parents grew up with in their own families of origin. Conversely, some house rules are the result of a deliberate process of information gathering, prayer, discussion, and counsel.

4) *Finally, determine your preferences.*   Each spouse may have different thoughts about how, when, and where the child should be educated.   Those preferences should be secondary to the principles found in the Bible.

Once you determine the Biblical principles, organizational norms, house rules, and your own preferences, you have the basis for making a good decision.

Tips to Assist in Discussing the Decision Making Process

1) Identify and clarify the decision that needs to be made. Humbly seek God's guidance through prayer.

2) Study the Word to determine if the decision involves biblical absolutes. If so, follow the scriptural principles laid out in the Bible.

3) If the decision does not involve biblical absolutes or if the Bible has no explicit command or principle about the decision, see if the church provides teaching or guidance on how to proceed.

4) Seek the counsel of someone spiritually mature in their Christian values and who you know to have knowledge or expertise in the area you are seeking guidance in.

5) Realize that some decisions and personal preferences have multiple options, any of which may be acceptable to God. In these cases, move to a greater authority such as determining biblical principles to help make the decision. In these cases, you can use biblical wisdom principles to make a decision.

6) Identify the needs of those who will be affected by the decision. Consider the balance of spiritual and emotional consequences of the decision.

7) Consider the short-term and long-term impacts of each option.

8) Evaluate pros and cons of the various aspects of the decision.

9) Remember that just because something happens easily or smoothly doesn't necessarily mean that it is good or right. Just because something is difficult, doesn't necessarily mean that it is bad either.

10) Implement your choice.

11) Re-evaluate the actual implications of your choice.

Discussion Starters

1) How do you go about making important life decisions? What criteria do you typically use?

2) What role do you see your partner having when you are making major decisions?

3) How do you plan on resolving situations where you both feel strongly about something and disagree on the approach to take?

Biblical References

Philippians 4:6-7, *"Do not be anxious about anything, but in every situation, by prayer and petition, with thanksgiving, present your requests to God. And the peace of God, which transcends all understanding, will guard your hearts and your minds in Christ Jesus."*

Proverbs 13:10, *"Pride only breeds quarrels, but wisdom is found in those who take advice."*

Joshua 24:15, *"But if serving the LORD seems undesirable to you, then choose for yourselves this day whom you will serve, whether the gods your ancestors served beyond the Euphrates, or the gods of the Amorites, in whose land you are living. But as for me and my household, we will serve the LORD."*

Philippians 2:3-4, *"Do nothing out of selfish ambition or vain conceit, but in humility consider others better than yourselves. Each of you should look not only to your own interests, but also to the interests of others."*

Chapter 26

Spiritual Beliefs and Developing a Personal Relationship with Christ

Introduction

Maximum joy, fulfillment, and blessing are only possible when a couple is right with God and on the same page spiritually with each other. In this chapter, we will focus on the following spiritual areas:

1) Issues to consider regarding differences in spiritual beliefs.
2) How to have a personal relationship with Jesus Christ.

Common Issues Regarding Spiritual Beliefs

Couples tend to have issues in the following areas:

1) Disagreement on core spiritual issues or beliefs.
2) Minimizing the importance of their spiritual differences or their partner's low level of commitment to God.
3) A willingness to live separate spiritual lives without fully considering the impact this is likely to have on their relationship and children.

Develop and Incorporate Your Own Story

Share your spiritual background with the couple. How did you come to faith in Jesus Christ? How has your personal relationship with Jesus impacted your marriage?

Tips on Discussing Spiritual Beliefs

Couples should want to reduce the potential negative impact of differences in spiritual beliefs on their life and marriage. It is prudent to discuss the following issues, as applicable, with your mentees before they proceed with marriage.

1) Identify what beliefs are very important to you. Are there issues that aren't negotiable? What issues are open to compromise?

2) What spiritual beliefs and practices do you want to teach your children? Will your spouse commit to supporting that? What happens if they change their mind?

3) How do your beliefs impact how each of you views marriage, roles, priorities, financial decision making, having children, and parenting?

4) What values, beliefs or preferences are you willing to yield on for the sake of your marriage?

5) Do you have the support of both of your parents? How important are spiritual beliefs to each of them? Are they likely to interfere with your decisions on what spiritual practices you observe or don't observe?

Agree not to pressure the other or make changes and commitments before you are both ready, even if it means delaying the marriage.

How to Have a Personal Relationship with Jesus Christ

If one or both of the individuals you are mentoring does not have a personal relationship with Jesus Christ, the following outline provides a guide for presenting how they can have that type of relationship and benefit from it as the centerpiece of their marriage.

1) Our sin has separated us from God.

God loves you and has a special plan for your life and marriage. But there is a problem in all of our lives called sin.

We all have sinned and are therefore separated from a holy and righteous God. Therefore we cannot know and experience God's love and plan for our life (including His plans for your marriage) through our own efforts.

"For all have sinned and fall short of the glory of God." (Romans 3:23)

"It's your sins that have cut you off from God..." (Isaiah 59:2a - NLT)

"For whoever shall keep the whole law, and yet stumbles at just one point, is guilty of breaking all of it." (James 2:10)

"For the wages of sin is death, but the gift of God is eternal life in Christ Jesus our Lord." (Romans 6:23)

Jesus Christ is God's only provision for our sin. Through Him you can know and experience God's love and plan for your life.

2) Jesus Died in Your Place.

"We all, like sheep, have gone astray, each of us has turned to his own way; and the LORD has laid on him the iniquity of us all." (Isaiah 53:6)

"God made him (Jesus) who had no sin to be sin for us, so that in him we might become the righteousness of God." (2 Corinthians 5:21)

"But God demonstrates his own love for us in this: While we were still sinners, Christ died for us." (Romans 5:8)

3) Jesus is The Only Way (A Bridge) To God.

"Jesus answered, 'I am the way and the truth and the life; no one comes to the Father except through me." (John 14:6)

4) Even Our "Good Works" Won't Save Us.

"For by grace you have been saved through faith, and that not of yourself, it is the gift of God, not by works so that no one can boast." (Ephesians 2:8-9)

5) We must confess our sins to God, turn away (repent) from them, and individually receive Jesus Christ as your personal Savior and Lord.

Then we can know and experience God's love and plan for our lives.

"If we confess our sins, he is faithful and just and will forgive us our sins and purify us from all unrighteousness." (1 John 1:9)

237

"Yet to all who received him, to those who believed in his name, he gave the right to become children of God." (John 1:12)

"Here I am! I stand at the door and knock. If anyone hears my voice and opens the door, I will come in and eat with him, and he with me." (Revelation 3:20)

6) **The Bible promises eternal life to all who personally receive Christ as Savior and commit to living your life under his Lordship.**

You can then start a new life (being "born again" spiritually) and know that you are going to Heaven.

*"God has given us eternal life, and this life is in the Son. He who has the Son has life; and he who does not have the Son of God does not have life. I write these things to you who believe in the name of the Son of God so that you may **know** that you have eternal life."* (1 John 5:11-13)

Encourage your mentees to make this decision to follow Christ today.

"I tell you, now is the time of God's favor, now is the day of salvation." (2 Corinthians 6:2b)

7) **If you would like to receive Jesus as your personal Lord and Savior, pray the following prayer (or something similar) with the person desiring to follow Jesus:**

"Dear God, I realize that I have sinned against You and that I can't save myself by my own works. I acknowledge that Jesus Christ died on the cross to take the judgment that I deserve and then rose from the dead in fulfillment of the scriptures. I want Jesus to be my Savior. I now turn from my sin, invite Him into my life to take control of it, and to be my Lord and Savior. Help me to live for You each day, as I put my trust in Jesus now. Amen."

Couple Exercises

List the spiritual goals you are individually committing to and committing to as a couple. Discuss them with each other.

1) Have the couple share their Christian testimonies and how they feel it will impact their marriage.
2) Discuss areas where you may want to serve together once married. What role will they each play in the ministry?
3) Are you both in agreement spiritually? Do your priorities build up or hinder each other?

Discussion Starters

1) How thoroughly do you understand each other's spiritual beliefs and views?
2) Where are you now and where have you been in your spiritual journey?
3) How does God's plan of salvation compare with what you had been taught?
4) What is the basis for a person's relationship with God?
5) Are you confident that you both have a passionate, living faith in Jesus Christ?

Recommended Resources

Graham, Billy. *How to Be Born Again*. Dallas, Tex.: Word Pub., 1989.

A similar presentation of the gospel message, in over 150 different languages, is available from several Christian organizations.[1]

Chapter 27

Developing Spiritual Intimacy in Marriage

"A cord of three strands is not quickly broken."
(Ecclesiastes 4:12b)

Introduction

The verse mentioned above provides a powerful word picture of a rope strengthened by three strands intertwined into a single cord. This symbolizes the strength and synergy that exists in a marriage (husband, wife, and God) when it is centered on God and His Word.

> *"What could be more exciting than two people coming together and entrusting their uncertain futures to God's purposes, bound by a common love for His Son? Now, I call that real romance."*
> ~ Beth Moore[1] ~

Intimacy in marriage begins with a spiritual relationship with God. The Apostle John writes, *"Dear friends, since God so loved us, we also ought to love one another. No one has ever seen God; but if we love one another, God lives in us and his love is made complete in us."* *(1 John 4:11-12)*

In this chapter, we will focus on two spiritual issues:

1) Developing spiritual intimacy in marriage.
2) Selecting a church to worship, learn and serve at together.

241

Developing a strong marriage relationship begins with a commitment to developing a strong relationship with God through Jesus Christ. As we mature in that relationship through obedience to God's Word and honor God together, the Holy Spirit brings spiritual maturity and intimacy to the marriage.

"...being confident of this, that he who began a good work in you will carry it on to completion until the day of Christ Jesus." (Philippians 1:6)

Common Issues Regarding Spiritual Intimacy
Couples tend to have issues in the following areas:

1) Differences in how spiritual beliefs are expressed in life and lived out in their marriage.
2) Difference in church preferences.
3) Uncertainty regarding what spiritual beliefs to pass on to their children.

Develop and Incorporate Your Own Story
Share what have you done as a couple to develop spiritual intimacy in your marriage. How do you keep your spiritual life alive individually and as a couple? Looking back, is there anything you would have done differently?

Tips for Discussing Spiritual Intimacy
Spiritual intimacy in marriage is about partnering with God, embracing His love, strength, and leadership, and applying that power in your marriage.

1) Spiritual intimacy is built on a decision to walk close to God in obedience, prayer, meditation on Scripture, fellowship with believers, and service to others. (Acts 2:42)

2) It's a willingness to make Jesus Christ the Lord of our lives (including your marriage) and looking to Him for direction in all of your decisions (e.g. which house to buy, what job to take, where to go on vacation, or which school is best for your children). (Matthew 7:21)

3) It's a willingness to allow God to help you overcome any sense of discomfort over sharing together spiritually and learning to see your marriage as a spiritual adventure.

4) It's realizing that God will often choose to direct the couple and change their hearts to be in agreement, rather than only speaking through one of them.

When we allow God to enter and rule in our marriages, the human relationship is transformed into a life-long covenant relationship with God. Our marriage is transformed into an adventure of lasting love and joy and lived out as a gift from our loving, Heavenly Father.

Initiating and Building Spiritual Intimacy
Building spiritual intimacy doesn't always come naturally, but it's worth the effort because spiritual intimacy:

1) Develops trust, oneness, and closeness.
2) Reduces conflict.
3) Provides a secure spiritual foundation for your home.
4) Helps you withstand the challenges of life.
5) Strengthens your marriage through a shared spiritual focus.
6) Infuses hope and joy deep into your marriage.
7) Develops a home environment where there is safety, peace, love, and forgiveness.
8) Establishes the groundwork for building a great spiritual legacy in your family.
9) Takes the focus off of "me."
10) Allows you to experience what God had in mind for your marriage!

Spiritual intimacy doesn't just happen. Couples need to make some specific decisions and be accessible to what God desires for their marriage.

Where to Start: Partnering with God
Engaging in a personal relationship with Jesus Christ is the first and most important step in initiating spiritual intimacy. It's vital that both people are in agreement spiritually. That means the mentees both need

to "do business" with God—they both need to submit to Him and follow Him.

Imagine a triangle. Optimally, in a Christian marriage relationship, God is at the top and the husband and wife are at opposite ends at the bottom. As you grow spiritually, you move upwards toward God and closer together as a couple.

If each mentee believes differently or are on opposite spiritual growth trajectories, they will not only grow apart relationally, but their spiritual growth is likely to stall as well.

The Lord waits to be invited into our life and marriage. He wants to become the third cord spoken of in Ecclesiastes 4:12. God created each of us in His image with a human spirit that was created to connect with the Spirit of the Living God.

Once you have entered into a personal relationship with Christ, you are ready to share your spiritual journey with your spouse. Together you will discover all that God has for you within the beautiful covenant of a Christian marriage.

Praying Together
Couple prayer is a vital ingredient to a committed Christian marriage. The most intimate thing a couple can do is pray together. When couples pray together, they help settle the issue of who is the Lord over their marriage.

Statistics show only 1 in 1,500 couples that pray together regularly will get a divorce, yet only 4% of Christian couples actually pray together on a regular basis.[3]

When couples neglect to pray together, they miss a *huge* opportunity for tapping into God's protection, guidance, and blessing for their marriage! Praying together is both a solvent and glue.[2] It dissolves resentments and bitterness and binds hearts together.

Swiss psychiatrist, Dr. Paul Tournier says, *"It is only when a husband and wife pray together before God that they find the secret of true harmony: that the difference in their temperaments, their ideas, and their tastes enriches their home instead of endangering it...When each of the marriage partners seeks quietly before God to see his own faults, recognizes his sin, and asks the forgiveness of the other, marital problems are no more...They learn to become absolutely honest with each other...This is the price to be paid if partners very different from each other are to combine their gifts instead of setting them against each other."[4]*

Praying together can be awkward at first because it seems so personal and risky. Praying together can make you feel vulnerable and inadequate. Prayer may be your most difficult step toward spiritual intimacy.

However, every marriage needs a place where two people can come together for a few quiet moments—a place where they have a unified focus: God. Couples who successfully develop this part of their spiritual life together often set a specific time of day (e.g. after dinner or before bedtime) to read the Bible and pray. By developing this habit, couples find that quiet place.

Growing Together Spiritually
Couples need to get involved in activities that will facilitate God-driven growth in their lives and in their marriage. These include:

1) Church attendance, active participation, and service utilizing your spiritual gifts and talents.
2) Joining a small group or individual Bible study.
3) Praying individually and together.

Where was Adam when Eve Sinned?
Real intimacy in marriage begins with a healthy relationship with God. When Adam and Eve lost fellowship with God through their sin, they also lost oneness with each other. Their intimacy was destroyed and they were "both naked and ashamed." When their intimate relationship with God was severed, so was their intimate relationship with each other.

Adam's failure to lead his wife and Eve's failure to consult her husband was a spiritual problem. Was Eve afraid that Adam wouldn't see things her way? Was Adam present but too passive to intervene or protect her? Was he spiritually disengaged and failed to see the threat that Satan posed to his wife?

Hindrances to Spiritual Intimacy

Remember, Satan is hard at work seeking to prevent fulfillment of your deepest needs for intimacy. He continually tries to hinder us with the fear of being transparent and through a husband's passivity towards being a godly leader. In doing so, he lures us into hiding our deepest needs from those we love most, and he leaves us vulnerable to spiritual attack. Satan is opposed to couples living transparent and engaged lives.

Nothing deepens intimacy like transparency and forgiveness. An attitude of forgiveness is the only thing that helps resolve past conflicts. Couples must openly face their fears and failures. They need to ask God to give them the spiritual strength to resolve any painful experiences in their past.

When couples fully discover God's supernatural love for themselves and for each another, they will begin to experience the oneness that God intended for their marriage. Then they can recapture some of what was lost in the Garden of Eden and express love, transparency, and trust in the oneness of marriage.

God's love enables spouses to develop spiritual intimacy as they are engage in fulfilling God's will for their marriage. Jesus said, *"But seek first his kingdom and his righteousness, and all these things will be given to you as well."* (Matthew 6:33)

Ask the Lord to help you both fulfill all of Christ's plans and desires for your marriage. Rely on the Holy Spirit to bring you closer together in that process.

Selecting a Church to Worship and Serve at Together

In addition to teaching the good news or gospel of salvation (as stated in Chapter 26, "How to Have a Personal Relationship with Jesus Christ"), select a church with the following core *beliefs and practices*:

1) The Scriptures (Old and New Testaments) are the complete, divinely inspired, infallible Word of God. The Bible is the supreme authority and guide for Christian faith and living.
2) There is one God, eternally existent in three persons: Father, Son and Holy Spirit.
3) Jesus Christ is the head of the church.
4) Heaven and Hell are real, literal places. Those who follow Christ will live with Him forever and those who reject Christ as Savior and Lord will be separated from Him forever.
5) Developing fully devoted followers of Christ.
6) Providing accountability and fellowship among believers.
7) Having a missionary and service focus that displays Christ's love to others locally and abroad.
8) Providing a strong teaching ministry for adults and children.
9) Having a style of worship that is relevant, spiritually engaging, and scripturally sound.

The church should be located reasonably close to your home so that you can actively participate and serve.

Couple Exercises

1) Discuss the specific steps you are taking and will take to build spiritual intimacy in your marriage.
2) After taking some time to adjust to married life, what are some ways you could cultivate spiritual intimacy through serving others together?

Discussion Starters

1) Have you experienced any tension in your relationship because of differences in your spiritual beliefs?
2) How do your spiritual beliefs bring you closer as a couple or push you apart?

3) How do you think your spiritual beliefs will help your relationship grow stronger as you face the trials of life together?
4) Have you given thought to how being dependent on God will affect you during difficult times?
5) Are your spiritual beliefs playing a major role in your commitment to each other?
6) How are your major decisions influenced by your spiritual beliefs?

Biblical References
Romans 12:6, *"We have different gifts, according to the grace given us. If a man's gift is prophesying, let him use it in proportion to his faith."*

1 Corinthians 14:12, *"So it is with you. Since you are eager to have spiritual gifts, try to excel in gifts that build up the church."*

2 Corinthians 6:14, *"Do not be yoked together with unbelievers. For what do righteousness and wickedness have in common? Or what fellowship can light have with darkness?"*

Recommended Resources
Kennedy, Nancy. *When He Doesn't Believe: Help and Encouragement for Women Who Feel Alone in Their Faith.* Colorado Springs, CO: WaterBrook, 2001.

Strobel, Lee, and Leslie Strobel. *Surviving a Spiritual Mismatch in Marriage.* Grand Rapids, MI: Zondervan, 2002.

Chapter 28

Marriage Expectations

Introduction

We all enter marriage with pre-conceived expectations that are formed through a wide variety of previous experiences and inputs from our families, culture, and the media. Expectations about love and marriage have a powerful impact on relationships.

To a large degree, couples will be happy or disappointed in life based on how well what is happening matches up with what they think should be happening. All married couples start out hoping for and believing they will experience the very best. Problems arise when these hopes and beliefs are not based on reality.

Until a person realizes that they might be holding their partner to an unfair or unreasonable standard, they are likely to feel disappointed when their partner doesn't read their mind, mend their childhood wounds, or fully contribute to a "perfect marriage."

Common Issues Regarding Expectations

Couples tend to need improvement in the following areas:

1) Thinking the euphoria of new love will never change or fade.

2) Guarded (and low) expectations for their marriage, based on what they have seen in others (lack of strong marriage role models).

3) Not realizing that their expectations will change or be uncovered during different stages of married life (e.g. buying and decorating their first home, having children, illness, empty-nest, etc.).

4) Settling for lower expectations for their marriage than God intended.

5) Fear of losing their individual identity once married.

6) Concern about divorce due to personal experience or from seeing the experiences of others.

> *"When a couple is still infatuated with each other, you don't need much because you're still enjoying that chemical high. You expect very little, you feel great, and you're spending a lot of time trying to please each other. But as the relationship deepens, expectations change. And when you're not getting those needs met, suddenly your partner can do little that pleases you - everything seems annoying. ... You may start arguing, but not about the real issues that are bothering you."[1]*

Develop and Incorporate Your Own Story
Share how your expectations as a couple have changed since your engagement period and through the different stages of your marriage (newlyweds, young parents, relocations, etc.).

Tips on Discussing Marriage Expectations
Share the following with your mentees:

1) Both will need to accept that there will be differences in marriage expectations. There is a need for both give and take.

2) Individuals need to be careful not to overlook areas where they need to personally develop by placing the burden for doing so on their spouse.

3) Recognize that there will be some irresolvable differences which you will just need to let go of. Neither of you married a perfect person.

4) Use disappointment as a signal. Let it inform you of a subconscious, unspoken, or unmet need. Every marriage has room for improvement.

5) Resist the temptation to compare your life situation with others. Everyone gets a "complete person" when they marry—not just the sanitized public image of someone you might hear about from others.

6) Use unmet expectations as a reminder to find your true completeness in Christ alone.

7) Focus more on gratitude in order to keep unmet expectations in their proper place.

8) Embrace God's view of marriage, and fight hard to build and protect it. Note that the Bible begins with a marriage (Adam and Eve), uses marriage to illustrate God's love for His people (Christ and the church), and ends with a marriage banquet feast in heaven (God with His people). This clearly reveals the importance that God places on the unique relationship of marriage!

9) Marriage should be wonderful. By God's design, you were created for companionship (Genesis).

10) Marriage is important to God's glory. Of all the things He could have chosen to illustrate His love for us, He chose marriage. Make yours an accurate picture of God's love to a watching and needy world.

11) We learn from others. Surround yourself with couples who share your religious values and are building strong marriages.

Couple Exercises

Select one or two of the following, based on the couple's specific needs in the area of expectations.

1) Ask the couple to list 3-5 expectations that they have for their marriage together (not just individually for their spouse). Discuss how realistic their expectations are.

2) Help the mentees identify the healthy expectations they can help satisfy for each other.

3) Help each person understand where their expectations came from by identifying where their major sources of input came from. How reliable are those sources?

4) Discuss how we know what God thinks about marriage. List 5-10 expectations that God has for their marriage. Have them share and discuss their lists.

5) Discuss some of the following unreasonable expectations with your mentees. Have them identify reasonable alternatives.

Unreasonable/Incorrect Expectations	Reasonable Expectations (Discussion points listed below, for the mentors use.)
My spouse will meet all of my social and emotional needs.	• There will be times when your spouse will disappoint and frustrate you. • You will need to maintain some individual friends as well as develop new couple friendships.
If we can maintain the same level of love we began with, our marriage will succeed.	• How love is expressed and received will vary over the course of a lifetime together. Sometimes it will be thrilling. Sometimes it will be comforting. Sometimes it will just be there. The goal is to nurture your marriage so your love grows richer and deeper.
I know everything there is to know about my spouse and my spouse knows everything about me.	• To succeed in marriage, you will need to regularly invest in learning how to be happily married during each stage of your lives together. • As you grow older, you change. The man or woman you married ten years ago is not the man or woman you are married to today. You need to be constantly learning about your spouse.

Unreasonable/Incorrect Expectations	Reasonable Expectations (Discussion points listed below, for the mentors use.)
Our marriage will be free from arguing.	▪ Conflict avoidance is a strong predictor of divorce. ▪ It is unrealistic to assume that marriage will solve your unique differences or grant you the power to unilaterally decide for your spouse.
What we have experienced as a couple so far can only get better once we are married.	▪ Every marriage goes through times of intense joy and intense sadness and disappointment. We're all human.
If we were meant for each other, this feeling of love that we have should never fade.	▪ Love is dynamic and multi-faceted. It will change over time and will take work in order to grow deeper.
Marriage will correct the problems we have had so far.	▪ Marriage doesn't resolve problems. It just magnifies them. ▪ Marriage will bring a new set of problems which will need to be managed and resolved.
Marriage will help us "grow up" and be more independent.	▪ In some ways, marriage may "force" you to grow up. In others, you will see a greater need to grow up. ▪ Independence from your parents will be a learned process for both you and your parents. ▪ You will always have someone in authority over you. That's life. ▪ Marriage isn't to be an escape from your parents.

Unreasonable/Incorrect Expectations	Reasonable Expectations (Discussion points listed below, for the mentors use.)
Our marriage will be just like (or unlike) my parents' marriage.	<ul><li>No two marriages are alike. Integrating each of your backgrounds and expectations will be a unique process.</li><li>Role expectations need to be discussed, selected, adapted, and honored.</li></ul>
We're in love and we know each other well. Getting married won't be a big transition for us.	<ul><li>When dating, you usually see their best face. Once married, you will see everything—every hour, every day, and every year.</li></ul>
Since he or she is my soul mate, we will always think alike.	<ul><li>If you always think alike, one of you isn't necessary.</li><li>If you learn how to resolve differences fairly and effectively, resolved conflict can actually strengthen your marriage.</li></ul>
Marriage is a risky proposition. We have a 50-50 chance of making it.	<ul><li>While all couples face the risk of divorce, you both can learn how to be successfully married by learning and using sound biblical and relational tools.</li></ul>
Once we are able to be with each other all the time, our relationship will get better.	<ul><li>Being together every day will present new challenges, especially during times of conflict or irritability.</li></ul>
My spouse and I will see most things alike.	<ul><li>God created you in His image, male and female. You are different in skills, emotions, roles, and so on, yet of equal value.</li></ul>
If he loves me, he will know what I'm thinking or feeling.	<ul><li>Men and women are different, and neither is a mind reader.</li></ul>
Marriage will cure my feelings of loneliness.	<ul><li>Without addressing the root cause for loneliness, lonely single people become lonely married people.</li></ul>

Unreasonable/Incorrect Expectations	Reasonable Expectations (Discussion points listed below, for the mentors use.)
Having children will make our marriage stronger.	▪ The addition of children to a marriage presents new challenges. If you want a lasting marriage, your children cannot always come first—your spouse does. ▪ The best gift you can give your children is building a strong marriage.
If my expectations aren't being met, I must have married the wrong person.	▪ If you are expecting the perfect mate, you will be disappointed. So will your spouse. ▪ Develop your marriage skills. Marriages do best when marriage expectations match a couple's marriage skills!
Once we are married, I will get him or her to church.	▪ It is often more difficult to affect a person's behavior after marriage. If they aren't willing before, it will be less likely after. ▪ Pray for your spouse and let him or her see the impact your faith has on how you live and love them.
When married, I can expect the same amount of attention, affection, and money spent on me as when we were dating.	▪ Time demands and priorities change throughout life. Successful couples learn to adapt to life changes.
My wife (husband) will do things just like mom (dad) did things (e.g. cook, fix things, house keeping).	▪ You didn't marry your parent; you married a unique individual who came from a different home.

Discussion Starters

1) Do you think you will ever have major problems or challenges in your marriage?
2) Can time alone resolve most of the problems married couples face?
3) Is love all that couples need in order to have a great marriage?
4) Is there anything that would cause you to question your love for each other?
5) Do you expect the difficulties you are having now will fade away after your wedding? If so, why?
6) Can your partner meet all of your needs for companionship? Why not?
7) How do you expect the romantic feelings you now have to change over time?

Biblical References

Reasonable marriage expectations focus on core values, such as:

1) *Faithfulness*

   "Many a man claims to have unfailing love, but a faithful man who can find?" (Proverbs 20:6)

   "She speaks with wisdom, and faithful instruction is on her tongue." (Proverbs 31:26)

2) *Respect*

   "... each one of you also must love his wife as he loves himself, and the wife must respect her husband." (Ephesians 5:33)

   "Teach the older men to be temperate, worthy of respect, self-controlled, and sound in faith, in love and in endurance." (Titus 2:2)

3) *Friendship*

   "A friend loves at all times ..." (Proverbs 17:17a)

   "If one falls down, his friend can help him up. But pity the man who falls and has no one to help him up!" (Ecclesiastes 4:10)

4) Romance

> *"Take me away with you--let us hurry! Let the king bring me into his chambers."* (Song of Songs 1:4)

> *"Let my lover come into his garden and taste its choice fruits."* (Song of Songs 4:16b)

5) Forgiveness

> *"Forgive us our debts, as we also have forgiven our debtors...For if you forgive men when they sin against you, your heavenly Father will also forgive you."* (Matthew 6:12, 14)

> *"Bear with each other and forgive whatever grievances you may have against one another. Forgive as the Lord forgave you."* (Colossians 3:13)

Chapter 29

Relationship Outlook

*Dating, Engaged, or Married...Building the Relationship
is the Foundation for Success.*

Introduction

Relational empowerment is the ability to develop and maintain healthy relationships with others. Unfortunately, being able to build and maintain healthy and satisfying relationships in the home or community does not happen automatically, whether we are religious or not. As a matter of fact, our natural disposition as people coupled with the conditioning of our society often makes our relationships a very troublesome and painful experience. Much of our suffering on a personal level is the direct result of the difficulties we encounter when trying to build or maintain relationships.

This mentoring session is designed to:

1) Share realistic and unrealistic expectations about love, relationships, and the challenges all people face in relationships.
2) Help the couple identify relationship skills they can use.
3) Provide steps that mentees can use in building strong, healthy relationships.

Common Issues Regarding Relationship Outlook

1) *Vulnerability.* Many people think that vulnerability is a sign of weakness. That's an especially popular opinion among Type

A personalities. They prefer maintaining a facade of strength and pretending to have it all together at all times. But that's not how God views vulnerability. He sees us as we really are. Any attempt to pass ourselves off as something else doesn't work with God. And expressing humility before God is what He recognizes and rewards.

With relationships, think of it this way: If you allow your vulnerability to show, you'll find that others will start to relate to you better. You may start to hear things like, "I thought I was the only one with that problem." That opens the door to some great discussion. And if you allow yourself to be more vulnerable with God, you'll find that such an attitude reaps its own rewards. Realize, too, that in this world you're never completely vulnerable. God is our ultimate protector—always has been and always will be.

2) *Unhealthy Relationships.* Chemistry buffs and pyrotechnic experts will tell you that certain chemicals should never be combined. A mixture that seems harmless can quickly become combustible and dangerous. The same warning applies to relationships. Certain people, when mixed together, create a volatile combination. For you, maybe it's a married woman or man at work who likes to flirt. Or maybe, it's a friend who knows how to talk you into things you shouldn't do. The question you need to ask is, "How can I steer clear of trouble and avoid danger?"

3) *Core Issues.* Core issues are those having to do with a person's basic identity, self-worth, and needs. Regardless of how important the other issues may be, compared to the core issues of a healthy identity and a genuine sense of personal worth, such issues are superficial. In fact, these other issues hinge on personal identification, self worth, and personal needs.

Similarly, husbands are often guilty of communicating with their wives on a "logical" level rather than considering her need for security (love, acceptance, and forgiveness). Proving that our opinion is "right" by the rules of logic completely misses the core issue of our spouse's personal needs and true identity. It is possible to be absolutely "right" and relationally wrong at the same time.

Wives also fall prey to the temptation of "nagging" their husbands into agreement rather than communicating while understanding his basic need for significance (importance, meaning, and adequacy) and respect.

Without addressing the basic personal needs and the assumptions we have concerning how those needs are met, it is impossible to experience anything but superficial communication. This is not to say that there is no overlap in both genders with security and adequacy needs...there is. Men, as well as women, seek and need security (love, acceptance, and forgiveness). Women, as well as men, seek and need significance (importance, meaning, and adequacy). But each gender approaches these differently.

The Three Steps to a Better Relationship with Your Partner: Trust, Give and Bless, and Forgive

1) Scripture says it and experience proves it. God is trustworthy. He is the essence of rock-solid dependability. Eternally devoted, He never leaves us in the lurch. As the children of God, this quality should also permeate our relationships. Does it? Are we there for friends even when it is inconvenient? Do we keep promises to our spouses and children? Do we stand by relatives, remaining dedicated to them even when they do annoying things or it is unpleasant to be around them? Resolve to do a better job today of letting God's consistent care and concern flow through you.

2) Consider how the Bible portrays God as often lovingly searching for people. From the Garden of Eden, where the Creator asks Adam, "Where are you?" to Jesus' stories of a lost sheep, a missing coin, and a wayward son, the picture is one of a caring Father wanting desperately to find His children. Imagine the difference it would make if we sought relationships (with our spouses, our children, our friends) with

such passion, seeking not to *get* something from them but to *give* and *bless*.

3) Have you ever seen a friendship ripped apart by betrayal or unresolved conflict? Have you ever wondered what you could do to bridge such serious rifts? In the book of Philemon, Paul offers a strategy for repairing broken relationships. As a follower of Christ, Philemon had a responsibility to forgive Onesimus just as he himself had been forgiven by God. Paul urges Philemon to do him a favor and give Onesimus another chance. What would happen if you used a similar strategy the next time you have an opportunity to serve as a peacemaker between two people?

Develop and Incorporate Your Own Story

Share a time when you felt you had to completely trust God and ask for forgiveness from your spouse. Tell how you approached the feeling of vulnerability and the outcome of the core issues that were involved.

Tips on Developing a Healthy Relationship Outlook

1) Give regular attention to your relationship—at least 15 minutes of meaningful dialogue each day. The focus of this dialogue should be on your feelings about each other and your life together.

2) Be curious about each other and give your relationship the same priority and attention you gave it when you were first dating—ask lots of questions.

3) Speak the "truth" in love. Speaking the truth in love is a biblical description of effective communication. In order to love others like Christ, we must develop this communication skill to such an extent that it becomes second nature to us.

4) Journal. Some people find it useful to practice "journaling" when trying to hear God's voice. This simply means spending time alone with God in prayer and writing down on paper what you think He is telling you. Try asking God what He thinks of you and who He has made you to be, and then write down the answers you receive.

5) Love others around you. Having heard God assure you of His love, ask Him to lead you in loving others around you. (Note the way your sense of personal security is enhanced by being used of God to love others.)

The stronger the approach a couple takes to strengthen their relationship, the more they will affect the outcome. The more constructive the approach they take, the greater the probability of success.

Couple Exercises
Here are two couple exercises that you can do with your couple.

Exercise 1: Important Topics for Discussion
Describe a recent situation in which your feelings were hurt by what someone said or did. What were you specifically feeling at the time (anger, rejection, fear)? Note the natural tendency to blame that person for the way you were feeling and to justify or rationalize your response to them. Now try to identify the false assumptions you were harboring when you were hurt by them. Note how much easier it is to blame them than it is to identify your own false assumptions.

Exercise 2: Scenario Communication
Be honest with God about the hatred you have inside for the one who hurt you. Express not only your hatred for the one who hurt you, but also all your justifications as to why you hate them. Confess the false assumptions discovered earlier (I wouldn't have a problem with my self-image if this person had not said that or done this, etc.). Ask God to forgive you for your unbelief about your own worth, the unforgiveness and judgment you harbor in your heart, and to cleanse you from any hatred in your soul. Allow God to affirm your worth and convince you that you are secure in His love and significant in His plan.

Discussion Starters

1) What area in your relationship do you find most difficult to express to your partner?
2) Do you sometimes feel your partner lacks respect for you and your dignity?

3) If you could share one new thing about yourself to your partner, what would it be?

Biblical References

Numbers 30: 1-3, *"Moses said to the heads of the tribes of Israel: "This is what the Lord commands: When a man makes a vow to the Lord or takes an oath to obligate himself by a pledge, he must not break his word but must do everything he said. When a young woman still living in her father's house makes a vow to the Lord or obligates herself by a pledge..."*

Ephesians 5: 31-33, *"For this reason a man will leave his father and mother and be united to his wife, and the two will become one flesh." This is a profound mystery—but I am talking about Christ and the church. However, each one of you also must love his wife as he loves himself, and the wife must respect her husband."*

2 Corinthians 6:14, *"Do not be yoked together with unbelievers. For what do righteousness and wickedness have in common? Or what fellowship can light have with darkness?"*

Recommended Resources

Stanley, Scott. *A Lasting Promise: a Christian Guide to Fighting for Your Marriage*. San Francisco: Jossey-Bass, 1998.

Townsend, John Sims. *Who's Pushing Your Buttons?: Handling the Difficult People in Your Life*. Nashville, TN: Integrity, 2004.

Wright, H. Norman. *Communication: Key to Your Marriage : a Practical Guide to Creating a Happy, Fulfilling Relationship*. Ventura, CA: Regal, 2000.

Burke, H. Dale. *Different by Design: God's Master Plan for Harmony between Men and Women in Marriage*. Chicago: Moody, 2000.

Parrott, Les, and Leslie L. Parrott. *Saving Your Marriage before It Starts: Seven Questions to Ask Before—and After—You Marry*. Grand Rapids, MI: Zondevan, 2006.

McNulty, James K., and Benjamin R. Karney. "Positive Expectations in the Early Years of Marriage: Should Couples Expect the Best or Brace for the Worst?" *Journal of Personality and Social Psychology* 86.5 (2004): 729-43.

Van, Epp John., and Epp John. Van. *How to Avoid Falling in Love with a Jerk: the Foolproof Way to Follow Your Heart without Losing Your Mind.* New York: McGraw-Hill, 2008.

Chapter 30

Building Trust in Your Relationship

Introduction

In order for a relationship to develop lasting intimacy, trust must be present. For a new couple, the relationship is at a fragile stage since there is a very limited history of trustworthy behavior. Trust isn't an emotion; it's a learned behavior that takes time and shared experiences to cultivate.

Even when trust is established, couples need to realize that trust is a perishable asset within a relationship. It must be consistently guarded, and maintained.

Common Issues Regarding Trust

1) An unwillingness to open up and be transparent.
2) Past experiences with deceitfulness between partners.
3) Fear of being hurt if one person trusts the other.

Develop and Incorporate Your Own Story

Share the things you do to maintain trust in your own marriage. If you have had a lapse in trust, share what you did in order to rebuilt trust in your marriage.

Tips to Assist in Discussing Trust Building

Here are ways to help build (or rebuild) trust in your relationship:

1) *Be Trustworthy*
   - Follow the Word of God in every area of your life. Live your life beyond reproach.

   - Develop a healthy sense of self respect. Build that on what God says about you and your worth rather than relying on what others might say. (See Chapter 9 – Dealing with Your Partner's Unique Traits - Partner Styles and Habits.)

   - Be a man or woman of your word. Establish a history of always being reliable and doing what you say. If you plan on changing direction, model trustworthy behavior by discussing it first.

   - Never lie to your spouse or others. If you do, you will leave them wondering what else you've been lying about. Watch out for the "little white lies." They aren't "little" in a marriage relationship, and they are also sin.

   - When there are trials in your relationship, meet them directly and assertively. You reinforce commitment and trust when you work through those times when things are the worst. (See Chapter 6 on Communication.) Procrastination and avoiding difficult conversations erodes trust in a relationship.

   - Be an open book with each other regarding your schedule, activities, and plans. Be the first one to inform them about things they might want to know. Talk to each other more and don't keep secrets.

   - Take full responsibility for your actions, develop your leadership skills with a mentor, and be proactive in looking out for the needs of your spouse and family.

   - Develop strong relational boundaries with friends of the opposite sex and any friends that your spouse has reservations about. Protecting your own marriage is paramount. Gary and Mona Shriver, in their book, *Unfaithful – Rebuilding Trust After Infidelity*[1], recommend protective "hedges" for your eyes (what you allow yourself to look at), your actions (compliments and hugs), and your mind (daydreaming about someone other than your spouse). Count the cost of sexual immorality before the fog of temptation hits.

▪ Apologize for past offenses; make restitution and demonstrate repentance. Then allow sufficient time for your spouse to see the changed behavior, and allow them to begin trusting again at a pace that they feel comfortable with. You can't force trust.

2) *Be Willing to Extend Trust*

▪ Be a good listener.

▪ Express your love in words and actions, and tell them of your commitment to your marriage.

▪ If you truly believe that your partner is a good willed person, extend them the "benefit of the doubt." Start from a point of trust and stay there unless or until they prove by their actions that they aren't behaving in a trustworthy manner. Extending trust is initially a step of faith.

▪ After your partner appropriately expresses sorrow for an offense, apply the process of forgiveness. (See Chapter 8 – Granting Forgiveness.) Don't bring up old issues again.

▪ Don't allow hurts from past relationships to contaminate your current relationship. You are now dealing with a different person who deserves to be treated for who they are, not judged for the actions of others.

▪ Be willing to work through problems in your relationship. Create an atmosphere that freely allows either of you to bring up issues that are troubling you without fear of how the other might respond.

▪ As appropriate, be willing to face your fears and take some risk. If after trying for a period of time, you are still wallowing in the pain of betrayal and unable to extend trust to your spouse, seek counseling together to help you both work through these issues.

▪ Be willing to extend grace to each other.

Listen to the questions your partner is asking (e.g. "Where have you been?" or "Why didn't you answer my call?"). They may indicate some concern about the level of trust in your relationship.

If you don't trust your spouse, it will create an environment of doubt and lead your partner to doubt you as well.

Couple Exercises

1) List five things your partner could do to establish a foundation of trust in your relationship. Discuss them together.
2) Share with your partner your expectations of trust. What does trust mean to you?
3) In what areas in your life does trust mean the most to you?

Discussion Starters

1) Describe a time when you felt that your trust had been betrayed by someone. How did you feel? How did you recover from it?
2) How was trust established in your family?
3) Is there an element of distrust that bothers you today? Why?

Biblical References

Matthew 5:37, *"Simply let your `Yes' be `Yes,' and your `No,' `No'; anything beyond this comes from the evil one."*

James 5:16a, *"Therefore confess your sins to each other and pray for each other so that you may be healed."*

1 Timothy 3:8-9, *"Deacons, likewise, are to be men worthy of respect, sincere, not indulging in much wine, and not pursuing dishonest gain. They must keep hold of the deep truths of the faith with a clear conscience."*
1 Timothy 3:11, *"...wives are to be women worthy of respect, not malicious talkers but temperate and trustworthy in everything."*

Recommended Resource

Jenkins, Jerry B. *Hedges: Loving Your Marriage Enough to Protect It.* Wheaton, IL: Crossway, 2005.

Part 7

REMARRIAGE AND STEPFAMILIES

Chapter 31

Remarriage

Introduction

Couples getting married for the first time in the United States have approximately a 45 to 50% chance of getting divorced. Remarried couples have an even greater divorce rate at about 60% with that rate increasing even more when children are involved. Why?

Compared to first marriages, remarriages tend to:

1) Involve more people with personality characteristics that are detrimental to successful marriage (e.g. selfishness, impulsivity, neuroticism).
2) Be more accepting of divorce as an option when there are marital problems.
3) Have less social support than first time marriages have.
4) Add additional pressure and baggage from the previous marriages (e.g. emotional pain, legal issues, child support, children visitation rights, etc.).

In addition, many remarried couples haven't yet learned to successfully resolve marital disagreements, and thus they are more prone to repeating behaviors that led to problems in their first marriage. This is likely to involve a greater commitment of time for all involved in the mentoring process.

As a mentor, you will first need to help the couple determine if there was a biblical basis for the divorce and if remarriage is a biblically supported option. Scriptural passages to consider are included at the end of this chapter.

Common Issues Regarding Remarriage

1) Insufficient time to heal from the prior divorce.
2) Unresolved issues or ongoing conflict with former spouse.
3) Lack of training in key marriage skills, such as communication, conflict resolution, finances, and so on.
4) Haste to get married due to loneliness, sexual temptation, and so on.
5) If this is a first marriage for one of the partners, they may be unaware of past issues or minimize them as not being relevant to their current relationship.
6) Lack of biblical justification for remarriage and wanting to remarry anyway.

Develop and Incorporate Your Own Story
If either of you have been remarried, share general lessons learned from your experience that may be relevant to the mentees.

Tips on Discussing Remarriage
Successful remarriages have several common characteristics. These couples:

1) Finished grieving their prior loss and are emotionally ready for this marriage. (Ongoing hostility with a former spouse indicates a problem in this area.)

2) Got pre-marital counseling or mentoring and are engaged with other groups that will provide encouragement, support, and accountability.

3) Learned from past mistakes and have a clear picture of their couple strengths and weaknesses.

4) Realistically faced the challenges ahead with reasonable expectations (e.g. adjusting to new family members and understand how challenging marriage can be).

5) Nurture their couple bond by setting time aside for themselves as a priority.

6) Start fresh in a new house and neighborhood.

7) Don't compare the new marriage with their old one.

8) Are open to personal change and relational compromise and adjustments.

9) Get financial counsel, especially when there are issues with alimony, child-support, or finances.

10) Form new routines and family traditions while flexibly adopting the best from each partner's experiences.

11) Work towards re-developing transparency and vulnerability in their marriage while openly acknowledging their hopes and fears.

12) Leave the negativity from their prior marriage behind.

Couple Exercises

Download a copy of "Questions Before Considering Remarriage" found in the Resources section of TheSolutionForMarriages.com and have the couple review and discuss it together. Debrief selected areas with them.

Discussion Starters

1) Have you both discussed the Property or Marital Settlement Agreement (or Marital Separation Agreement) from the past marriage(s)?

2) What impact do you think this agreement will have on your relationship? Your children? Your finances?

3) Do you think a Pre-Marital Agreement is necessary for your relationship/marriage? Why or Why not?

Biblical References
Is there a biblical option for this remarriage? Some verses that apply
to this are:

1) Matthew 5:31-32
2) Matthew 19:1-12
3) Mark 10:1-12
4) Luke 16:18
5) 1 Corinthians 7:10-16

Recommended Resource
Rosberg, Gary, and Barbara Rosberg. *Divorce Proof Your Marriage.*
Wheaton, IL: Tyndale House, 2004.

Chapter 32

Stepfamilies[1]

Introduction

Many experts agree that unrealistic expectations for stepfamily life often set couples up for great disappointment. While all new marriages involve different people and different dynamics, it is not uncommon for individuals to slip into the same old patterns and routines (e.g. being avoidant during conflict), especially in the midst of the stress of blending two families.

Christian blended families are becoming more and more common in our society. This chapter looks at the unique challenges that stepfamilies face and helps prepare the mentee couple for that.

Common Issues Regarding Stepfamilies

1) Managing the roles and expectations of father vs. stepfather and mother vs. stepmother.
2) Couples not recognizing the level of challenge involved with integrating two families.
3) Children coming between the parent and stepparent in matters of house rules, discipline, and so forth.

Tips on Discussing Stepfamilies

When two families form one blended family, they often struggle with the integration because they come from two different households and different sets of rules. A crucial point to the stepfamily success is to set up rules for discipline and be consistent with the rules for all children involved. Rules should not be permitted to be stretched or broken nor should children be permitted to maneuver one parent against another.

A stepfamily often experiences times when the child or children visit the noncustodial parent. As stepparents, we should strive to be good examples of godliness and manage ourselves with integrity.

Below is a list of common unrealistic and realistic expectations for both parents and children.

Common Expectations	
Unrealistic	**Realistic**
Love will happen instantly between all family members.	Love may or may not happen between stepfamily members. It will take time for relationships to develop; some will bond quickly, others slowly.
We'll do marriage better this time around.	Individuals who have experienced a breakup or divorce often have learned tough lessons from the past. But a new marriage cannot be compared to a prior one. It involves different people and different marital dynamics.
'Blending' is the goal of this stepfamily.	When relationships "blend," they are equal and everyone feels connected. It's common for couples to want their family to "blend" quickly. But the truth is, some stepfamily members may never "blend," while others form close bonds.
A child's expectation: My stepparent will not try to act like my parent.	Sometimes stepparents want so badly to be accepted that they try to manage the children as a biological parent would. Unfortunately, the children will still notice the difference.

Common Expectations	
Unrealistic	**Realistic**
A child's expectation: When my stepparent does discipline me, they will act just like my biological parent.	What's familiar to children is their biological parent's parenting style. A different parenting style and different rules can be difficult to adjust to. Before marriage, try to bring each household's rules in line with each other (e.g. same bedtime, curfew, etc.). After marriage, each parent should strive to be the authority with their own children and agree to the same rules for everyone.

Couple Exercises

A stepmother expressed the following expectations two years into her remarriage:

1) I thought my husband would appreciate how overwhelming and difficult it would be for me to care for his children.
2) I thought that raising his children would fulfill my need to be a mother.
3) I thought I would have more say in the children's visitation schedules (e.g. when we watch them for their mother, when they spend the night at a friend's house, etc.).
4) I expected to fit in, to be welcomed by his children, and to be treated well.
5) I expected to immediately take priority over all his other relationships, even his children.

How do you identify with her desires? How realistic do you believe them to be? Discuss as a couple.

Discussion Starters

1) What have you each done to fully understand and prepare for the realities of life in a blended family?
2) What do you see as the major challenges you are likely to face in adjusting as a blended family?

3) How aware are you of the stress your couple relationship is likely to experience?
4) How much have you talked about the new and unique parenting responsibilities you will have?
5) What discipline scenarios have you discussed? Are you in agreement on discipline for your children? Your partner's children?

Additional discussion items can be found in Chapter 31, Remarriage.

Biblical References
1 Timothy 3:4, *"He must manage his own family well and see that his children obey him with proper respect."*

Titus 2:3-5, *"Likewise, teach the older women to be reverent in the way they live, not to be slanderers or addicted to much wine, but to teach what is good. Then they can urge the younger women to love their husbands and children, to be self-controlled and pure, to be busy at home, to be kind, and to be subject to their husbands, so that no one will malign the word of God."*

Recommended Resources
Deal, Ron L. *The Smart Stepfamily*. Minneapolis, MN: Bethany House, 2006.

Part 8

SUPPLEMENTAL MATERIALS FOR MENTORS

Mentors' Letter to the Parents[1]

On the next page is an example of a letter that we write to the mentee's parents which serves the following purposes:

1) Provides another perspective on the relationship between the parents and their son or daughter and possible insights into the mentee's family of origin.
2) Helps prepare the parents for letting go of their son or daughter and to recognize the new family unit.
3) Highlights any areas that may need your attention during your mentoring sessions.
4) Solicits the parent's prayer support.
5) Provides an opportunity for the parents to share a special word of encouragement that you can then share with the couple.

A copy can be downloaded from the Resources section of TheSolutionForMarriages.com

Mentors' Names
Address

Dear Parents of *John Smith*,

We are privileged to have the opportunity to mentor *John and Jane*, and believe that it is important to include parents as we help them prepare for a fulfilling and Christ honoring marriage through our pre-marriage mentoring program.

You have invested much of your love, time, energy and, finances in raising and training *John* which has enabled him to come to this point in life. You know *John* perhaps better than anyone else, and we would like to have and benefit from your perspective as we meet with them over the next few months.

Please reply to the following questions by e-mail to *mentors@ emailaddress.com* or returning them to *John* so that your comments may be shared and discussed in our future premarital mentoring sessions.

1) Describe your past and current relationship with your son.
2) Describe your current relationship with your future daughter-in-law.
3) What do you see as your role in helping your son form a new, independent household as God instructs them to do in Genesis 2:24?
4) What would respect from your son and daughter-in-law look like to you after they are married?
5) How frequently would you like to talk to and/or see the newly married couple?
6) How would you like holiday time to be handled by each of the families involved?
7) What are your hopes and prayers for this couple as they come together in marriage?

Thank you for your input to this mentoring process. We appreciate your prayers for each of us as we work with *John and Jane*.

Blessings,

Mary and Mike Mentors

The 3-6 Month Post-Marriage Follow-up

Introduction

Ongoing expert coaching is critical for helping couples gain the skills needed for a successful marriage. After giving time for the "honeymoon phase" of marriage to wane, consider investing one more session into the lives of your mentees.

We recommend meeting with your mentee couple 3-6 months after their wedding. See how they are doing, applaud their success together, and offer to help them with any issues that have developed in their relationship.

Tips for Conducting the Follow-up Meeting

The following set of questions can serve as a guide. Pick the ones that you feel are most relevant.

1) How is an "ideal" marriage different from what your marriage is like today?

2) Now that you are more familiar with your spouse, you may be tempted to say or do things that you wouldn't have done during your engagement. How are you each handling that temptation?

3) Matthew 7:24-27 describes wise and foolish builders. In what specific areas are you building your marriage on a firm foundation?

4) Have you discovered any likes, dislikes, or habits that your spouse has that you were not aware of before marriage?

5) Have you discovered any problems that originated before your marriage that are now manifesting themselves in your relationship?

6) What challenging situations have you encountered that have drawn you closer together in marriage?

7) How has leaving your parents been working out? How have the holidays gone? Do you both feel that your family was fairly treated?

8) How is your relationship with your in-laws? Parents? Have all parties been able to or allowed to "leave and cleave?"

9) How is work going for you? How does it impact your relationship?

10) How are your finances? Are things different than you expected before getting married?

11) Have either of you tried to change something about your spouse? In what ways?

12) Are there any activities in your spouse's life that you feel are consuming too much of their time?

13) Have you been able to accept and appreciate advice from each other?

14) What has been you biggest fight or area of disagreement so far? Do you both feel the issue(s) have been fully and fairly resolved?

15) How has your relationship with God changed now that you're married? In what areas have you and your spouse been able to grow together spiritually?

16) What spiritual disciplines (prayer, Bible study, obedience, church involvement) have been easy to implement or maintain since you got married? Which have been most challenging for you to maintain? Do you have a plan to address any gaps?

17) What could we do to improve the marriage mentoring process you experienced?

18) In what ways did you feel under-prepared for marriage? Well prepared?

Mentors, make note of any constructive suggestions your mentees have, and incorporate them into your future mentoring sessions.

Couple Exercises

1) Have the couple share a few enjoyable and memorable memories from their first three months of marriage.

2) What specific seminars or marriage training will the couple take during the coming year?

3) What specific activities will the couple take during years 2-5 to keep their relationship fresh and/or to prepare for parenting?

Encourage the couple to continue to build their marriage upon the foundation of God's Word. Remind them of Ecclesiastes 4:9-12. That is where their true security comes from.

Write to us at info@TheSolutionForMarriages.com with your recommendations for marriage enrichment options.

Check the Resources section of TheSolutionForMarriages.com for enrichment recommendations as they become available.

Mentoring Program Evaluation[1]

Introduction
In the spirit of continuous improvement, mentors should seek feedback from those they mentor so an individual and a church's mentoring process can be refined for maximum impact. The following form is intended to be used for this purpose.

A copy of this evaluation form is available in the Resources section of
TheSolutionForMarriages.com

Premarital Couple's Evaluation of Mentoring Experience
(To be completed once premarital portion of mentoring is complete)

Premarital Couple's Names:

_____   _____
First   Last

_____   _____
First   Last

Marriage Mentor Couple's Names:

_____   _____
First   Last

How many sessions did you have with your Marriage Mentors: _____

Overall, was the mentoring a positive experience? Yes _____ No _____
Somewhat _____

What topics did you find most helpful?_____
_____
_____

What topics do you feel should have been discussed, but weren't?
_____
_____

What areas of sharing did you find most difficult? Why? _____
_____
_____

Have you seen your relationship improve due to the mentoring? If so, how? _____
_____
_____

Do you feel ready for marriage? _____
_____
_____

How could your overall mentoring experience have been improved? _____
_____
_____

Is there anything that you would still like to discuss with the pastor/marriage ministry leader? _____
_____
_____

Signature of Premarital Couple:

Partner 1: _____   Date: _____

Partner 2: _____   Date: _____

How Relationships Are Impacted by Cohabitation

Introduction

Have you ever snuck a look at a gift you were going to receive ahead of time (e.g. finding a birthday present and looking at it before your birthday)? Did knowing ahead of time spoil the surprise on the day you were to receive it? Living together is like opening a wonderful gift ahead of its intended time. It is un-wrapping a special gift, peeking at it too soon, and then having to live with the consequences.

Cohabitation rates have skyrocketed since the 1960s when Western cultures began to cast off traditional sexual mores, but the same period also saw a correlating upsurge of divorce. This section looks at how a couple may have decided to cohabitate, issues that this has raised, and the impact cohabitation has had on their relationship.

Tips for Discussing Cohabitation

While virtually all studies show that cohabitation is detrimental to the marriage relationship, about two-thirds of married couples cohabit before marriage in the United States. Here are some relationship areas that researchers have found to be impacted by cohabitation.

Note that some recent studies[1] have yielded conflicting results for *engaged* couples that live together but have a specific wedding date scheduled. We recommend that mentors always address this topic from both a spiritual perspective and a relational perspective. Even if there wasn't such a negative effect on couples, cohabitation is still morally wrong.

Higher Break up or Divorce Rates - The Myth of "Testing the Relationship" First

Today, a majority of young people believe that living together first is helpful in determining if a marriage is likely to last. Nothing could be further from the truth. While it might seem reasonable to "try the shoe on before deciding if you'll buy it," it's impossible to "practice" permanence. Marriages aren't shoes. Shoes can be thrown away without anyone getting hurt.

By its very nature, trying out a relationship through cohabitation results in a self-serving, performance-based relationship. That's a far cry from the commitment-based, covenant relationship of a true marriage. When cohabiting, couples usually focus on obtaining satisfaction *from* the other person. Marriage requires spouses to focus on providing satisfaction *for* the other person and receiving satisfaction as a by-product.

1) Living together sets up a couple for failure. Cohabitation increases the divorce rate of those who eventually marry to about 65%.[2] Others estimate the increase in divorces after cohabitation at 50 to 100% higher than for couples who have not lived together.[3] This effect was noted in studies conducted in the United States, Canada, New Zealand, and several European countries.[4] Why is this so? Cohabiting couples fail to realize that what is *not* being tested is commitment—the very glue that holds a marriage together.

2) The risks are even greater for African-American couples. As reported in the *Journal of Marriage and the Family*, 70% of both white and black cohabiters believed they would eventually marry their partner. In reality, only 60% of whites and less than 20% of black cohabiters eventually married.[5]

3) For those couples living together, the question is not will they stay together, but how long will it be before they break up. Out of 100 cohabiting couples, 40 break up before getting married, and (with higher divorce rates) 45 of the 60 who do marry get divorced. This leaves only 15 of 100 couples still together ten years later. Cohabitation isn't a "trial marriage" but rather a "trial divorce."[6]

4) A University of Western Ontario study of over 8,000 ever-married men and women found a direct relationship between cohabitation and divorce. It was determined that cohabitation "has a direct negative impact on subsequent marital stability," because living in such a union "undermines the legitimacy of formal marriage" and "reduces commitment of marriage."[7]

5) Dr. Scott Stanley from the University of Denver reported in his book, The Power of Commitment, that "men were

less dedicated in their marriages if they had lived with their partners before marriage."[8] If a couple lives together before marriage, both partners are more likely to cheat on the other after marriage.

6) The longer the cohabitation experience, the more likely married individuals are to question the value of marital permanence. Couples who do not cohabit prior to marriage, on the other hand, are more likely to accept that various small stressors are part of the normal cost of commitment to marital permanence.[9]

Adverse Psychological Impact

1) Cohabiting women have rates of depression three times higher than married women (National Institute for Mental Health).[10] The longer couples cohabit, the greater the likelihood of depression.[11]

2) A study by the National Council on Family Relations (n=309 newlywed couples) found those who cohabited were less happy in marriage.[12]

3) Our discussions with cohabiting couples indicate that women tend to view living together as a stepping stone to marriage while the appeal to their male partners were the conveniences of readily available sex and shared expenses. This difference in perspective often leads to grave disappointment to cohabiting women.

Reduced Communication

1) Dr. Catherine Cohan and Stacey Kleinbaum of Pennsylvania State University interviewed 92 couples married less than 2 years and found that those who lived together for *just one month* before marriage displayed poorer communication and problem-solving skills than those who did not live together. "In general, they discovered that those who lived together before marriage were more verbally aggressive, more hostile, and less supportive than those who waited until marriage to live together. The problem, according to the authors, could be

that those living together without the benefit of marriage have less commitment to one another and so they don't work at their marriage as much. They summed up their research by saying, 'We just know that people who lived together first had poorer communication skills.'"[13]

2) 60% of those who had cohabited before marriage were more verbally aggressive, less supportive of one another, and more hostile than the 40 % of spouses who had not lived together.[14]

3) People who lived together before marriage have more negative communication in their marriages than those who did not live together.[15]

Reduced Relationship Quality

1) Cohabitation is associated with lower levels of relationship satisfaction.[16]

2) Cohabitation is associated with higher perceived relationship instability.[17]

3) Cohabitation is associated with lower levels of dedication to the partner for both men and women.[18]

4) Conventional wisdom says it is acceptable to have a "trial period" to "test drive a car before you buy it." For marriage, however, just the opposite is true! "A newly married couple makes a more deliberate effort to accommodate each other because they know their relationship will be for life. They want to build compatibility, not test it."[19] As Proverbs 14:12 reminds us, "There is a way that seems right to a man, but in the end it leads to death."

5) The longer couples live together before marriage, the earlier disillusionment develops in the marital relationship along with lower the marital quality and commitment. [20]

Increased Aggression

1) Cohabitation is associated with greater likelihood of domestic aggression.[21]

2) A woman who lives with a man is three times more likely to be physically abused than a married woman, and if the cohabitating couple breaks up, the woman is 18 times more likely to be harmed than a married woman.[22]

3) Physical intimacy is a mistaken attempt to quickly build emotional bridges, but relationships built on such an inadequate foundation eventually collapse. A study at Penn State University comparing the relationship qualities of 682 cohabiters and 6,881 married couples, 19 to 48 years of age, found that cohabiters argue, shout, and hit more often than married couples.[23]

4) 60% of test subjects who had cohabited before marriage were more verbally aggressive, less supportive of one another, and more hostile than the 40% of spouses who had not lived together.[24]

Handling of Property
Economic forces often contribute to a couple deciding to cohabit.

1) "A couple dates, they get sexually involved, and they find themselves spending a great deal of time together, including many nights. Sooner or later it dawns on them that they can do what they're doing much cheaper by sharing a residence and other living expenses. Their thinking has severed the moral connection between sex and marriage so the economic aspect of their relationship becomes the dominant consideration."[25]

2) For most cohabiting couples, money and property tend to remain either 'his' or 'hers', rather than 'ours'. As a result, there is limited shared financial goal setting and planning with less importance placed on how he or she spends their own money. This mindset misses the economic synergy that is present in most marriages.

Adverse Impact on Children

1) "Compared with children in married stepfamilies, children in cohabiting homes are more likely to fail in school, run

afoul of the law, suffer from depression, do drugs, and—most disturbingly—be abused. (Note that children in in-tact, married homes do best on all these outcomes.) In the words of an Urban Institute study, "cohabiting families are not simply an extension of traditional married biological or blended families. Indeed, a recent federal report on child abuse found that children in cohabiting stepfamilies were 98% more likely to be physically abused, 130% more likely to be sexually abused, and 64% more likely to be emotionally abused, compared with children in married stepfamilies."[26]

2) Research reported on a web site for husbands and fathers showed:[27]

   ▪ Since cohabiting couples are more likely to break up than married couples, children are five times more likely to experience the trauma of a breakup of their parents (Journal of Marriage and Family).
   ▪ Children are 50 times more likely to be abused when they are not living with two biological or adoptive parents (U.S. Census data).
   ▪ Even factoring in socioeconomic and mental health differences, cohabiting couples' children are twice as likely to suffer from psychiatric disorders, diseases, suicide attempts, alcoholism, and drug abuse.
   ▪ Children are more likely to suffer the negative effects of poverty and low socioeconomic status.
   ▪ Children are more likely to have difficulties forming healthy relationships.

3) Parents who cohabited have greater difficulty establishing moral guidelines for their children, especially when they reach the dating age.

Spiritual Issues

Last but not least, the Bible says in Hebrews 13:4, *"Marriage should be honored by all, and the marriage bed be kept pure, for God will judge the adulterer and all the sexually immoral."* God has so much more in store for the couple who will stay pure in their earthly relationships. He also desires to forgive the couple who is willing to repent (turn away) of their sin, and start their relationship anew.

The biblical commitment is always to sexual purity as God's will for our lives. Pastor Jeff VanGoethem says, "The simple truth is that the practice of cohabitation does not follow God's wisdom on how to establish permanent love relationships. Little wonder they fail at the rate they do."[28]

In couples we have mentored, there is a dramatic difference in the spiritual and relational vitality observed between those who have had sex outside marriage and those who enter marriage as virgins.

Whether one looks at cohabitation from a biblical or secular perspective, the overwhelming evidence suggests that living together is not wise.

Cohabitation Without Sex[29]

While most couples living together before marriage are sexually involved, what about a cohabiting couple that is not sexually active? For example, how do you mentor a couple that lives together for financial reasons but chooses to abstain from sex until marriage?

While we applaud a couple's decision to abstain sexually before marriage, there are still several good reasons why a couple shouldn't live together before marriage.

1) *The first issue is temptation.* Let's face it; living together, sharing a house, or sharing a bed is not the best way to fight temptation. If you are serious about saving all sexual activity for marriage, the last thing you should do is move in with the person you love and are sexually attracted to. When you live together before marriage, you increase your exposure and vulnerability to temptation. *"Can a man scoop fire into his lap without his clothes being burned?"* (Proverbs 6:27). In a cohabiting arrangement, ask yourself, are you truly relating to each other like brother and sister with absolute purity? *"Treat younger men as brothers... and younger women as sisters, with absolute purity."* (1 Timothy 5:1-2)

2) *Next is the matter of your testimony.* The Bible says to avoid even the *appearance* of evil (Ephesians 5:3; 1 Thessalonians

296

5:22). What kind of example does cohabitation set for others who are watching? How will those, who do not know about your commitment to abstain sexually, view your relationship to each other and to Christ? The testimony of our lives affects how people view Christ, the church, and God's design for marriage. Many have rejected Christianity because they don't see people who call themselves Christian living it out. Living together presents a poor testimony for Christ and His church. *"...I urge you to live a life worthy of the calling you have received."* (Ephesians 4:1b)

You also present a stumbling block to others who may be encouraged to follow in your footsteps without abstaining from sex. *"...make up your mind not to put any stumbling block or obstacle in your brother's way."* (Romans 14:13b)

3) *Thirdly there is the trivialization of marriage.* Living together trivializes marriage by detracting from the sacredness that God ordained for marriage alone. Living together prematurely adopts the social and some of the relational aspects of marriage and therefore dishonors it. This goes against Hebrews 13:4 which says, *"Let marriage be honored by all."* It's sad to hear a couple who cohabited and then gets married say, "It's not that different." They have lost out on an important part of the joy and uniqueness of the marriage relationship which God intended for them.

Additionally, the trivialization effect has been found to adversely impact the couple's relational dynamics in several areas.

4) *When you get married, you are likely to have more difficulty with the transition.* While abstaining sexually before marriage is always a wise choice, the limited difference in living arrangements between the day before and the day after the wedding can make it more difficult to suddenly "let go" sexually after abstaining during cohabitation.

If you ever decide to break your engagement, your heartache, financial, and even legal complications will be that much greater since you have emotionally and physically bonded to a greater extent than you would have if you didn't cohabit.

Discussion Starters

1) How are you dealing with the challenges of living together?
2) How familiar are you with the research on the impact of cohabitation on a couple's long-term prospects for lasting relationship?
3) How has living together impacted your level of lifelong commitment to each other?
4) Has your level of confidence in the strength of your relationship changed since you began cohabiting?
5) Was the step you took to live together something you specifically planned, or did you just drift into that decision?
6) How did you reconcile your religious teaching and spiritual beliefs with your decision to cohabitate?
7) How have your families reacted to your decision to live together?

Recommended Resources

McManus, Michael J., and Harriett McManus. *Living Together: Myths, Risks & Answers*. New York: Howard, 2008.

Whitehead, Ph.D, Barbara Dafoe, and David Popenoe. "Publications - Special Reports, The National Marriage Project, U.Va." *University of Virginia*. University of Virginia, 28 Apr. 2004. http://www. virginia.edu/marriageproject/pdfs/print_whitehead_testimonial.pdf.

Institute for American Values, and National Center for African American Marriages and Parenting. *The Marriage Index A Proposal to Establish Leading Marriage Indicators*. 1st ed. Poulsbo, WA: Broadway Pubns, 2009.

Additional Information on Pornography for Mentors

The Pornography Industry

Pornography is basically equivalent to prostitution. No matter how one might rationalize it, the user is paying or engaging a stranger to have sex so you can watch them do it. The more porn people consume the more porn that is being made. All porn consumers have a hand in making the industry grow. No man would ever want his sister or daughter to be a porn star, so why is it okay for someone else's sister or daughter?

Former workers in the pornography industry have described the prolific social degradations of drug use (forced and voluntary), rape, sexual abuse, humiliation, degradation, and bondage that is common in the industry. The vast majority of participants resort to drugs in order to numb the emotional and physical pain that these women are subjected to. This is a most extreme form of women abuse!

The pornography industry recognizes the reality of the "Law of Diminishing Returns" even if its users don't. If one looks at the evolution of pornography over the past several decades, what used to be classified as "hard core" is now labeled "soft core" and is embedded and widely accepted in our porn-saturated media and culture.

In the recent past, "...pornography usually meant the explicit depiction of sexual intercourse between two aroused partners, displaying their genitals. 'Softcore' meant pictures of women...in various states of undress, breasts revealed.

"Now hardcore has evolved and is increasingly dominated by ...scripts fusing sex with hatred and humiliation. Hardcore pornography now explores the world of perversion, while softcore is now what hardcore was a few decades ago, explicit sexual intercourse between adults, now available on cable TV. The comparatively tame softcore pictures of yesteryear...now show up on mainstream media ...including television, rock videos, soap operas..."[1]

Common Reasons and Excuses for Using Porn

According to a Kinsey Institute survey[2] which asked "Why do you use porn?" respondents said:

1) To masturbate/for physical release (72%).
2) To sexually arouse themselves and/or others (69%).
3) Out of curiosity (54%).
4) Because I can fantasize about things I would not necessarily want in real life (43%).
5) To distract myself (38%).

But much like getting high, reality has a way of creeping back in. Almost without fail, moments after climax, feelings of shame, guilt, and inadequacy return as the person attempts to hide his or her tracks.

The Bio-chemical Basis for Sex Addiction

When a man looks at a sexually oriented image, there are hormones released that hold his attention. These hormones affect his thinking long after the images are gone. Most men can distinctly remember the first time they saw a naked woman or pornographic materials.

> *"Porn is a whispered promise. It promises more sex, better sex, endless sex, sex on demand, more intense orgasms, and experiences of transcendence."*
> ~ William M. Struthers[3] ~

"Frequent pornography users develop new maps in their brains based on the pictures and videos they see. Those news maps develop a 'hunger to be stimulated,' so much so that the men at their computers are likes rats in a lab cage, 'pressing the bar to get a shot of dopamine or its equivalent.'"[4]

Pornography de-sensitizes men so much that images the addict once considered disgusting become appealing as they desperately seek the same "high" but now must resort to something new.

"Porn use has many of the same properties as drug use...Despite being ingested through the eyes and ears... porn stimulates the reward and

pleasure centers in the brain, instantly and dramatically, increasing the production of dopamine, a neurotransmitter associated with both sexual arousal and drug highs. In addition, using porn for sexual stimulation has been shown to increase production of other "feel-good" chemicals, such as adrenaline, endorphins, testosterone, and serotonin; with sexual climax, it releases powerful hormones related to falling in love and bonding, such as oxytocin and vasopressin.

"Porn wasn't just operating like a drug—it was operating like a designer drug, able to give the use...novelty, excitement, escape, mastery, and (with orgasm) relaxation.

"My newfound knowledge of pornography's drug-like effects helped me bring more compassion to the issues porn users faced...I started recommending that clients supplement their individual and couples counseling work with attending 12-step sexual addiction recovery programs, such as Sex Addicts Anonymous, Sexaholics Anonymous, and Recovering Couples Anonymous...I began encouraging intimate partners to attend Codependents of Sex Addicts meetings and to check out supportive websites, such as www.pornaddicthubby.com... support groups can be critical to successful recovery, helping overcome social isolation and shame, building accountability supports, and sharing triumphs."[5]

"During sexual process, the brain begins narrowing its focus as it releases a tidal wave of endorphins and other neurochemicals like dopamine, norepinephrine, oxytocin and serotonin. These "natural drugs" produce a tremendous rush or high. When these chemicals are released during healthy marital intimacy we refer to them as "the fabulous four" because of the myriad positive benefits they generate between husband and wife. When they are released during pornography use and other sexual addiction behaviors, we call them "the fearsome four" due to the severe addiction and many negative consequences they produce in the brain and nervous system.... the neurochemical release triggered by pornography viewing is so intense, many scientists refer to it as an "erototoxin" and the most powerful drug in history...

"Imagine taking the most powerful drug in history and making it instantly available at the push of a button, at little or no cost. Your drug use is secret, and the drug dealers come to you! That's exactly what the Internet has done with pornography. It's what we call the "4 A's of the Internet"-Accessible, Affordable, Anonymous and Aggressive."[6] Mary Anne Layden, co-director of the Sexual Trauma and Psychopathology Program at the University of Pennsylvania's Center for Cognitive Therapy, called porn the *"most concerning thing to psychological health that I know of existing today."*[7]

"The internet is a perfect drug delivery system because you are anonymous, aroused and have role models for these behaviors. To have drug pumped into your house 24/7, free, and children know how to use it better than grown-ups know how to use it -- it's a perfect delivery system if we want to have a whole generation of young addicts who will never have the drug out of their mind."[8]

Time to Recovery

The time it takes for a porn addicted person to recover depends on many factors, including:

1) Degree of damage done (personal, relational, economic, etc.).
2) Personality.
3) Degree of motivation for change.
4) Amount, type, and frequency of counseling used.
5) Accountability structures in place and used.
6) Level of active engagement by the recovering addict with his or her accountability partners.

State Marriage Handbooks (USA)

Several states have published marriage handbooks as a free public resource. Some of these are well done while others are lacking in scope, content, and/or time-tested values.

This list is provided as a resource to our readers, and is not specifically endorsed by us. Feel free to use these as you see fit since they were developed through public financing and are in the public domain.

See the Resources section of TheSolutionForMarriages.com for periodic updates to this list.

Alabama

http://www.aces.edu/pubs/docs/H/HE-0829/HE-0829.pdf
The handbook includes information about money, balancing work and family, responsibilities in the home, children, and in-laws. The resource also addresses substance abuse, gambling, mental health problems, sexual infidelity, and other issues that hurt relationships.

Colorado

http://www.smartmarriages.org/colorado.handbook.html
Apparently no longer being produced and distributed, this handbook included information on communication skills, dealing with conflict, and understanding expectations.

Florida

http://www.flclerks.com/PDF/2000_2001_pdfs/7-99_VERSION_Family_Law_Handbook.pdf
The *Family/Marriage Law Handbook* is required by the State of Florida to be read by all marriage license applicants before the marriage license is issued.

Louisiana

http://www.dss.state.la.us/assets/docs/searchable/OFS/GuideMarriageChild/MarriageMatters.pdf

This graphically appealing handbook offers creative pop quiz exercises for couples. It includes information about handling conflict and techniques for developing listening skills.

Oklahoma
http://www.marriageok.net/MarriageOKMagazine.pdf
This handbook has extensive information about marriage license requirements, benefits of a healthy marriage, special issues with marrying young, conflict resolution, and parenting skills.

Texas
http://www.oag.state.tx.us/AG_Publications/pdfs/marriage.pdf
This handbook offers a workbook style interaction with couples and addresses personality differences, conflict issues, communication skills, children, money, and faith issues.

Utah
http://extension.usu.edu/files/publications/publication/
Marriage_2007.pdf
Based on the Alabama handbook as a model, this resource provides basic tips for managing relational expectations, discussing shared goals, and handling issues related to finances, parenting, in-laws, and remarriage.

Certificate of Completion

"Marriage Preparation"
Is Awarded to

Mentees' Names

For successful completion of the "Preparation for Marriage" Mentoring Program, which includes a minimum of 12-hours of mentoring, personal couples homework, and a demonstration of this couple's commitment to seek God's direction and follow His holy design for marriage according to His Word.

_____   _____
Date   Mentors' Name

A copy of this Certificate of Completion form is available in the Resources section of TheSolutionForMarriages.com

Notes

Chapter 1: The Art of Marriage Mentoring

1. Wages, S. A. & Darling, C. A. (2004) Evaluation of a Marriage Preparation Program (PREPARE) Using Marriage Mentors. Marriage & Family Journal 7(2), 103-121.
2. Robert Oglesby, Director, Center for Youth & Family Ministry, Abilene Christian University, Abilene, TX.
3. McClurkan, J. S., The Effect of Couple-to-couple Mentoring on Weak Marriage Relationships, 2003. http://www.marriageteam.org/Coaching_studies.html
4. McManus, Mike and Harriet, Living Together, Myths, Risks & Answers, Howard Books, New York, 2008, Pg. XVIII.

Chapter 2: The First Meeting with Your Mentees

1. Knutson, Luke, and Dr. David H. Olsen. *A Christian Journal* 6.4 (2003): 529-46. *Prepare-Enrich*. Life Innovations, Inc., Minneapolis, MN. https://www.prepare-enrich.com/pe_main_site_content/pdf/research/aacc_study_2003.pdf
2. For more information, see www.marriageteam.org and www.marriagesavers.org

Chapter 3: Potential Background Areas to Discuss

1. Items listed in the left column of this table are based on the Customized Version of Life Innovations' PREPARE/ENRICH Facilitator Report. Some areas may not apply to the specific couple you are mentoring.

Chapter 4: Managing and Coping With Stress – The Personal Stress Profile

1. Schermerhorn, John R., Richard Osborn, and James G. Hunt. *Organizational Behavior*. 9th ed. New York: Wiley, 2005
2. Holmes TH, Rahe RH (1967). "The Social Readjustment Rating Scale". J Psychosom Res 11 (2): 213–8. Commonly known as the Holmes and Rahe Stress Scale. Adapted by authors for use in mentoring.

Chapter 5: Emotional Stability

1. Self talk is anything we verbally or silently say to ourselves. Self talk can be positive (for encouragement or motivation) or negative (expressing criticism or pessimism).

2. Http://stresscourse.tripod.com/id97.html. ChristianityToday.com, Magazines, News, Church Leadership & Bible Study. http://www. christianitytoday.com/ct/2008/march/18.28.html.

Chapter 6: Communication

1. For more on the Imago Dialogue, go to http://gettingtheloveyouwant.com/ articles/imago-dialogue-101
2. Adapted from Paterson, Randy, Ph.D., The Assertiveness Workbook, MJF Books, New York, NY, 2000, Pg. 33.
3. Self disclosure is the sharing of personal information that others would be unlikely to know or find out. Self-disclosure creates an environment of mutual trust, which benefits both individuals. When we confide in others, they increasingly confide in us.
4. Olson, David H. L., and Amy K. Olson. *Empowering Couples: Building on Your Strengths*. Minneapolis, MN: Life Innovations, 2000. Pg. 31.

Chapter 7: Conflict Resolution

1. Portions adapted from Apostolic Christian Counseling and Family Services, Conflict Resolution Skills in Marriage, 2008.
2. Nicholson, David. *What You Need to Know before You Fall in Love*. Nashville, Tenn.: Thomas Nelson, 1995.
3. Gottman, John, and Nan Silver. *The Seven Principles for Making Marriage Work*. New York, NY: Three Rivers, 1999.27
4. Anderson, Kerby. "Abuse and Domestic Violence." *Abuse and Domestic Violence-Probe Ministries*. Probe Ministries, 2003. http://www.probe. org/site/c.fdKEIMNsEoG/b.4219479/k.7FEF/Abuse_and_Domestic_ Violence.htm
5. Hegstrom, Paul. *Angry Men and the Women Who Love Them: Breaking the Cycle of Physical and Emotional Abuse*. Kansas City, MO: Beacon Hill of Kansas City, 1999.
6. Gottman, John Mordechai, and Nan Silver. *The Seven Principles for Making Marriage Work*. New York: Three Rivers, 1999.

Chapter 8: Granting Forgiveness – What It Is, What It Isn't and How to Do It Well

1. Portions adapted from Apostolic Christian Counseling and Family Services, Forgiveness; What It Is, What It Isn't, & How To Do It, 2008.
2. Jeffress, Robert. "Chapter 2." *When Forgiveness Doesn't Make Sense*. Colorado Springs, CO: WaterBrook, 2000. 102.
3. www.*gettingtheloveyouwant.com/articles/imago-dialogue-101*
4. Worthington, Everett L., and Everett L. Worthington. *Forgiving and Reconciling: Bridges to Wholeness and Hope*. Downers Grove, IL: InterVarsity, 2003.

5. Ibid, 102
6. Ibid, 224-226

Chapter 9: Dealing with Your Partner's Unique Traits – Partner Style and Habits

1. Rogers, Carl R. *Client-Centered Therapy: Its Current Practice, Implications, and Theory*. Boston: Houghton Mifflin, 1965.
2. Glenn, John. *The Alpha Series: the Gift of Recovery*. Bloomington, IN: Author House, 2006.
3. Cornwell, Erin York, and Linda J. Waite. "Social Disconnectedness, Perceived Isolation, and Health among Older Adults." *Journal of Health Social Behavior* March.50(1) (2009): 31-48. http://www.ncbi.nlm.nih.gov/pmc/articles/PMC2756979/.
4. The Solomon Syndrome is defined as our need/desire for "worthiness". An example is thinking, "I will be worthy *if…*" Solomon attempted to fill the voids in his life with many "ifs" including material things, wives, castles and more, but none worked. It was only when he turned to God that his life become complete.

Chapter 10: Financial Management

1. Blue, Ron, and Jeremy White. *Faith-based Family Finances*. Carol Stream, IL: Tyndale House, 2008.
2. Peterson, Karen S. "Adults Should Know Status of Parents." *USA Today* [Franklin, TN] 12 Mar. 1992.
3. Rockefeller, Sr., John D. *Give Him the First Part*. Campus Crusade for Christ International, 25 May 2011. http://www.ccci.org/training-and-growth/devotional-life/todays-promise/tp0525.htm.

Chapter 11: Finding Common Ground – Leisure Activities

1. Jaynes, Sharon. *Becoming the Woman of His Dreams: Seven Qualities Every Man Longs For*. Eugene, OR: Harvest House, 2005. 11.

Chapter 12: Developing Sexual Fulfillment & Intimacy in Marriage (Discussed with the Couple Together)

1. Rainey, Dennis, and Barbara Rainey. "November 9." Moments Together for Couples. Ventura, CA: Regal, 1995.
2. *Sex, A Study of the Good Bits of Song of Solomon*. By Mark Driscoll. Edinburgh, Scotland. Presentation.
3. Gardner, Tim Alan, *Sacred Sex*, WaterBrook Press, Colorado Springs, CO, 2002. 15.
4. Ibid., pg. 17.

5. Adapted from Family Life, *Weekend to Remember* Conference Manual (1985): 86.
6. "Dissatisfied, Ladies? Tips to Reach the Big O." MSNBC, 02 Nov. 2007.
7. House, H. Wayne. "Should Christians Use Birth Control?" *Christian Research Institute and the Bible Answer Man, Hank Hanegraaff.* Christian Research Institute. Web. 30 Aug. 2011. http://www.equip.org/articles/should-christians-use-birth-control-.
8. From the Mayo Clinic web site http://www.mayoclinic.com
9. Rainey, Dennis, Barbara Rainey, and Robert G. DeMoss. *Rekindling the Romance: Loving the Love of Your Life.* Nashville, TN: Thomas Nelson, 2004. 76.

Chapter 13: Developing Sexual Fulfillment & Intimacy in Marriage Preparation for Sex and Sexual Expectations (Men's Session)

1. Masters, William H., Virginia E. Johnson, and Robert J. Levin. *The Pleasure Bond: a New Look at Sexuality and Commitment.* Toronto, NY: Bantam, 1976. 113-14.

Chapter 14: Developing Sexual Fulfillment & Intimacy in Marriage Preparation for Sex and Sexual Expectations (Women's Session)

1. Dennis Rainey, Affair Proof Your Marriage, Family Life, http://www.familylife.com/site/apps/nlnet/content3.aspx?c=dnJHKLNnFoG&b=3781253&ct=4638395
2. Barbara Rainey, Why Sex is so Important to You Husband, Family Life, http://www.familylife.com/site/apps/nl/content3.asp?c=dnJHKLNnFoG&b=3584679&ct=4638039

Chapter 15: The Dangers of Pornography

1. Adapted from "Danger Ahead! Avoiding Pornography's Trap." *The New Era Magazine,* Volume 10, Number 10, Oct. 2002: 36.
2. "The Social Costs of Pornography." *The Witherspoon Institute*: 13. Princeton, NJ. 2010.
3. Internet Pornography Statistics, 2008. Also applies to the next item listed in the text.
4. Ibid. 2006.
5. MSNBC.com survey (2000) conducted by Dr. Alvin Cooper, San Jose Marital Services and Sexuality Center, San Jose, CA.
6. "Facts." Communicating With Women - News. Every Man's Battle. 19 July 2011. http://www.everymansbattle.com/gethelp/pastors/facts.html.
7. Kuchment, Anna. "The Tangled Web of Porn in the Office." Newsweek - National News, World News, Business, Health, Technology, Entertainment, and More - Newsweek. The Newsweek/Daily Beast Company LLC, 29 Nov. 2008. http://www.newsweek.com/2008/11/28/the-tangled-web-of-porn-in-the-office.html.

8. Ropelato, Jerry. "Internet Pornography Statistics." Top Ten Reviews. Net Nanny. http://internet-filter-review.toptenreviews.com/internet-pornography-statistics.html.

9. "Relationships in Focus, Sexual Addiction: Real problem or Convenient Excuse?" *Today in Dixie*, 31 Mar. 2010.

10. Maltz, Wendy. "Out of the Shadows." *Psychotherapy Networker Magazine* 2009:7.

11. LaRue, Jan. "Senate Subcommittee Hears Experts on Pornography Toxicity." Dr. Judith Reisman. 2 Dec. 2004. http://www.drjudithreisman.com/archives/2005/12/senate_subcommi.html.

12. Satinover, Dr. Jeffrey. "Statement on Pornography to the US Congress." Diss. Princeton University, 2004. *Pornography|Citizens for Community Values*. Citizens for Community Values, Nov. 2004. http://www.ccv.org/wp-content/uploads/2010/04/Jeffrey_Satinover_Senate_Testiomony-2004.11.17.pdf

13. "Pornography: Society at Risk." LDS Resources on Pornography. LDS & The Philippines Alliance Against Pornography, 2006. http://mentalhealthlibrary.info/library/porn/pornlds/pornldsauthor/links/philippine/pornx.htm.

14. Maltz, Wendy. "Out of the Shadows." Psychotherapy Networker. 2009. http://www.psychotherapynetworker.org/magazine/currentissue/694-out-of-the-shadow

15. Hart, Archibald D. *The Sexual Man*. Dallas: Word Pub., 1994, Pg. 89.

16. Thomas, Gary L. "Slaying the Secret Sin." http://www.garythomas.com/slaying-the-secret-sin

17. Patrick Carnes, Pine Grove Behavioral Health & Addiction Services

18. Kennedy, John W. "Help for the Sexually Desperate," *ChristianityToday.com, Magazines, News, Church Leadership & Bible Study*. Christianity Today, 7 Mar. 2008. http://www.christianitytoday.com/ct/2008/march/18.28.html.

19. McDowell, Sean, and Pamela Paul. "What's The Big Deal with Pornography?" *How Porn Became the Norm*. Planet Wisdom. http://www.planetwisdom.com/seanmcdowell/article/whats_the_big_deal_with_pornography/.

20. Our observations are also confirmed by a study published in *Sexual Addiction and Compulsivity*, which found 68% of couples in which one person was addicted to Internet porn, resulted in one or both partners losing interest in sex. After getting a porn fix, a person often feels more depressed and lonely because the only intimacy they can get is with a magazine or a video. This leaves one feeling empty inside as pornography becomes a crutch and saps their confidence.

21. Wang, Laurie. "The Effects of Internet Pornography." *Power to Change*. Power To Change, 18 Sept. 2009. http://powertochange.com/discover/sex-love/effectsofporn/.

22. A claim made by the American Academy of Matrimonial Lawyers. "Behavior: The Porn Factor." *Time Magazine* 19 Jan. 2004.

23. Zillmann, Dolf, and Jennings Bryant. "Pornography and Sexual Callousness, and the Trivialization of Rape." *Journal of Communication* 32.4 (1982): 10-21.

24. Kennedy, John W. "Help for the Sexually Desperate," *ChristianityToday. com, Magazines, News, Church Leadership & Bible Study*. Christianity Today, 7 Mar. 2008. http://www.christianitytoday.com/ct/2008/ march/18.28.html

25. Since this is an area with many new resources becoming available, be sure to check TheSolutionForMarriages.com for the latest recommendations. One such site is http://www.settingcaptivesfree.com

26. Piper, John. "How to Kill Sin, Part 1 - Desiring God." *Killing Sin.* Desiring God, 02 Feb. 2002. http://www.desiringgod.org/resource-library/ sermons/how-to-kill-sin-part-1.

Chapter 16: Breaking Free from Pornography A Five Step Process for Victory"

1. Kennedy, John W. "Help for the Sexually Desperate." *Christianity Today* 07 Mar. 2008. http://www.christianitytoday.com/ct/article_print. html?id=53974

2. This helpful concept is based on the "Every Man's Battle" book and workshop by Steve Arterburn of New Life Ministries.

Chapter 17: Testing Before Marriage (STDs)

1. We are grateful to have had this section reviewed for medical accuracy by Dr. John Li, M.D. and Dr. Celeste Li, M.D.

2. Crouse, Janice Shaw. *Gaining Ground, a Profile of American Women in the Twentieth Century: Trends in Selected Indicators of Women's Well-being.* Washington, D.C.: Beverly LaHaye Institute, 2001.

3. World Health Organization "Global Prevalence and Incidence of Selected Curable Sexually Transmitted Infections Overview and Estimates," 2001.

4. Crouse, Janice Shaw. *Gaining Ground, a Profile of American Women in the Twentieth Century: Trends in Selected Indicators of Women's Well-being.* Washington, D.C.: Beverly LaHaye Institute, 2001.

Chapter 18: Family of Origin

1. This chapter draws on materials published by Life Innovations. Used with permission.

2. Olsen, PhD, Dr. David H., and Dr. Peter Larsen, Ph.D. *Couple Checkup*™ *Discussion Guide with Biblical References*. Minneapolis, MN: Life Innovations, 2010.

3. From a special edition by Olsen, PhD, David H. "Journal of Family Therapy" *Circumplex Model of Marital & Family Systems.* University of Wyoming - Dept of Agriculture & Applied Economics,

1999. http://agecon.uwyo.edu/eruralfamilies/ERFLibrary/Readings/CircumplexModelOfMaritalAndFamilySystems.pdf.

4. Adapted from Hendrix, PhD, Harville, and Helen LaKelly Hunt, PhD. "Imago Couples Therapy; Relationship Therapy; Education Worldwide." *Couples Therapy and Workshops from Imago Relationships Intnl.* Imago Relationships International. http://gettingtheloveyouwant.com/articles/an-introduction-to-imago.

5. Ibid.

6. Adapted from Skomal, Lenore. "Two First Borns? Bad Match: Birth Order Can Indicate Whether Your Marriage Will Work Out - or Not." *Divorce360.com | Divorce Advice, News, Blogs and Community.* Divorce360.com, 24 June 2008. http://www.divorce360.com/divorce-articles/news/trends/two-first-borns-bad-match.aspx?artid=586.

7. Ibid.

Chapter 19: Boundaries & Your Couple and Family Map

1. This chapter draws extensively on materials published by Life Innovations. Used with permission.

Chapter 20: Handling Cultural Différences

1. In this chapter, "cultural" is broadly used to include race, religion, country of origin, etc.

2. Romano, Dugan. *Intercultural Marriage: Promise and Pitfalls,* 3rd ed. Boston & London: Intercultural, a Division of Nicholas Brealy, 2008. 142.

3. Numbers 12:1 says, *"Miriam and Aaron began to talk against Moses because of his Cushite wife, for he had married a Cushite."* God punishes Miriam for this discrimination in verse 10 by turning her skin white with leprosy. The people of Cush, a region south of Ethiopia, were known for their black skin. In J. Daniel Hays' book, From Every People and Nation: A Biblical Theology of Race (Downers Grove, Ill.: InterVarsity Press, 2003), he writes that Cush "is used regularly to refer to the area south of Egypt…where a Black African civilization flourished for over two thousand years. Thus it is quite clear that Moses marries a Black African woman." (p. 71).

4. Romano, Dugan. *Intercultural Marriage: Promise and Pitfalls,* 3rd ed. Boston & London: Intercultural, a Division of Nicholas Brealy, 2008. 151.

5. Exercise is adapted from Crohn, Joel. *Mixed Matches: How to Create Successful Interracial, Interethnic, and Interfaith Relationships.* New York: Fawcett Columbine, 1995. 69-70.

Chapter 21: Managing Wedding Planning Boundaries

1. This material is from The First Dance (www.thefirstdance.com), a DVD resource that we highly recommend for engaged couples, by Elizabeth Thomas and Bill Doherty, Ph.D. Used with permission.

Chapter 23: Protecting Your Relationship – The Internet, Social Media and Friends

1. www.myfoxaustin.com/.../Special-Report-Social-Media-and-Divorce-20110203-ktbcw
2. "Divorce Facebook Study Shows Social Networking Often Leads to Breakups." *Facebook Is Blamed in a Growing Number of Divorce Cases, Study Shows.* PR News Channel, 05 Mar. 2011. http://www.prnewschannel.com/absolutenm/templates/?a=3582&z=4.

Chapter 24: Biblical Roles of Husbands and Wives

1. Piper, John, and Wayne A. Grudem. "Chapter 3, Male-Female Equality and Male Headship." *Recovering Biblical Manhood and Womanhood: A Response to Evangelical Feminism.* Wheaton, IL: Crossway, 1991. 99.
2. Piper, John, and Wayne A. Grudem. "Chapter 1, Male-Female Equality and Male Headship." *Recovering Biblical Manhood and Womanhood: A Response to Evangelical Feminism.* Wheaton, IL: Crossway, 1991. 29.
3. Ibid., pg. 36.
4. Ibid., pg. 37.
5. Scott. "WoW - Love, Respect and Submission." *Journey to Surrender.* Journey to Surrender, 8 June 2011. http://www.surrenderedmarriage.org/2011/06/wow-love-respect-and-submission.html?utm_source=feedburner.
6. Piper, John, and Wayne A. Grudem. "Chapter 1, Male-Female Equality and Male Headship." *Recovering Biblical Manhood and Womanhood: A Response to Evangelical Feminism.* Wheaton, IL: Crossway, 1991. 52.
7. Driscoll, Mark, Complimentarianism, http://theresurgence.com/2009/03/29/complementarianism.
8. Köstenberger, Andreas J., and David W. Jones. *God, Marriage & Family: Rebuilding the Biblical Foundation.* Wheaton, IL: Crossway, 2004. 29.

Chapter 25: Decision Making In Marriage

1. Adapted from Apostolic Christian Counseling and Family Services. "Roles, Responsibilities, and Decision Making In Marriage." (2008)
2. Ibid.

Chapter 26: Spiritual Beliefs and Developing a Personal Relationship With Christ

1. For on-line presentations of the Gospel in over 150 different languages, go to *The Four Spiritual Laws - In Your Language!* Global Media Outreach, 2007-2008. http://www.4laws.com/laws/languages.html.

Chapter 27: Developing Spiritual Intimacy in Marriage

1. Moore, Beth. *To Live Is Christ: Embracing the Passion of Paul.* Waterville, Me.: Walker Large Print, 2008.
2. Price, Rev. Bill. "Bible Prayer Fellowship - About Us." *Bible Prayer Fellowship - Teaching United Prayer*. Bible Prayer Fellowship - Teaching United Prayer, 2011. http://www.praywithchrist.org/aboutus.php.
3. Stoop, Jan, and David A. Stoop. *When Couples Pray Together: Creating Intimacy and Spiritual Wholeness*. Ann Arbor, MI: Vine, 2000. 9.
4. Burns, Jim. "Grow Towards Spiritual Intimacy in Your Marriage." *Grow Toward Spiritual Intimacy in Your Marriage*. Christianity.com. http://www.christianity.com/Home/Christian%20Living%20Features/1407864/

Chapter 28: Marriage Expectations

1. Love, Patricia, and Jo Robinson. Hot Monogamy: Essential Steps to More Passionate, Intimate Lovemaking. New York: Plume, 1995.

Chapter 30: Building Trust In Your Relationship

1. Shriver, Gary, and Mona Shriver. *Unfaithful: Rebuilding Trust after Infidelity*. Colorado Springs, CO: Cook Communications Ministries, 2005. 189-202.

Chapter 32: Stepfamilies

1. This chapter is adapted from Deal, Ron L. *The Smart Stepfamily*. Minneapolis, MN: Bethany House, 2006. and Einstein, Elizabeth, and Linda Albert. *Strengthening Your Stepfamily*. Atascadero, CA: Impact, 2006.

Part 8: Supplemental Materials for Mentors

Mentors' Letter to the Parents

1. Adapted from Prokopchak, Steve, and Mary Prokopchak. *Called Together:* Shippensburg, PA: Destiny Image, 2009.

Mentoring Program Evaluation

1. Adapted from the form used by Christ Fellowship Church, Palm Beach Gardens, FL.

How Relationships Are Impacted by Cohabitation

1. Jason, Sharon. "Cohabiting Has Little Effect on Marriage Success." USA Today. USA Today, 14 Oct. 2010. http://www.usatoday.com/news/health/2010-03-02-cohabiting02_N.htm
2. Binstock, Georgina, and Arland Thornton. "Separations, Reconciliations, and Living Apart in Cohabiting and Marital Unions." *Journal of Marriage and Family* 65.2 (2003): 432-43.
3. Hill, PhD, John R., and Sharon G. Evans, MA. "Effects of Cohabitation Length on Personal and Relational Well Being." Alabama Policy Institute, 3 Aug. 2006. http://www.alabamapolicy.org/pdf/cohabitation.pdf.
4. Bennett, Neil G., Ann Klimas Blanc, and David E. Bloom. "Commitment and the Modern Union: Assessing the Link between Premarital Cohabitation and Subsequent Marital Stability." *American Sociological Review* 53.1 (1988): 127-38. http://www.jstor.org/pss/2095738; T. K. Burch & A. K. Madan, Union Formation and Dissolution: Results from the 1984 Family History Survey (Ottawa: Statistics Canada, Catalogue No. 99-963) (1986); Catherine Cohan & Stacey Kleinbaum, "Toward a greater understanding of the cohabitation effect: Premarital cohabitation and marital communication." *Journal of Marriage and the Family* 64 (2002): 180-192; D. M. Fergusson, L. J. Horwood, & F. T. Shannon, "A proportional hazards model of family breakdown." *Journal of Marriage and the Family* 46 (1984) 539-549; and Zheng Wu, "Premarital cohabitation and post marital cohabiting union formation." *Journal of Family Issues* 16 (1995) 212-232.
5. Susan L. Brown, "Union Transitions Among Cohabiters: The Significance of Relationship Assessment and Expectations." *Journal of Marriage and the Family* 62 (2000): 833-846.
6. McManus, Michael J., and Harriett McManus. Introduction. *Living Together: Myths, Risks & Answers*. New York: Howard, 2008. 60-61.
7. Hall, David R., and John Z. Zhoa. "Cohabitation and Divorce in Canada." *Journal of Marriage and the Family* May (1995): 421-27.
8. Stanley, Scott. *The Power of Commitment: a Guide to Active, Lifelong Love*. San Francisco: Jossey-Bass, 2005. 152.
9. Hill, PhD, John R., and Sharon G. Evans, MA. "Effects of Cohabitation Length on Personal and Relational Well Being." Alabama Policy Institute, 3 Aug. 2006. 12.
10. All About Cohabitating Before Marriage, Psychological Reasons, http://members.aol.com/cohabiting/index.htm July 1999
11. Hill, PhD, John R., and Sharon G. Evans, MA. "Effects of Cohabitation Length on Personal and Relational Well Being." Alabama Policy Institute, 3 Aug. 2006. 3.

12. McManus, Michael J. *Marriage Savers: Helping Your Friends and Family Stay Married*. Grand Rapids, MI: Zondervan Pub. House, 1993.
13. Gordon, Serena. ""Marriage" - Jim L. Wilson." *Sermons.Logos.com*. Fresh Ministry, Jan. 2009. http://sermons.logos.com/submissions/80537-Marriage.
14. Catherine Cohan & Stacey Kleinbaum, "Toward a greater understanding of the cohabitation effect: Premarital cohabitation and marital communication." *Journal of Marriage and the Family* 64 (2002): 180-192.
15. DeMaris, A., and G. R. Leslie. "Cohabitation with Future Spouse: Its Influence upon Marital Satisfaction and Communication." *Journal of Marriage and Family* 46 (1984): 77-84.
16. Stafford, Laura, Susan L. Klein, and Caroline T. Rankin. "Married Individuals, Cohabiters, and Cohabiters Who Marry: A Longitudinal Study of Relational and Individual Well-Being." *Journal of Social and Personal Relationships* April.21 (2004): 231-48.
17. Dush, Claire M. Kamp, Catherine L. Cohan, and Paul R. Amato. "The Relationship Between Cohabitation and Marital Quality and Stability: Change Across Cohorts?" *Journal of Marriage and Family* 65.3 (2003): 539-49.
18. Stanley, S. M., S. W. Whitton, and H. J. Markman. "Maybe I Do: Interpersonal Commitment and Premarital or Non-marital Cohabitation." *Journal of Family Issues* 25 (2004): 496-519.
19. Harley, Jr., Ph.D, William F. "Meet Dr. Harley." *Marriage Builders ® - Successful Marriage Advice*. Marriage Builders ®. 27 June 2011.. http://www.marriagebuilders.com/graphic/mbi2000_meet.html.
20. DeMaris, Alfred, and William MacDonald. "Premarital Cohabitation and Marital Instability: A Test of the Unconventionality Hypothesis." *Journal of Marriage and the Family* 55 (1993): 399-407.
21. Downridge, Douglas A., and Silvia S. Halli. ""Living in Sin" and Sinful Living: Toward Filling a Gap in the Explanation of Violence against Women." *Aggression and Violent Behavior* November-December 5.6 (2000): 565-83. *Science Direct*. Science Direct, 16 Nov. 2000. http://www.sciencedirect.com/science/article/pii/S1359178999000038.
22. McManus, Mike. "Articles: Better Together? Only in Holy Matrimony, Not in Cohabitation." *Marriage Resources for Clergy @ Marriageresourcesforclergy.com*. Marriage Resources for Clergy, 13 Mar. 2008. http://www.marriageresourcesforclergy.com/site/Articles/articles017.htm.
23. Brown, S., and A. Booth. "Cohabitation versus Marriage: A Comparison of Relationship Quality." *Journal of Marriage and Family* 58 (1996): 667-68.
24. Catherine Cohan & Stacey Kleinbaum, "Toward a greater understanding of the cohabitation effect: Premarital cohabitation and marital communication." *Journal of Marriage and the Family* 64 (2002): 180-192.

25. VanGoethem, Jeff. *Living Together: a Guide to Counseling Unmarried Couples*. Grand Rapids, MI: Kregel Academic & Professional, 2005. 48-49.
26. Wilcox, Ph.D, W. Bradford. "Why the Ring Matters." *New York Times* [New York] 20 Dec. 2010. http://www.nytimes.com/roomfordebate/2010/12/19/why-remarry/why-the-ring-matters
27. www.husbandsanddads.com
28. VanGoethem, Jeff. *Living Together: a Guide to Counseling Unmarried Couples*. Grand Rapids, MI: Kregel Academic & Professional, 2005. 105.
29. Adapted from RayFowler.org. Used with permission. http://www.rayfowler.org/2008/06/19/living-together-without-sex/

Additional Information on Pornography for Mentors

1. Doige, MD, Norman. "Cohabitation versus Marriage: A Comparison of Relationship Quality." (2008). *NoPornNorthHampton*. NoPornNorthHampton, 13 Mar. 2010. http://nopornnorthampton.org/2010/03/13/norman-doidge-acquiring-tastes-loves-neuroplasticity-sexual-attraction-love.aspx.
2. "Do You Use Porn? A Survey from the Kinsey Institute." *American Porn*. WBGH Foundation, Feb. 2002. http://www.pbs.org/wgbh/pages/frontline/shows/porn/etc/surveyres.html.
3. Struthers, William M. *Wired for Intimacy: How Pornography Hijacks the Male Brain*. Downers Grove, IL: IVP, 2009. 69.
4. Bodo, Cristian. ", Does Sex Addiction Have Any Basis in Science?" *American Sexuality Magazine*. AlterNet.org, 18 Dec. 2008. http://www.alternet.org/sex/114024/does_sex_addiction_have_any_basis_in_science/?page=1.
5. Maltz, Wendy. "Out of the Shadows." *Psychotherapy Networker Magazine* 2009: 7. http://www.psychotherapynetworker.org/magazine/currentissue/694-out-of-the-shadow
6. http://www.netnanny.com/learn_center/article/175
7. Singeal, Ryan. "Internet Porn: Worse Than Crack?" *Wired.com*. Wired.com, 19 Nov. 2004. http://www.wired.com/science/discoveries/news/2004/11/65772.
8. Ibid.

About the Authors

Jeffrey Murphy committed his life to following Jesus Christ at the age of 17. He married the woman he had been praying for, Glynis McKay, at the age of 23. After a few years of wedded bliss, their marriage began a downward spiral as a result of being inadequately trained in the skills necessary for a successful marriage, the demands of a budding career, the arrival of two children, and their own selfishness and immaturity.

It was out of this despair, that Jeff and Glynis began their quest to learn how to be successfully married—a journey that has now continued for over 26 years. They are very thankful for the FamilyLife® *Weekend to Remember* conference, which they attended for several years before becoming the New Jersey conference co-chairmen. While learning new marriage skills, they began sharing them with other couples in small group studies and investing their time in marriage ministry through their local church. Over the years as they mentored many couples, they continued to field test and refine their mentoring approach and the resources they use, which have been integrated into this book. Glynis is the author of chapter 14 of this book.

After 30 years at Johnson & Johnson, Jeff retired and moved to Florida with Glynis where they continue to invest in marriage mentoring initiatives while enjoying special times with their daughter Laura, son-in-law Chad, granddaughter Willow, and their son Steven and his wife Allison who reside in Texas. They also enjoy posting marriage tips on Twitter as @MarriageMentor.

Jeff holds a Bachelors degree in Engineering from Stevens Institute of Technology and a Masters of Business Administration from Seton Hall University. He is certified by Life Innovations as a PREPARE/ENRICH Marriage Mentor and a PREPARE/ENRICH Seminar Director.

Chuck Dettman came to know Christ at age 11. He learned the meaning of *"obedience"* from personal experience while straying from Jesus during his early adult years. He rededicated his life to Jesus after hearing "his story" told by another Christian veteran who suffered similar hurts and anguish. Romans 6:21 asks us, *"What benefit did you reap at that time from the things you are now ashamed of? Those things result in death!"*

Mae and Chuck met in 7th grade, dated in High School, and married in 1969 just prior to Chuck's Viet Nam tour.

They began mentoring in home Bible studies and saw how their Christ-centered relationship was "different" from others. Though far from "perfect," their marriage and commitment to Christ demonstrated a peace and happiness that intrigued other couples. This became the opportunity to mentor other couples and to teach them to *work* at their relationship and *grow* their *love* for one another (with Christ) each day.

Chuck and Mae have two adult children, Glynn and Barbara, and seven grandchildren.

Executive Director and Founder of Today's Promise, Inc., Chuck is an ordained minister with more than 12-years in couple and professional life-coaching experience. Chuck has become one of the premier marriage, relationship, budget and career coaching mentors in the nation—having been recognized by the NY Times, CBS Evening News, and the Harvard School of Business, among others. Chuck holds a Bachelor of Science in Business and Finance from Barry University, graduating Cum Laude. He was formerly employed by the U.S. Under Secretary of the Treasury in local banks as a loan officer, Junior Vice President, and Auditor which provided unprecedented exposure to the financial industry.

He holds many certifications including a former Florida State teaching certificate as an Occupational Therapist for Secondary Education and a Certified Crown Financial Budget Coach/Counselor. He is a Certified Marriage Mentor for PREPARE/ENRICH marriage preparation, and he coaches those already married. He holds certification as a Seminar Director for PREPARE/ENRICH, providing training to clergy, professional counselors, and mentor couples. He proudly serves as a 15th Judicial Circuit Court Registered Provider for marriage education, qualifying couples for discounted marriage licensure. He is a Master Instructor for START SMART, a premarital training course that teaches specific skills to seriously dating or engaged couples. An instructor for PICK a Partner also known as *"How to Avoid Marrying a Jerk(ette),"* a class that instructs unmarried individuals in how to best prepare for future committed relationships.

The Solution for Marriages incorporates many of their latest approaches which have proven to be successful in helping couples build the foundation for life-long, satisfying marriages.

Made in the USA
Charleston, SC
07 November 2011